跨文化交流入门

主　编　许力生
编　者　傅　政　吴丽萍

INTERCULTURAL COMMUNICATION

ZHEJIANG UNIVERSITY PRESS
浙江大学出版社

序

放眼今天的世界,“全球化”已成不可抗拒的趋势,其浪潮汹涌澎湃,欲将世界各地不同文化的人群统统卷入其中。不管愿意不愿意,几乎谁都不可避免地要和来自不同文化背景的人们进行交往,跨文化交流正在成为越来越普遍的日常现实。

然而,文化之间的差异却往往会给交际造成意想不到的困难与问题,误解、困惑、矛盾甚至冲突也因此时有发生。不同文化群体的人们能否在“地球村”这个人类拥有的唯一家园中和平共处,共同努力来解决关系人类生存的一系列问题,在很大程度上要取决于我们能否有效地进行交往并逐步相互理解。

因此,培养跨文化意识,发展跨文化交流能力,学会与来自不同文化背景的人进行交往,对于生活在21世纪、肩负着人类未来希望的年轻学子来说,就显得尤为重要。不管他们所学专业是什么,将来从事何种职业,具备超越文化局限的眼光和意识,拥有跨文化交流的知识和技能,可以说都是十分必要的,其意义无论怎么强调都不过分。

这部英文教材《跨文化交流入门》,比较系统、全面地介绍了跨文化交流及其相关问题,并提供大量实际案例分析,使理论与实践有机地结合在一起。我们希望,这部教材能够有助于大学生们认识人类交际活动的重要性、丰富性、复杂性,了解文化差异对交际活动的制约和影响,使他们可以一方面提高运用英语获取知识信息、表述意见观点、分析问题和解决问题的技能水平,另一方面又能对跨文化交流有较为全面的了解与认识,形成和发展对文化差异的敏感和宽容以及处理文化差异问题的灵活性,全面提高综合素质,最终具备与不同文化背景人们进行广泛、深入国际交流的能力。本书也适合一切具有中级及以上英语水平、对跨文化交流感兴趣的学生和其他人士阅读、学习。

由于编者的水平和能力有限,书中疏漏与谬误仍在所难免,敬请使用者批评指出,以便今后进一步改进和完善。

编　者

2017 年 3 月于浙江大学

CONTENTS

Chapter 1 Communicating in the Global Village

Our most basic common link is that we all inhabit this planet.

—John F. Kennedy

Chapter 1 Communicating in the Global Village

Preview Questions

1. What problems have you ever had when communicating with others?

2. How would you communicate with someone who does not share the same experiences with you?

3. Why do you think we have to study intercultural communication?

Text A

What Is Intercultural Communication

With the world becoming smaller, many young people decide to continue their studies abroad. Studying in a different country is something that sounds very exciting to young people. Many of those who leave their home to study in another country think that they are going to have a lot of fun. Certainly, it is a new experience, which brings them the opportunity of discovering new things and a feeling of freedom. In spite of these advantages, there will also be some problems and difficulties when they are actually involved in intercultural communication.

Intercultural communication is communication between members of different cultures. This definition is simple, but the process is complex. Intercultural communication involves differing perceptions, attitudes, and interpretations. We know that even two people from the same culture can have communication problems.

Suppose that you're planning to study in a country about which you know very little. You are sophisticated enough to expect that the spoken language and probably some gestures will be different. You know, too, that customs will be different, but you are not sure exactly what this will mean. At least there will be interesting things to take pictures of or write home about. The climate and foods will be different, of course, but these differences are attractions and are not really problems.

From the moment you arrive, your cultural and personal background will influence everything you expect and a great deal of what you do and do not do. Most of the people you meet will be similarly influenced by their own backgrounds, culturally, socially, and personally.

If some of the people you meet think you act a little strangely, they may never know whether you are peculiar, or whether most people from your country are strange, or whether all "foreigners" are strange.

Most of what you do in a foreign country will be "what comes naturally," which means what you have always done or seen others do back home. Most of our behavior is outside of our awareness so that "normal behavior" means behavior according to the norms of our culture and not what is done everywhere or done "naturally." Still, to the extent that you are aware of the possibilities of different behavior in the land you are visiting, you may be unusually self-conscious of some of this "normal behavior."

Cultures do not communicate; individuals do. Everyone has a unique style of communication, but cultures determine a general style for their members. The relationship of the individual to his culture is **analogous to** that between an actor and his director. The actor puts his own personality into his acting but is nevertheless influenced by the director. We are not always aware of the subtle influences of our culture. Likewise, we may not perceive that others are influenced by their cultures as well.

Problems and misinterpretations do not result every time members from two cultures communicate. However, when cultural conflicts do arise, they may be perceived as personal rather than cultural. In the following example it is a cultural misunderstanding that creates negative feelings and confusion:

> Yaser, an international student from Jordan, first met Steve in their chemistry class at an American university. He was excited to get to know an American, for he wanted to learn more about American culture. Yaser hoped that he and Steve would become good friends.
>
> At first, Steve seemed very friendly. He always greeted Yaser warmly before class. Sometimes he offered to study with Yaser, and even invited Yaser to eat lunch with him. But after the semester was over, Steve seemed more distant. The two former classmates didn't see each other very much at school. One day Yaser decided to call Steve. Steve didn't seem very interested in talking to him. Yaser was hurt by Steve's change of attitude. "Steve said we were friends," Yaser complained. "And I said friends were friends forever."

This misunderstanding was due to Yaser's failure to understand that for Americans a friendship may be superficial, casual, situational as well as deep and enduring. If he had known more about American culture, he could have avoided misunderstanding Steve.

Some misunderstandings are insignificant and can be easily ignored or remedied. Other conflicts are more serious in that they can cause misinterpretations and create **persistent** negative attitudes toward foreigners.

Difficulties in intercultural communication arise when there is little or no awareness of **divergent** cultural values and beliefs. In cross-cultural interaction, speakers sometimes assume that what they believe is right, because they have grown up thinking their way is the best. This ethnocentric assumption can result in negative judgments about other cultures.

In the following example, two women demonstrate that they cannot understand each other's points of view. In Rosamine's culture children live with their parents until marriage because dependence on parents is considered positive. In Merita's culture children leave home when they are eighteen because independence and self-reliance are considered positive.

ROSAMINE: I think it's terrible that in your country children leave their parents when they're so young. Something that shocks me even more is that many parents want their children to leave home. I can't understand why children and parents don't like each other in your country.

MERITA: In your country parents don't allow their children to become independent. Parents keep their children protected until the children get married. How are young people in your country supposed to learn about life that way?

Both women are insensitive to each other's values concerning family life. They have been raised and conditioned according to cultural norms. Therefore, each has a different view of what is right.

Preventing cultural conflicts is possible with increased awareness of our own attitudes as well as sensitivity to cross-cultural differences. Developing intercultural sensitivity does not mean that we need to lose our cultural identities—but rather that we recognize cultural influences within ourselves and within others.

(Based on D. R. Levine & M. B. Adelman: *Beyond Language*, Chapter 9)

Notes

sophisticated 老练的,富有经验的
analogous to... 与……相似的
persistent 持续存在的
divergent 有分歧的;有差异的
ethnocentric 有种族或民族优越感的
identity 身份,特性

Questions

1. What kind of problems are people likely to meet when they visit a foreign country?

2. How can you understand the sentence "The definition of intercultural communication is simple, but the process is complex"?

3. What may lead to problems or difficulties in intercultural communication?

Text B

The Era of Intercultural Communication

In the past most human beings were born, lived, and died within a limited geographical area, never encountering people of other faces and/or cultural backgrounds. Such an existence, however, no longer prevails in the world. Even members of once isolated groups of people now frequently have contact with members of other cultural groups.

H.M. McLuhan characterized today's world as a "global village" because of the rapid expansion of worldwide transportation and communication networks. We can now board a plane and fly anywhere in the world in a matter of hours. Communication satellites, sophisticated television transmission equipment, and the World Wide Web now allow people throughout the world to share information and ideas at the same time.

Nowadays, people all over the world are faced with the same environmental issues, such as pollution, that affect all cultures. It has become clear that pollution does not observe geographic and cultural boundaries. We are beginning to realize that we must work together to solve these problems or face common disasters.

As the population of the world has increased, it has become more difficult to remain detached and isolated from global tensions and conflicts. When people of different nationalities and ethnic origins, who frequently speak different languages and hold different convictions, attempt to work and live together, conflicts can easily arise. Recent events have shown that hostility anywhere has the potential to become hostility everywhere.

And we should not forget that the reality of a global economy makes today's contacts far more commonplace than in any other period of the world's history. Multinational corporations now participate in various international business arrangements. Each country's economy is now tied to the economic fortunes of others. This means that it would not be unusual for you to work for an organization that does business in many countries or for you to conduct business in remote parts of the world.

In a world of international interdependence, the ability to understand and communicate effectively with people from other cultures takes on extreme urgency. However, we may find intercultural communication different from communication within our own cultural group. Even if we overcome the natural barriers of language difference, we may fail to understand and to be understood. Misunderstanding may even become the rule rather than the exception. And, if we are unaware of the significant role culture plays in communication, we may place the blame for communication failure on other people.

It is recognized widely that one of the characteristics separating humans from other animals is our development of culture. The development of human culture is made possible through communication, and it is through communication that culture is transmitted from one generation to another. Culture and communication are intertwined so closely that E. Hall maintains that "culture is communication" and "communication is culture."

In other words, we communicate the way we do because we are raised in a particular culture and learn its language, rules, and norms. Because we learn the language, rules, and norms of our culture by a very early age (between five and ten years old), however, we generally are unaware of how culture influences our behavior in general and our communication in particular.

When we communicate with people from other cultures, we often are confronted with languages, rules, and norms different from our own. Confronting these differences can be a source of insight into the rules and norms of our own culture, as well as being a source of frustration or gratification.

Therefore, in order to minimize misunderstandings when we communicate with people from other cultures, what we have to learn is to understand culture, communication, how culture influences communication, and the process of communication between people from different cultures. Such knowledge is extremely important. In fact, it is necessary if we are to comprehend fully the daily events of today's multicultural world. It will help us analyze our intercultural encounters in order to determine where misunderstandings occur and determine how these misunderstandings can be minimized in future interactions. This is important not only to decrease misunderstandings but also to make the world a safer place for all of us to live.

(Adapted from W. B. Gudykunst & Y. Y. Kim: *Communicating with Strangers*, Introduction)

Notes

prevail 盛行,流行

H. M. McLuhan 麦克卢汉 (1911—1980), 加拿大传播学家

the rule rather than the exception 常态而非例外

intertwine 紧密相连

E. Hall 霍尔(1914—2009),美国人类学家

gratification 满意;喜悦

Questions

1. Which changes have occurred to people's way of life in the modern era? Which factors lead to these changes?

2. Why is intercultural understanding important in modern society?

3. How can you understand the relationship between communication and culture in this global era?

Exploration

"Where are you from?" This is what people often ask each other. Why do you think people do it? Nowadays people are much more mobile than before. It is natural that people from different places have to work and live together. Suppose you are a native of the place where you are now, how would you view and treat people who have come from other places and look somewhat different from you do? If you are not a native of the place, how would you like to be treated by the local people?

Intercultural communication includes communication between people of different groups living within the same society. The social harmony that we are striving to achieve depends very much on communicating successfully with one another. Are there any people in our society who have lived among us but seldom been treated seriously by us? Are you curious about how people of other social groups live? Do you often communicate with persons belonging to a different social group? How do you usually do when communicating with them?

Cases for Discussion

Case 1

Professor Lin has published a book on the differences between Chinese and American culture. One day, he met Andrew who was teaching English in China. When Andrew found that Professor Lin was the author of the book that he had been trying to buy, he asked Professor Lin whether Professor Lin had any spare copies that he could buy because all the bookstores he went to had run out of the book.

Professor Lin promised that he would send Andrew a copy of his book. A week later, Andrew received a book along with a note that said the book was a gift. Andrew was uncomfortable about this and called Professor Lin to thank him.

Questions

1. Why was Andrew uncomfortable when receiving the book and the note sent by Professor Lin?
2. If you were Professor Lin, what would you do to avoid this?

Case 2

A young Japanese student came to the United States, and he was overwhelmed by the cordial reception he was given. He said, "The American people are wonderful. They are so warm, so friendly—much beyond my expectations."

Some time later while traveling in the West, this same young man had dinner with an American family and remarked that he greatly admired the country's efficiency, organization, and accomplishment. But, he said, there was one thing he would never quite understand, and that was why Americans were so cold and distant. His host was deeply hurt.

The point here is that both the first and last statements by the young man are typical. Very often, upon arrival in this country the foreign visitors are astonished by the warmth and friendliness of the American people. But often after a few months they begin to feel homesick and lonely, and they blame the Americans for causing these feelings by being cold. Now, why is this?

Questions

1. What had made the Japanese young man change his view about Americans?
2. What can you infer about American friendship based on this case?

Case 3

An American university student Tom is active in a foreign student club at his university and has several good friends from different countries. One of them tells Tom his parents and sister will be visiting, and he asks Tom if he would like to meet them. Tom invites all of them to visit his home one afternoon.

They arrive and present him with a nicely wrapped gift. Tom tells them they needn't have brought anything, but thanks them and proceeds to open the gift, which turns out to be a very pretty vase from their country. He thanks them again. He senses some awkwardness and realizes that he has not offered them anything to drink. "Would you like coffee or tea or a soft drink?" he asks. They all refuse. Things seem more awkward now. But he talks a little of their country, about studies at the university, about the cost of living, and eventually the father whispers something to his son. "I think we must be leaving to return to the hotel," he says. Everybody stands up, shakes hands, and they start to leave. "Please come and visit again," Tom says as he stands up and watches the family walk to the door, open it, and disappear down the hall.

Two days later, in a very indirect way, Tom learns from another friend that the visitors thought he was a rude host.

Questions

1. Why is Tom considered a rude host by his visitors? Try to figure out at least three things among the following Tom does that are regarded to be impolite.

a. Tom invites them to visit his home but does not invite them to have dinner with him.

b. Tom opens the gift as soon as he is presented with it.

c. Tom thanks them only twice for the gift.

d. Tom does not make a second offer of drinks when they refuse the first.

e. Tom talks about the cost of living in the U.S.A.

f. Tom does not ask them to stay longer when they say they must be leaving.

g. Tom does not go out to see them off.

h. Tom does not promise to return them a visit later.

2. How can you explain the fact that Tom is misunderstood when he actually wants to be kind and friendly to the visitors?

Readings for Further Study

1
Discovering Problems in Intercultural Communication

While visiting Egypt, Richard, an engineer from the United States, was invited to a spectacular dinner at the home of an Egyptian friend. And what a dinner it was! Clearly the host and hostess had gone out of their way to entertain him. Yet, as he was leaving their home he made a special effort to thank them for their dinner and sensed something he said was wrong. Something about his sincere complements was misunderstood.

In Japan he had an even less pleasant experience though he thought he had handled it well. A number of serious mistakes had occurred in a project he was supervising. While the fault did not lie with any one person, he was a supervisor and at least partly to blame. At a special meeting called to discuss the problem, poor Richard made an effort to explain in detail why he had done what he had done. He wanted to show that anybody in the same situation could have made the same mistake and to tacitly suggest that he should not be blamed unduly. He even went to the trouble of distributing materials which explained the situation rather clearly. And yet, even during his explanation, he sensed that something he was saying or doing was wrong.

Even in England where he felt more at home, where he had no problems with language, this kind of misunderstanding occurred. He had been invited to take tea with one of his colleagues, a purely social, relaxed occasion. Tea was served along with sugar and cream. As he helped himself to some sugar and cream, he again sensed he had done something wrong. But what went wrong?

We should know that in Egypt as in many cultures, the human relationship is valued so highly that it is not expressed in an objective and impersonal way. While Americans certainly value human relationships, they are more likely to speak of them in less personal, more objective terms. In this case, Richard's mistake might be that he chose to praise the food itself rather than the total evening, for which the food was simply the setting or excuse. For his host and hostess it was as if he had attended an art exhibit and complimented the artist by saying,

"What beautiful frames your pictures are in."

In Japan the situation may be more complicated. For this example we can simply say that Japanese people value order and harmony among persons in a group, and that the organization itself—be it a family or a corporation—is more valued than the characteristics of any particular member. While this feeling is not alien to Americans—or to any society—Americans stress individuality as a value and are apt to assert individual differences when they seem justifiably in conflict with the goals or values of the group. In this case, Richard's mistake was in making great efforts to defend himself. Let the others assume that the errors were not intentional, but it is not right to defend yourself, even when your unstated intent is to assist the group by warning others of similar mistakes. A simple apology and acceptance of the blame would have been appropriate.

When it comes to England, though there are some significant differences in language and language style, we expect fewer problems between Americans and Englishmen than between Americans and almost any other group. In this case we might look beyond the gesture of taking sugar or cream to the values expressed in this gesture: for Americans, "Help yourself"; for the English counterpart, "Be my guest." American and English people equally enjoy entertaining and being entertained but they differ somewhat in the value of the distinction. Typically, the ideal guest at an American party is one who "makes himself at home," even to the point of answering the door or fixing his own drink. For persons in many other societies, including at least this English host, such guest behavior is presumptuous or rude.

In analyzing apparent problems of communication across cultures, it is all too tempting to look first for difficulties posed by language misinterpretation or assume some nonverbal indiscretion. But we have tried to suggest through these brief discussions of Richard's problems that the misunderstanding or misbehavior more likely resides elsewhere, in the subtler but consistent cultural patterns of behavior that become understandable when we appreciate difference in cultural values. Thus what we first need, in attempting to analyze any such situation, is not necessarily more language skills or more information about a particular culture, but rather an openness to alternatives to our own conventional behavior. If we appreciate the logic of our own actions, we can more quickly imagine alternatives equally consistent with other values.

Notes

spectacular 相当丰盛的；壮观的
tacitly 心照不宣地，不言而喻地
unduly 过度地
alien 相异的，不熟悉的
justifiably 正当地；情有可原地
presumptuous 专横的
indiscretion 不慎重；不明智

Questions

1. Why were Richard's sincere compliments misunderstood in the Egyptian family?

2. What was wrong in the way Richard dealt with the problem in Japan?

3. Which behavior was considered improper in England when Richard was taking tea?

4. Do you think it is always right or possible for us to do as the Romans do when in Rome?

2
Communicating across Cultures in Today's World

Many years ago, the word "neighbor" referred to people very much like one's self—similar in dress, in diet, in custom, in language—who happened to live next door. Today relatively few people are surrounded by neighbors who are cultural **replicas** of themselves. Tomorrow we can expect to spend most of our lives in the company of neighbors who will speak in a different tongue, seek different values, move at a different pace, and interact according to a different norm. Within a decade or two the probability of spending part of one's life in a foreign culture will exceed the probability a hundred years ago of ever leaving the town in which one was born.

The technological feasibility of such a global village is no longer in doubt. The means already exist: in telecommunication systems linking the world by satellite, in aircraft capable of moving people faster than the speed of sound, in computers which can **disgorge** facts more rapidly than men can formulate their questions. The methods for bringing people closer physically and electronically are clearly at hand. What is in doubt is whether the erosion of cultural boundaries through technology will bring the realization of a dream or a nightmare. Will a global village be a mere collection or a true community of men? Will its residents be neighbors capable of respecting and utilizing their differences, or clusters of strangers living in ghettos and united only in their **antipathies** for others?

It has taken centuries to learn how to live harmoniously in the family, the tribe, the city state, and the nation. And now we are forced into a great leap from the mutual suspicion and hostility that have marked the past relations between peoples into a world in which mutual respect and comprehension are requisite.

Even events of recent decades provide little basis for optimism. Increasing contact has brought no **millennium** in human relations. If anything, it has appeared to intensify the divisions among people rather than to create a broader intimacy. Every new reduction in physical distance has made us more painfully aware of the psychic distance that divides people and has increased alarm over real or imagined differences. Wider access to more people will be a doubtful victory if human beings find they have nothing to say to one another or cannot stand to listen to each other.

In the world of tomorrow we can expect to live—not merely vacation—in societies which seek different values and abide by different codes. There we will be surrounded by foreigners for long periods of time, working with others in the closest possible relationships. If people currently show little tolerance or talent for encounters with alien cultures, how can they learn to deal with constant and inescapable coexistence?

Anyone who has truly struggled to comprehend another person—even those closest and most like himself or herself—will appreciate the immensity of the challenge of intercultural communication. Human understanding is by no means guaranteed because communicators share the same dictionary. (Within the United States, where people inhabit a common territory and possess a common language, mutual understanding among Mexican Americans, White Americans, Black Americans, Indian Americans—to say nothing of old and young, poor and rich, male and female, pro-establishment and anti-establishment cultures—is a **sporadic** and unreliable occurrence.)

As we move or are driven toward a global village and increasingly frequent cultural contact, we need more than simply greater factual knowledge of each other. We need, more specifically, to identify what distinguish one culture from another. For to grasp the way in which other cultures perceive the world, and the assumptions and values that are the foundation of these perceptions, is to gain access to the experience of other human beings. Access to the world view and the communicative style of other cultures may not only enlarge our own way of experiencing the world but enable us to maintain constructive relationships with societies that operate according to a different logic than our own.

When people communicate between cultures, where communicative rules as well as the substance of experience differs, the problems multiply. But so, too, does the number of interpretations and alternatives. If it is true that the more people differ the harder it is for them to understand each other, it is equally true that the more they differ the more they have to teach and learn from each other. To do so, of course, there must be mutual respect and sufficient curiosity to overcome the frustrations that occur as they **flounder** from one misunderstanding to another.

(Adapted from D. C. Barnlund: *Communication in a Global Village*)

Notes

replica 一模一样的人或物	millennium 幸福时代
disgorge 交出，拿出	sporadic 偶尔发生的
antipathy 反感，厌恶	flounder 胡乱地说话或做事

Questions

1. Why does the author say a global village is technologically feasible now?

2. According to the author, can technological progress really bridge the gap in intercultural communication?

3. What should people be armed with in cultural contact of the global village?

Summary

1. The rapid expansion of worldwide transportation and communication network results in a global village, where people from different cultures are coming into more contact with one another than ever before.

2. Intercultural communication is communication between members of different cultures. Misunderstandings and conflicts are likely to arise in this process when there is little or no awareness of diverse cultural values and beliefs.

3. As people are driven toward a global village and confronted with increasingly frequent intercultural encounters, it is necessary to enhance their intercultural awareness and sensitivity.

4. In a world of international interdependence, the ability to understand and communicate effectively with people from other cultures takes on extreme urgency.

Chapter 2 Communication

Every tale can be told in a different way.

—Greek proverb

Chapter 2 Communication

Preview Questions

1. What roles does communication play in our life?
2. Can you define in your own words what communication is?

Text A

A Wide-Angle View of Communication

From birth to death, all types of communication play an integral part in your life. Whatever your occupation or leisure-time activities is, communication of one form or another has a role. In fact, if people were asked to analyze how they spend most of their waking day, the prime responses would be "communicating" or "being communicated to." In reality, communication is our link to the rest of humanity.

But what is communication? And what is it we seek to accomplish with it? Let us begin to answer these questions by examining what we consider to be the essential ingredients of communication.

Senders and receivers

Communication involves people who send and receive messages, sometimes simultaneously. This means that the role of sender or receiver is not restricted to any one party to the communication process; instead, we play both roles.

There are times when it seems as if communication is predominantly one way: receivers of messages fail to react; senders of messages fail to consider the reactions of the receiver before sending another message. But for communication to be effective, the messages people send to others should, at least in part, be determined by the messages received from them.

Field of experience

We each carry our field of experience with us wherever we go. When the people communicating have had similar life experiences, chances are they will be able to relate to each other in an effective way. However, to the extent that their life experiences have been different, they will probably have difficulty interacting with or understanding each other. As our storehouses of experience diverge, it becomes harder for us to share meaning. Conversely, as storehouses of experience converge, the sharing of meaning becomes easier.

Messages

The message is the content of a communicative act. People communicate a wide variety of messages. Some of these messages are private (a smile accompanied by an "I love you"), while others are directed at millions (a network television show, a mass-market paperback). Some messages are sent intentionally (I want you to know), while others are sent accidentally (I didn't realize you were watching me). But as long as someone is there to interpret the results of a sender's efforts, a message is being sent. Thus, we can say that everything a sender does or says has potential message value.

Consequently, whether you smile, listen, renew a magazine subscription, watch a particular TV program, or turn away from a person, you are communicating some message, and your message is having some effect.

Channels

We may send our messages to receivers through a variety of sensory channels. We may use sound, sight, smell, taste, touch, or any combination of these to carry a message. Some channels are more effective at communicating messages than others, and the nature of the channel selected affects the way a message will be processed. The impact of a message changes as the channel used to transmit it changes. Experience shows that most of us have channel preferences; that is, we prefer to rely on one or more channels while disregarding others. Which channels are you most attuned to? Why? Adept communicators are channel switchers who recognize that human communication today is an ever-expanding, multichanneled event.

Noise

Noise is anything that interferes with the ability to send and/or receive messages. Thus, while noise could be sound, it does not necessarily have to be sound. It could also be physical discomfort (a headache), psychological makeup (a poor self-concept, an inflated ego, or a high level of defensiveness), semantic misunderstandings (as when people give different meanings to words and phrases or use different words and phrases to mean the same thing), or the environment (a sparsely furnished room, a dimly lit office).

The important point to remember is that noise can function as a communication barrier. As noise increases, the chances for effective communication usually decrease, and as noise decreases, the chances for effective communication usually rise.

Feedback

Feedback returns information to the sender of a message, thereby enabling the sender to determine whether the message was received or correctly understood. There are at least three ways of looking at feedback.

First, it can be positive or negative. Positive feedback encourages sources to continue sending similar messages. In contrast, negative feedback discourages sources from encoding similar messages.

Second, feedback can be immediate or delayed; and third, it can be free or limited. In an immediate and free feedback condition, the reactions of the receiver are directly and freely communicated to and perceived by the source. At a political rally a speaker knows immediately whether the audience in the hall is friendly or unfriendly. In contrast, if you want to communicate your opinion of a newspaper article to the editor, before your views are received by the intended party, and printed, several days or perhaps even weeks might elapse.

Feedback serves useful functions for both senders and receivers: it provides senders with the opportunity to measure how they are coming across, and it provides receivers with the opportunity to exert some influence over the communication process.

Effect

Every communication has an outcome; that is, it has some effect on the persons who are a party to it, though the effect may not always be immediately observable. The consequence may be monetary, cognitive, physical, or emotional. For example, people may profit from the communication, or learn something, or alter their appearance or self-image.

Context

Finally, every communication takes place in some context, or setting. Sometimes, the context is so natural that we fail to notice it; at other times, the context makes such an impression on us that we make a conscious effort to control our behavior because of it. For example, consider the extent to which your behavior would change if you were to move from a park to a political rally, to a movie theater, to a funeral home. Every context provides us with rules or norms for interaction. Sometimes place, time, and the people with us affect us without our being aware of it.

Notes

predominantly 主要地
diverge 歧义；背离
converge 会合；集中
attune to 习惯于，适应于
adept 熟练的；内行的
inflated ego 膨胀的自尊心
defensiveness 戒备心
semantic 语义上的

Questions

1. What do you think of the integral part that communication plays in our life?

2. What are the essential ingredients of communication? What kind of function does each serve in the communicative process?

3. What can be done to improve human communication in modern life?

Text B

Defining Communication

Communication is complex and multidimensional, then it can be defined in the following way: "Communication is a dynamic, systematic process in which meanings are created and reflected in human interaction with symbols."

Communication is a dynamic process

First, and perhaps most important, communication is an ongoing activity. It is not fixed. Communication is like a motion picture, not a single snapshot. A word or action does not stay frozen when we communicate; it is immediately replaced with yet another word or action. We constantly are affected by other people's messages and, as a consequence, are always changing.

Second, communication is dynamic because once a word or an action is employed, it cannot be retracted. Once an event takes place, we cannot have it over—perhaps we can experience a similar event, but not an identical one. An Asian proverb makes much the same point: "Once the arrow has been shot it cannot be recalled."

Third, all the elements of communication constantly interact with each other. We send words, create actions, watch the response of those around us, and listen to our partners all at the same time.

Finally, communication is dynamic because inattention pervades our communication behavior. Briefly survey your own actions and you will realize that your mind often does not like what it is doing and hence dashes from idea to idea, seeking something it does like. We often shift topics in the middle of a sentence, and research shows that when we listen, our attention span is brief. This trait of communication is so common that in Buddhist writing it is said, "The mind is fickle and flighty. It flies after fancies wherever it likes: it is difficult indeed to restrain."

Communication is systemic

Communication does not occur in a vacuum, but rather is part of a larger system.

We send and receive messages not in isolation, but in a specific setting. Put more simply, setting and environment help determine the words and actions we generate and the meanings we give the symbols produced by other people. Dress, language, topic selection, and the like are all adapted to context.

Elements associated with the systemic nature of communication are place, occasion, time, and number of participants. Even though these are found in all communication encounters, culture influences how we respond to them. Either consciously or unconsciously, we know the prevailing rules, many of which are rooted in our culture. For example, nearly all cultures have religious buildings, but the rules of behavior in those buildings are culturally based. In Mexico, men and women go to church together and remain quiet. In Iran, men and women do not worship together, and chanting instead of silence is the rule.

The occasion of the communication encounter also controls the behavior of the participants. You know from your own experience that an auditorium can be the occasion for a graduation ceremony, play, dance, or memorial service. Each of these occasions calls for a distinctly different type of behavior, and each culture has its own specifications for these behaviors.

The influence of time on communication is so subtle that its impact is often overlooked. How do you feel when someone keeps you waiting for a long time? Do you respond to a phone call at 2:00 a.m. the same way you do to one at 2 p.m.? Do you find yourself rushing the conversation when you know you have very little time to spend with someone? The answers to these questions show that the clock often controls our actions. Every communication event takes place on a time-space continuum and the amount of time allotted, whether it be for social conversation or a formal speech, affects that event. Cultures as well as people use time to communicate.

The number of people with whom you communicate also affects the flow of communication. You feel and act differently if you are speaking with one person, in a group, or before a great many people. Cultures also respond to changes in number. For example, people in Japan find group interaction much to their liking, yet feel extremely uncomfortable when they have to give a formal public speech.

Communication is symbolic

Part of our definition calls attention to the fact the humans are symbol-making creatures. We employ symbols to share our internal states. Other animals may participate in the communication process, but none of them has our unique communication capabilities: through millions of years of physical evolution, and thousands of years of cultural evolution, we are able to generate, receive, store, and manipulate symbols. This sophisticated system allows us to use a symbol—be it a sound, a mark on paper, a stature, Braille, a movement, or a painting—to represent something else.

Although all cultures use symbols, they usually assign their own meanings to them. Not only do Mexicans say *perro* for dog, but the image they form when they hear the sound is quite different from the one Americans form. In addition to having different meanings for symbols, cultures also use these symbols for different purposes. In America and much of Europe, the prevalent view is that communication is used to get things done. In contrast, people in Japan and China believe information is internalized by most members of the culture, so not much needs to be coded. Symbols are at the core of communication and symbols, by virtue of their standing for something else, giving us an opportunity to share our personal realities.

(Adapted from L. A. Samovar et al.: *Communication between Cultures*, Chapter 2)

Notes

multidimensional 多维的
snapshot 快照
pervade 渗透;弥漫
The mind is fickle and flighty. 思维是变化多端,反复无常的。
chanting 有节奏地、反复地唱或喊
Braille 盲文
internalized 内在化的,同化的
by virtue of 由于,因为;借助,凭借

Questions

1. What does the author mean by saying "communication is complex and multidimensional"?

2. How do you understand the relationship between communication and culture? Can you provide an example to show this kind of relationship?

3. Why is using symbols very essential to communication?

Exploration

The danger of misinterpretation is greatest among people who actually speak different native tongues, or come from different cultural backgrounds.

Apart from language differences and nonverbal misinterpretations, there may be a lot of pitfalls in the intercultural communication.

For instance, many people naively assume there are sufficient similarities among peoples of the world to make communication easy. We are likely to expect that since the foreign person is dressed appropriately and speaks our language, he or she will have similar thoughts and feelings as we have.

Besides, the tendency to assume that our own culture or way of life is the most natural is another pitfall. It will prevent us from comprehending thoughts and feelings of other people from their point of view.

Try to find out what other pitfalls that may exist in intercultural communication.

Cases for Discussion

Case 1

English is widely used all over the world. Sometimes its use as a second or foreign language may cause problems in communication. For instance, we can find commercial signs written in English in many different countries, some of which can be quite misleading and funny as well.

Read the following and guess the meaning that is originally intended to convey.

1. Is forbidden to steal hotel towels please. If you are not a person to do such a thing please not to read notice. *(From a Tokyo hotel)*

2. The lift is being fixed for the next day. During that time we regret that you will be unbearable. *(In a Bucharest hotel lobby)*

3. Our wines leave you nothing to hope for. *(On the menu of a Swiss restaurant)*

4. It is forbidden to enter a woman even a foreigner if dressed as a man. *(In a Bangkok temple)*

5. Ladies are requested not to have children at the bar. *(In a Norwegian cocktail lounge)*

6. We take your bags and send them in all directions. *(In a Copenhagen airline office)*

7. It is strictly forbidden on our black forest camping site that people of different sex, for instance, men and women, live together in one tent unless they are married with each other for that purpose. *(A sign posted in a German park)*

8. Specialist in Women and Other Diseases. *(A sign outside a doctor's office in Rome)*

Questions

1. What corrections will you make on the above mistranslations?

2. Have you ever found some similar cases of mistranslation in our life? If you have, what are they?

Case 2

In intercultural communication, even simple things such as saying "yes" or "no" are very important, for in different cultures a "yes" may mean different things, and there are different ways of saying "no".

Once, an American businessman was reviewing an important contract with his Japanese counterpart.

"We've got to work together," the American said.

"Hai," the Japanese smiled. (Hai is the Japanese word for yes.)

"We're going to try for a 50-50 partnership," the American said.

"Hai."

"We will use American know-how and a Japanese work force."

"Hai."

After this exchange, the American executive might very well assume he had a hard and fast agreement. But nothing could be further from the truth.

When he said hai, the Japanese businessman was simply telling the man across the table that he heard what he was saying. There was no agreement.

Questions

1. Can you find some cases in which 是 in Chinese does not mean "yes" in English?
2. How would you put the following into Chinese?

   1) —Please don't say that.

   —Yes, I will.

   2) —I know what he wants.

   —Yes?

   —Money!

   3) —Waiter!

   —Yes, sir.

   4) —Yes?

   —I'd like two tickets, please.

   5) —Everything will be all right soon, yes?

Case 3

Wan is a student who is taking several classes at an American university. He does not know any of the students in his classes so he decides to join a club of the university. He chooses the ping-pong club since he really enjoys the game. At the beginning of the first club meeting, a student named George begins talking to him.

George: Hi. How ya doing?

Wan: Uh, fine.

George: Ya been here before?

Wan: No.

George: Ya play a lot ping-pong?

Wan: Yes.

George: Well, this is the place to come.

Wan: *(No response. He is silent.)*

George: Uh, what classes are you taking?

Wan: Electronics, Computer 1A... *(George interrupts)*

George: I'm taking computer 1A, too. Are you in the class that meets on Mondays and Wednesdays at 10 a.m.?

Wan: Yes.

George: Umm. I have not seen you before. Do you like the class?

Wan: Yes, I do. *(Long silence)*

George: Um, uh, do you belong to any other clubs?

Wan: No.

George: I'm in a couple of others. *(Long pause.)*

Wan: *(He says nothing.)*

George: *(Looking at the ping-pong tables)* I see they're starting to play. You gonna play a game?

Wan: Yes.

George: Okay. Talk to you later. *(George walks away.)*

Questions

1. There is a lot of silence in the conversation. How do you think each person feels when there is silence? Why are George and Wan having difficulties talking to each other?

2. George says, "Talk to you later." Do you think George is really planning to talk to Wan later? What does this sentence mean?

Readings for Further Study

1
Understanding Aspects of Communication

Everyone communicates and has a notion of what communication is and how it takes place. Our purpose here is to **specify** our notions about the nature of communication.

Communication involves the use of symbols. Symbols are things used to stand for, or represent, something else. Symbols are not limited to words; they also include nonverbal displays and other objects (e.g., the flag). The important thing to remember is that symbols are symbols only because a group of people agree to consider them as such. There is no natural connection between any symbol and its **referent**; the relationships are **arbitrary** and vary from culture to culture.

Since it is impossible to transmit electrical impulses directly from one person's brain to that of another person, it is necessary for us to put out ideas into codes that can be transmitted. Encoding refers to the process of putting our thoughts, feelings, emotions, or attitudes, for example, into a form recognizable by others. The symbols used may be written, verbal, nonverbal, mathematical, or musical, to cite only a few. We refer to the encoded set of symbols as a message. Decoding is the process of perceiving and interpreting, or making sense of, incoming messages and stimuli from the environment. How we encode and decode messages is influenced by our experiential background, including not only our unique individual experiences but also our shared group and cultural ones.

We view communication as a process, without a beginning, an end, or a fixed sequence of events. It is not static, at rest. It is moving. The ingredients within a process interact: each affects all of the others. Viewing communication as a process, therefore, allows for recognition of its continuity, complexity, unrepeatability, and irreversibility.

Viewing communication as a process also forces us to recognize that the encoding and decoding of messages take place simultaneously. We do not simply encode a message and then wait for a response to decode. Rather, we continually are encoding and decoding information simultaneously whenever we communicate. The information we decode influences what we encode, and what we encode influences how we decode incoming stimuli.

Not only do the environment and objects in it influence our communication, but our perceptions of the environment also influence the way we behave. We view communication as a transaction and this implies that the people with whom we communicate influence our communication and we influence theirs.

Although messages can be transmitted from one person to another, meanings cannot. Since meanings are not determined solely by the message, the net result of any communication is a partial difference between the meanings held by the communicators. In other words, the meaning of the message one person encodes is never exactly the same as the meaning another person decodes. To say that meaning in communication is never totally the same for all communicators is not to say that communication is impossible or even difficult—only that it is imperfect.

We also have to remember that one cannot not communicate. Any behavior, or the absence of any behavior, communicates something if there is someone in the environment to notice the behavior, or its absence. Many intercultural misunderstandings, in fact, are due to the unintentional behavior of a person from one culture being perceived, interpreted, and reacted to by a person from another culture. In other words, behavior that was not meant to communicate was interpreted by another person and influenced the messages that person sends.

Consider an example of a businessperson from the United States negotiating a contract in an Arab culture. During the course of a meeting, the businessperson from the United States crosses her or his legs and in the process points the sole of her or his shoe toward an Arab. The person from the United States, in all likelihood, will not attach any meaning to this. The Arab, in contrast, could very likely interpret this behavior as an insult and react accordingly. Showing the sole of the foot does not mean anything in the United States. In Arab cultures, however, showing the sole of the foot to another person is considered an insult. The misunderstanding can only be explained by looking at behavior that was not intended to be meaningful.

(Adapted from W. B. Gudykunst & Y. Y. Kim: *Communicating with Strangers*, Introduction)

Notes

specify 详细说明	irreversibility 不可逆转性
referent 所指;指称对象	transaction 交易
arbitrary 任意的	

Questions

1. What is communication characterized by?

2. What kind of human behavior may cause misunderstandings in intercultural communication? What should people do to avoid them?

3. What are the aspects of communication discussed in the passage?

2
Communication and Its Characteristics

We begin with a basic assumption that communication has something to do with human behavior and the satisfaction of a need to interact with other human beings. This last aspect is known as communication hunger. Almost everyone needs social contact with other people, and this need is met through the exchange of messages that serve as bridges to unite otherwise isolated individuals.

Messages come into being through human behavior. When we talk, we obviously are behaving; when we wave, smile, frown, walk, shake our heads, or gesture, we also are behaving. Frequently these actions are messages; they are often used to communicate something to someone else. Before these behaviors can be called messages, they must meet two requirements. First, they must be observed by someone and second, they must elicit meaning. Another way to say this is that any behavior to which meaning is attributed is a message.

Attribution means that we take meaning which we already have and assign or attach it to behavior we observe in our environment. We might imagine that stored somewhere in our brain is a meaning reservoir in which we have stored all of the meanings we possess. These various meanings have developed throughout our lifetime as a result of our culture acting upon us as well as the result of our individual experiences within that culture. Meaning is relative to each of us in that we are all unique human beings with unique backgrounds and experiences.

When we encounter a behavior in our environment, we dip into our unique meaning reservoir and select from it the meaning we believe has the highest probability of being the most appropriate for the behavior we encounter and the social context in which the behavior occurs. Sometimes this works quite well, but at other times it lets us down and we misinterpret a message; we attribute the wrong meaning to the behavior we have observed.

Communication can thus be defined as a behavior-affecting process in which one person (a source) intentionally encodes and transmits a message through a channel to an intended audience (receivers) in order to induce a particular attitude or behavior. Communication is complete only when the intended audience receives the message, attributes meaning to it (decodes it), and is affected by it.

There are several other characteristics that, when understood, help clarify how communication actually operates.

First, communication is an on-going, ever-changing activity. As participants in communication we constantly are affected by other people's messages and, as a consequence, we undergo continual change. This means that as we go through life we do so as a continually changing individual.

A second characteristic of communication is its interactive nature. Communication must take place between source and receiver. Usually this implies two or more people. In this situation communication is characterized by the fact that both parties bring to a communication event their own unique backgrounds and experiences.

Third, communication is irreversible. Once we have said something and someone else has received and decoded the message, we cannot **retrieve** the message. We may send other messages in attempts to modify the effect, but we cannot eliminate it. This is one of the big problems that occur when we unconsciously or unintentionally send a message to someone.

Fourth, communication takes place in both physical and social context. When we interact with someone it is not in isolation but within a specific physical surrounding. The physical surrounding includes specific physical objects such as furniture, window coverings, floor coverings, lighting, noise levels, **acoustics**, presence of absence of physical **clutter**, as well as competing messages. Many aspects of the physical environment can and do affect communication. The comfort or discomfort of a chair, the color of walls, or total atmosphere of a room are but a few.

Social context defines the types of social relationships that exist between source and receiver. In American culture people pay much less attention to **hierarchies** than people do in other cultures. Nevertheless, such differences as teacher-student, employer-employee, parent-child, admiral-seaman, senator-citizen, friend-enemy, physician-patient, and judge-attorney affect the communication process. And, quite frequently, the physical surroundings help define the social context. The employer may sit behind a desk while the employee stands before the desk to receive an admonition.

No matter what the social context, there will be some effect on communication. This social environment reflects the way people live, how they come to interact with and get along in their world. In short, this social environment is culture, and if we truly are to understand communication, we must also understand culture.

(Adapted from L. A. Samovar et al.: *Understanding Intercultural Communication*, Chapter 1)

Notes

otherwise isolated individuals 原本孤立的	acoustics 音响效果
elicit 引出	clutter 杂物
retrieve 找回,收回	hierarchy 等级

Questions

1. Can you give an example from your life experiences to show that communication is an ever-changing activity?

2. What can we do about it when we unconsciously or unintentionally send a message to others?

3. How is communication influenced by physical as well as social context?

Summary

1. Communication plays an integral part in human life. It involves the following essential ingredients: senders and receivers, field of experience, messages, channels, noise, feedback, effect and context. All these ingredients are interacted with each other.

2. Communication is complex and multidimensional. It is a dynamic, systemic process in which meanings are created and reflected in human interaction with symbols.

3. Although all cultures use symbols, cultures have different meanings for symbols, and also use these symbols for different purposes.

4. How people encode and decode messages in communication is influenced by their backgrounds, including not only their unique individual experiences but also their shared group and cultural backgrounds.

Chapter 3 Culture

Human beings draw close to one another by their common nature, but habits and customs keep them apart.

—Confucian saying

Chapter 3 Culture

Preview Questions

1. What does the term "culture" or 文化 usually mean to you?
2. What behaviors of ours are innate and what are learned in the cultural environment?

Text A

What Is Culture

We now move from communication to culture. The transition should be a smooth one, for as Hall reminds us, "Culture is communication and communication is culture."

People learn to think, feel, believe, and act as they do because of the messages that have been communicated to them, and those messages all bear the stamp of culture. This omnipresent quality of culture leads Hall to conclude that "there is not one aspect of human life that is not touched and altered by culture." In many ways, Hall is correct: culture is everything and everywhere. And more important, at least for our purposes, culture governs and defines the conditions and circumstances under which various messages may or may not be sent, noticed, or interpreted. Remember, we are not born knowing how to dress, what toys to play with, what to eat, which gods to worship, or how to spend our money and our time. Culture is both teacher and textbook. From how much eye contact we employ in conversations to explanations of why we get sick, culture plays a dominant role in our lives. When cultures differ, communication practices may also differ. In modern society, different people communicate in different ways, as do people in different societies around the world; and the way people communicate is the way they live. It is their culture. Who talks with whom? How? And about what? These are questions of communication and culture. Communication and culture are inseparable.

Because culture conditions us toward one particular mode of communication over another, it is imperative that we understand how culture operates as a first step toward improving intercultural communication.

As was the case with communication, many definitions have been suggested for culture. They range from all-encompassing ones ("it is everything") to narrower ones ("it is opera, art, and ballet"), but none of them seems to be able to tell us everything about culture. The following definitions are just some of the well-known ones.

"Culture may be defined as what a society does and thinks." (Sapir, 1921)

"What really binds men together is their culture—the ideas and the standards they have in common." (R. Benedict, 1935)

"Culture is man's medium; there is not one aspect of human life that is not touched and altered by culture. This means personality, how people express themselves, (including shows of emotion), the way they think, how they move, how problems are solved, how their cities are planned and laid out, how transportation systems function and are organized, as well as how economic and government systems are put together and function." (Edward T. Hall, 1959)

"By 'culture', anthropology means the total life way of a people, the social legacy the individual acquires from his group. Or culture can be regarded as that part of the environment that is the creation of man." (Clyde Kluckhohn, 1965)

"A culture is a collection of beliefs, habits, living patterns, and behaviors which are held more or less in common by people who occupy particular geographic areas." (D. Brown, 1978)

"...culture is the collective programming of the mind which distinguishes the members of one group or society from those of another." (G. Hofstede, 1984)

"Culture is a mental set of windows through which all of life is viewed. It varies from individual to individual within a society, but it shares important characteristics with members of a society." (L. Beamer & I. Varner, 1995)

It is believed that culture evolved to serve the basic needs of laying out a predictable world in which each of us is firmly grounded and thus enable us to make sense of our surroundings. Thus, the influence of culture becomes habitual and subconscious and makes life easier, just as breathing, walking and other functions of the body are relegated to subconscious controls, freeing the conscious parts of the brain of this burden and releasing it for other activities.

In addition to making the world a less perplexing place, cultures have become people's primary means of satisfying three types of needs: basic needs (food, shelter, physical protection), derived needs (organization of work, distribution of food, defense, social control), and integrative needs (psychological security, social harmony, purpose in life). Each culture offers its people a number of options for satisfying any particular human need. Some of these options are widely shared across cultures, but many others are not. In other words, ends in themselves are far more universal than the roads taken to achieve those ends since the roads are determined locally in the specific culture.

(Based on L. A. Samovar et al.: *Communication between Cultures*, Chapter 2)

Notes

omnipresent 无所不在的	a predictable world 一个可预见的世界
imperative 必要的，迫近的	perplexing 使人困惑的
all-encompassing 包容一切的	

Questions

1. Which of the definitions given above do you prefer? Why?
2. What havc you lcarned from those definitions about culture?
3. Can you give some examples to show how culture serves basic human needs?

Text B

Culture as a Way to Satisfy Our Human Needs

A culture can also be understood as a particular way to satisfy our human needs.

All human beings have certain basic needs. Everyone of us needs to eat and to make friends, for instance. Abraham Maslow, a psychologist, has suggested that people all over the world share five basic needs:

1. The physiological needs. Our fundamental needs for things that keep us alive, things such as food, water, air, rest, clothing, and shelter, all necessary to sustain life. These needs come first. We must meet them or we will die.

2. The safety needs. First we need to stay alive, and then we need to be safe. There are two kinds of safety needs: the need to be physically safe and the need to be psychologically secure. That is why various insurance programs are becoming increasingly popular nowadays.

3. The belongingness needs. Once we are alive and safe, we then try to satisfy our social needs, the needs to be with and accepted by other people. For example, the need for friendship is universal.

4. The esteem needs. These are needs for recognition, respect, reputation. The needs involve self-esteem (thinking well of ourselves) and the esteem of others. Efforts to achieve, to accomplish, and to master things and people are often efforts to gain respect and attention from others and from ourselves.

5. The self-actualization needs. The highest need of a person is to actualize oneself, to reach one's full potential, to become all that he or she might be. Very few people ever satisfy this need completely, partly because we are too busy trying to satisfy our lower needs.

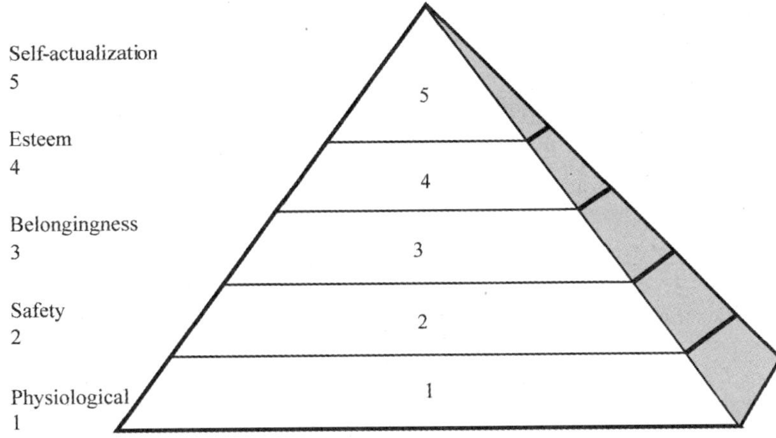

According to Abraham Maslow, people satisfy those needs in the order mentioned above. A good way to visualize the order is to think of a pyramid, as shown above(p.35). People are always trying to climb the pyramid. You have to climb over the first step before you can get to the second. You must pass the second before you reach the third, and so on.

Though the basic human needs are often said to be universally the same, people all over the world satisfy these needs in different ways. Each culture offers its people a number of options for satisfying any particular human need. Some of these options are widely shared across cultures, but many others are not. Just as Maslow has stated, ends in themselves are far more universal than the roads taken to achieve those ends since the roads are determined locally in the specific culture.

Every culture has its ways of doing things in daily life, such as ways of eating, drinking, dressing, finding shelter, making friends, marrying, and dealing with death. People have to learn the cultural ways of their community to satisfy their basic human needs. These ways are not something that the people in the group are born with. Instinctive behavior, on the other hand, is a pattern of behavior that an animal is born with. Spiders spinning their webs is an example. The mother spider does not teach her babies how to spin webs. (In fact, she is not even there when they are born.) Young spiders know how to do it when they are born.

As humans, we learn some of the ways of our culture by being taught by our parents or teachers. We learn more of the ways of our culture by growing up in it. We see how other people in our culture do things, and we do them the same way. We even learn how to think and feel in this way. Since we learn the ways of taking care our basic needs in the cultural group in which we grow up, our own culture seems very natural to us. We feel in our hearts that the way that we do things is the only right way to do them. Other people's cultures often make us laugh or feel disgusted or shocked.

Take eating as an example. All individuals must eat in order to survive, but what people eat, when they eat, and the manners in which they eat are all patterned by culture. No society views everything in its environment that is edible and might provide nourishment as food. Americans eat oysters but not snail. The French eat snails but not locusts. The Zulus eat locusts but not fish. The Jews eat fish but not pork. The Hindus eat pork but not beef. The Russians eat beef but not snakes. The Chinese eat snakes...

We all have ideas about what kinds of foods are good to eat. We also have ideas about what kinds of food are bad to eat. As a result, people from one culture often think the foods that people from another culture eat are disgusting or nauseating. When the famous boxer Muhammad Ali visited Africa, for example, one member of his group was shocked to see someone pick a butterfly and eat it. Many people would find it disgusting to eat rats, but there are many different cultures whose people regard rats as appropriate food.

Some people in Africa think African termites make a delicious meal. Many other people would probably be sick if they had to eat termites, but one hundred grams of termites contain more than twice as many calories and almost twice as much protein as one hundred grams of cooked hamburger. However, food likes and dislikes do not always seem related to nutrition. For example, broccoli is first on the list of the most nutritious common vegetables, but it is twenty-first on the list of vegetables that Americans like most to eat. Tomatoes are sixteenth on the list of most nutritious vegetables, but they are first on the list of vegetables that Americans like most to eat.

Dislike is not the only reason why some cultures will not eat a certain food. In some cultures, certain foods are taboo. Sometimes the food taboos may be so strong that just the thought of eating forbidden foods can cause an individual to feel ill. A Hindu vegetarian would feel this way about eating any kind of meat, an American about eating dogs, and a Muslim or orthodox Jew about eating pork.

However, we have to remember that, most of the time, the different ways that are the customs of different cultures are neither right nor wrong. It is simply that different people do the same things in different manners.

Notes

Abraham Maslow 亚伯拉罕·马斯洛(1908—1970),美国心理学家
actualize 实现
visualize 使可见,使直观化
edible 可食用的
nourishment 养料,养分
oyster 牡蛎
locust 蝗虫
Zulus(非洲东部) 祖鲁人
nauseating 令人作呕的
Muhammad Ali 穆罕默德·阿里(1942—2016),美国黑人拳王
termite 白蚁
calory 卡(路里)(热量单位)
protein 蛋白质
nutrition 营养
Hindu 印度人(的)
Muslim 伊斯兰教信徒
orthodox Jew 正统派犹太教徒

Questions

1. Do you agree that our lower needs always have to be satisfied before we can try to satisfy the higher needs?

2. What examples can you give about how people of different cultures achieve the same ends by taking different roads?

Exploration

Culture is reflected in the meanings people attach to various aspects of life: their way of looking at the world and their values, that is, what they consider as "good" and as "evil," what they consider as "true" and as "false," what they consider as "beautiful" and as "ugly," etc.

Do you think there is a universal concept of beauty? What do you think of the various beauty contests that seem to be very popular now in our society? What cultural values underlie these beauty contests and what influences do they have upon people, especially young people? Do you agree with those people who see such beauty contests as cultural threats to their traditional values? Why or why not?

Cases for Discussion

Case 1

Janice is a young American engineer working for a manufacturing joint venture near Nanjing. She and her husband George, who is teaching English at a university, are learning Chinese and enjoying their new life. They have been eager to get to know Chinese people better so were pleased when Liu, Janice's young co-worker, invited them to her home for dinner.

When Janice and George arrived, Liu introduced them to her husband Yang, and asked them to sit down at a table before 8 plates of various cold dishes. And a half-hour later she came back and sat down and the three began to eat. Yang came in from time to time to put dish after dish on the table. Most of the food was wonderful but neither George nor Janice could eat the fatty pork in pepper sauce or the sea cucumbers, and there was much more than they could eat. They kept wishing Yang would sit down so they could talk to him. Finally he did sit down to eat a bit, but quickly turned on the TV to show them all its high tech features. Soon it was time to go home.

Janice and George felt slightly depressed by this experience, but returned the invitation two weeks later. They decided to make a nice American meal and felt lucky to find olives, tomato juice, crackers and even some cheese in the hotel shop. They put these out as appetizers. For the main course they prepared spaghetti and a salad with dressing made from oil, vinegar, and some spices they found in the market.

When Liu and Yang arrived and began to have dinner, they took small bites of the appetizers and seemed surprised when both George and Janice sat down with them. They ate only a little spaghetti and did not finish the salad on their plates. George urged them to eat more but they refused and looked around expectantly. After a while, George cleared the table and served coffee and pastries. Yang and Liu each put four spoons of sugar into their coffee but did not drink much of it and ate only a bite or two of pastries.

After they left, George and Janice were upset, "We left their place so full that we couldn't walk but they're going to have to eat again when they get home. What went wrong?"

Notes

sea cucumber 海参
spaghetti 意大利面条
appetizer 开胃菜
pastry 酥皮点心

Questions

1. Why did Janice and George feel somewhat depressed by their experience of having dinner at Liu's home?

2. Why did Yang and Liu eat very little when they were invited by Janice and George for dinner?

Case 2

Peter and Li Hua were talking when a friend of Li Hua passed by.

"Hi, Xu Jia, when are we going to meet? You've been back from the States for two weeks by now!" Li Hua greeted him aloud.

"How about this Saturday? I'm sorry I've been really busy. There are so many friends I have to see."

When Xu Jia left, Peter could not help asking, "Is he a good friend of yours?"

"Oh, yes, we're the best of friends. He went to the States for half a year, and came back a while ago."

"If you're best friends, how come he said he needed to see others first?" Peter could not understand.

Questions

1. How will you define the word "friend" or "friendship" in your own words?
2. Can you find out the reason why Peter could not understand?

Case 3

An American woman was staying overnight for the first time with a Japanese family. After dinner, she and her hosts sat in the living room and discussed a variety of things: the family's trips abroad, things the guest should be sure to see while in Japan, etc. As the night wore on, the hosts politely and repeatedly asked if she wanted to take her bath. The guest replied that she was in no hurry and could wait until later. As a result, cross-cultural misunderstanding occurs.

Questions

1. Why did the Japanese hosts repeatedly ask the American woman to take her bath?
   A. The Japanese didn't like to have someone stay overnight at their home without the person thoroughly cleaning him-or herself.
   B. Taking a bath is usually one of the important ways the Japanese entertain their guests.
   C. The guest should take her bath first so that the family members could take theirs and then retire.
   D. The Japanese thought that the American woman was just being polite when she replied that she could wait until later.
2. What did the American woman fail to realize?

Readings for Further Study

1
Aspects of Culture

All men undergo the same life experiences such as birth, helplessness, illness, old age, and death. The biological potentialities of the species are the blocks with which cultures are built. The facts of nature also limit culture forms. No culture provides patterns for jumping over trees or for eating iron ore.

There is thus no "either-or" between nature and that special form of nurture called culture. Culture determinism is as one-sided as biological determinism. The two factors are interdependent. Culture arises out of human nature, and its forms are restricted both by man's biology and by natural laws. When a man eats, he is reacting to an internal "drive," namely, hunger contractions consequent upon the lowering of blood sugar, but his precise reaction to these internal stimuli cannot be predicted by physiological knowledge alone. Whether a healthy adult feels hungry twice, three times, or four times a day and the hours at which this feeling recurs is a question of culture. What he eats is of course limited by availability, but is also partly regulated by culture. Such selective, discriminative use of the environment is characteristically cultural.

Culture is created and transmitted by people. However, culture, like well-known concepts of the physical sciences, is a convenient abstraction. One never sees gravity. One sees bodies falling in regular ways. Similarly, one never sees culture as such. What is seen are regularities in the behavior or artifacts of a group that has adhered to a common tradition. The regularities are due to the existence of mental blueprints for the group.

Culture is a way of thinking, feeling, believing. It is the group's knowledge stored up (in memories of people; in books and objects) for future use. We study the products of this "mental" activity; the overt behavior, the speech and gestures and activities of people, and the tangible results of these things such as tools, houses, cornfields, and what not. It has been customary in lists of "culture traits" to include such things as watches or lawbooks. This is a convenient way of thinking about them, but in the solution of any important problem we must remember that they, in themselves, are nothing but metals, paper, and ink. What is important is that some men know how to make them, others set a value on them, are unhappy without them, direct their activities in relation to them, or disregard them.

The members of all human societies face some of the same unavoidable dilemmas, posed by biology and other facts of the human situation. This is why the basic categories of all cultures are so similar. Human culture without language is unthinkable. No culture fails to provide for aesthetic expression and aesthetic delight. Every culture supplies standardized orientations toward the deeper problems, such as death. Every culture is designed to perpetuate the group and its solidarity, to meet the demands of individuals for an orderly way of life and for satisfaction of biological needs.

However, the variations on these basic themes are numberless. Some languages are built up out of twenty basic sounds, others out of forty. Each culture dissects nature according to its own system of categories.

A culture is learned by individuals as the result of belonging to some particular group, and it constitutes that part of learned behavior which is shared with others. It is our social legacy, as contrasted with our organic heredity. It is one of the important factors which permits us to live together in an organized society, giving us ready-made solutions to our problems, helping us to predict the behavior of others, and permitting others to know what to expect of us.

(Adapted from C. Kluckhohn: *Mirror for Man*, Chapter 2)

Notes

contraction 收缩	solidarity 团结
aesthetic 美学的	

Questions

1. Why is the concept of "culture" important and useful?
2. How is culture related to nature? And how does culture affect human life?
3. How can culture be acquired in one's life?

2
High-Context and Low-Context Cultures

Edward Hall has observed that meaning and context are **inextricably** bound up with each other. While a linguistic code can be analyzed on some levels independent of context, in real life the code, the context, and the meaning can only be seen as different aspects of a single event.

He then defines the two key terms in the following manner:

A high-context (HC) communication is one in which most of the information is either in the physical context or internalized in the person, while very little is in the coded, explicit, transmitted part of the message. A low-context (LC) communication is just the opposite; i.e., the mass of the information is vested in the explicit code. Twins who have grown up together can and do communicate more economically (HC) than two lawyers in a courtroom during a trial (LC).

He categorizes cultures as being either high or low context, depending on the degree to which meaning comes from the settings for the words being exchanged. Hall maintains that although no culture exists exclusively at one end of the scale, most cultures can be placed along a scale showing their ranking on this particular dimension: some are high while others are low. (see the Table at P.44). American culture, while not on the bottom, is toward the lower end of the scale. China, the possessor of a great and complex culture, is on the high-context end of the scale.

In high-context cultures (Native American, Latin American, Japanese, Republic of Korea's (ROK's) as well as Chinese), people are very **homogeneous** with regard to experiences, information networks, and the like. As a result, for most normal transactions in daily life they do not require, nor do they expect, much in-depth, background information. Meaning, therefore, is not necessarily contained in words. In high-context cultures, information is provided through gestures, the use of space, and even silence. Meaning is also conveyed through status (age, sex, education, family background, title, and affiliations) and through an individual's informal friends and associates.

In low-context cultures (German, Swiss as well as American), the population is less homogeneous. This lack of a large pool of common experiences means that "each time they interact with others they need detailed background information." In low-context cultures, the verbal message contains most of the information and very little is embedded in the context or the participants.

This characteristic manifests itself in a host of ways. For example, the Asian mode of communication is often indirect and implicit, whereas Western communication tends to be direct and explicit—that is, everything needs to be stated. High-context cultures tend to be more aware of their surroundings and their environment and do not rely on verbal communication as their main information channel. In high-context cultures, so much information is available in the environment that it is unnecessary to verbalize everything. For instance, statements of affection, such as "I love you," are rare because the message is conveyed by the context.

In addition, members of low-context cultures expect messages to be detailed, clear-cut, and definite. If there are not enough data, or if the point being made is not apparent, members of these cultures will ask very blunt, even curt, questions. They feel uncomfortable with the vagueness and ambiguity often associated with limited data. On the other hand, high-context people are apt to become impatient and irritated when low-context people insist on giving them information they don't need.

Another problem is that people in high-context cultures perceive low-context people, who rely primarily on verbal messages for information, as less credible. They believe that silence often sends a better message than words, and anyone who needs words does not have the information. As the Indonesian proverb states, "Empty cans clatter the loudest."

Unless people from different cultures are aware of these subtle differences, communication misunderstandings between low-and high-context communicators can result. Japanese communicate by not stating things directly, while Americans usually do the opposite—"spell it out." The former is looking for meaning and understanding in what is not said. The latter places emphasis on sending and receiving accurate messages directly, usually by being articulate with words.

(Adapted from L. A. Samovar et al.: *Communication between Cultures*, Chapter 3)

Cultures arranged along the High-Context and Low-Context Dimension

High-Context Cultures
Japanese
Chinese
Rok's
African American
Native American
Arab
Greek
Latin
Italian
English
French
American
Scandinavian
German
German-Swiss
Low-Context Cultures

Notes

inextricably 无法摆脱地

affiliation 社会关系

homogeneous 同种类的，同性质的

Questions

1. Why are context, code, and meaning different aspects of a single event?

2. What is high-context communication and what is low-context communication?

3. What are the major differences between a high-context culture and a low-context one? How can people from these two different cultures avoid misunderstanding in communication?

Summary

1. Culture can be defined in many ways. This indicates that culture is all-inclusive； it is everything and everywhere.

2. Culture manifests itself in patterns of language and in forms of activity and behavior that act as models for both the common adaptive acts and the styles of communication.

3. A culture is learned by individuals as the result of belonging to some particular group， and it constitutes that part of learned behavior which is shared with others. It is our social legacy， as contrasted with our organic heredity.

4. Culture affects people in a deterministic manner from birth to death and the effect is found in everyday modes of behavior and in communication practices. When cultures vary， communication practices also vary.

Chapter 4 Cultural Differences

One man's meat is another man's poison.

—English proverb

Chapter 4 Cultural Differences

Preview Questions

1. In what aspects do you think our culture is different from other cultures?

2. Do you sometimes compare one culture with another? If you do, how do you usually do that?

Text A

Basic Differences between Cultures

There are so many dimensions on which cultures may differ. Then, how can we compare one culture with another to find out their similarities and differences?

American anthropologists, Clyde and Florence Kluckhohn, along with their fellow anthropologist Frederick Strodtbeck, have provided us with one of the needed tools for comparing cultures. Looking at the phenomenon of culture, they came up with five basic questions that get at the root of any culture's value system.

1. What is the character of innate human nature?	=Human nature orientation
2. What is the relation of Man to Nature?	=Man-Nature orientation
3. What is the temporal focus (time sense) of human life?	=Time orientation
4. What is the mode of human activity?	=Activity orientation
5. What is the mode of human relationships?	=Social orientation

The chart which follows (P.49) is an adaptation and simplification of one developed by Kluckhohns and Strodtbeck. It indicates the range of possible responses to the five orientations.

Orientation Beliefs & Behaviors

Human Nature →	Basically Evil	Mixture of Good And Evil	Basically Good
Relationship of Man to Nature →	Man Subjugated by Nature	Man in Harmony with Nature	Man The Master of Nature
Sense of Time →	Past-Oriented	Present-Oriented	Future oriented
Activity →	Being (Stress on who you are)	Growing (Stress on self-development)	Doing (Stress on action)
Social Relationships →	Authoritarian	Group-Oriented	Individualistic

Consider for a moment the five orientations. How would you describe the attitude of the majority of Americans toward each? Let's take a look at each of the five orientations to determine where a typical middle-class American might be expected to fit.

In respect to HUMAN NATURE, average, middle-class/mainstream Americans are generally optimistic, choosing to believe the best about a person until that person proves otherwise. We would place average Americans in the right-hand column (basically good) as far as Human Nature Orientation goes.

The Kluckhohns, however, placed Americans in the left-hand column (basically evil), citing the Christian belief in original sin. This may have been accurate reading for the 1950's, though we have our doubts. Certainly, whether Americans see human nature as good or evil, it is fair to say they accept it as changeable.

In the MAN-NATURE orientation, Americans see a clear separation between man and nature (this would be incomprehensible to many Orientals) and man is clearly held to be in charge. The idea that man can control his own destiny is totally alien to most of the world's cultures. Elsewhere people tend to believe that man is driven and controlled by Fate and can do very little, if anything, to influence it. Americans, on the other hand, have an insatiable drive to subdue, dominate, and control their natural environment.

Concerning orientation toward TIME, Americans are dominated by a belief in progress. They are future-oriented. This implies a strong task or goal orientation. They are very conscious too, that "time is money," and therefore not to be wasted. They have an optimistic faith in the future and what the future will bring. They tend to equate "change" with "improvement" and consider a rapid rate of change as normal.

As for ACTIVITY, Americans are so action-oriented that they cannot even conceive what it would be like to be "being—oriented." Indeed, they are hyperactive. They believe in keeping busy and productive at all times—even on vacation. As a result of this action-orientation, Americans have become very proficient at problem solving and decision making.

Their SOCIAL orientation is toward the importance of the individual and the equality of all people. Stress on the individual begins at a very early age when the American child is encouraged to be **autonomous**. It is an accepted rule that children (and adults) should make decisions for themselves, develop their own opinions, solve their own problems, have their own possessions. Friendly, informal, outgoing, and **extroverted**, Americans scorn rank and authority, even when they are the ones with the rank and authority. American bosses are the only supervisors in the world who would insist on being called by their first names by their subordinates. With a strong sense of individuality, family ties in America are relatively weak, especially when compared to the rest of the world.

Now, we come up with a picture of the American value system that looks like this:

		Basically Good (changeable)
		Man The Master of Nature
		Future -Oriented
		Doing
		Individualism

Let's look at the value systems of several other societies and compare them with the American system. We see many of the world's "traditional" cultures as follows:

Basically Evil		Mixture Good/Evil		
	unchangeable		unchangeable	
Man Subjugated by Nature				
Past-Oriented				
Being				
Authoritarian				

Here's how we view Arab cultures from a generalized perspective. There would be important variations, of course, from one specific culture to another—Egyptian, Saudi, Lebanese, etc. Notice that in one category—man-nature relationships—the Arabs seem to fall more or less equally into two of the classifications.

	Neutral		
		unchangeable	
Man Subjugated by Nature	Man in Harmony with Nature		
Past-Oriented			
Being			
Authoritarian			

Here's how we see the Japanese (a very complex culture and even more "contradictory" than the Arabs):

	Mixture Good/Evil		
		unchangeable	
	Man in Harmony with Nature		
Past-Oriented			Future-Oriented
	Self Development		Doing
Authoritarian	Group-Oriented		

The Kluckhohn chart only compares cultures on five basic orientations. It does not claim, therefore, to tell you everything about every conceivable culture. We have to recognize that models of this kind are over-simplifications and can only give approximations of reality. Their use is in giving rough pictures of the striking contrasts and differences of underlying values between cultures.

Even though the values may be in the process of marked change due to rapid modernization, they have a way of persisting in spite of change. The evolution of values is a slow process, since they are rooted in survival needs and passed on, from generation to generation.

(Adapted from L. R. Kohls: *The Survival Kit for Overseas Living*)

Notes

original sin 原罪
insatiable 难以满足的，贪得无厌的
hyperactive 极度活跃的
autonomous 自治的；自主的
extroverted 外向的

Questions

1. How is the mainstream American culture different from other traditional cultures, such as Eastern cultures?

2. How would you explain the fact that contradictory values may exist in the same culture?

3. Do cultural values change as time changes? Give some examples.

Text B

Cultural Dimensions

Hofstede, a well-known scholar of communication studies, has identified four value dimensions that have a significant impact on behavior in all cultures. These dimensions are individualism-collectivism, uncertainty avoidance, power distance, and masculinity and femininity. Hofstede's work was one of the earliest attempts to use extensive statistical data to examine cultural values. During the 1980s, he surveyed over a hundred thousand workers in multinational organizations in forty countries. After careful analysis, each country was assigned a rank in each category, depending on how it compared to the other countries. The results yielded a clear picture of what was valued in each culture.

Individualism and collectivism

Although we speak of individualism and collectivism as if they are separate entities, it is important to keep in mind that all people and cultures have both individual and collective dispositions. In cultures that value individualism, the individual is the single most important unit in any social setting, regardless of the size of that unit, and the uniqueness of each individual is of paramount value. An "I" consciousness prevails: competition rather than cooperation is encouraged; personal goals take precedence over group goals; people tend not to be emotionally dependent on organizations and institutions; and every individual has the right to his or her private property, thoughts, and opinions. Theses cultures stress individual initiative and achievement, and they value individual decision making.

Collectivism is characterized by a rigid social framework that distinguishes between in-groups and out-groups. People count on their in-group (relatives, clans, organizations) to look after them, and in exchange for that they believe they owe absolute loyalty to the group.

Collectivism means greater emphasis on (a) the views, needs, and goals of the in-group rather than oneself; (b) social norms and duty defined by the in-group rather than behavior to get pleasure; (c) beliefs shared with the in-group rather than beliefs that distinguish self from the in-group; and (d) great readiness to cooperate with in-group members.

In collective societies, a "we" consciousness prevails: identity is based on the social system;

the individual is emotionally dependent on organizations and institutions; the culture emphasizes belonging to organizations; organizations invade private life and individuals trust group decisions.

Uncertainty avoidance

At the core of uncertainty avoidance is the inescapable truism that the future is unknown. Though we may all try, none of us can accurately predict the next moment, day, year, or decade. As the American playwright Tennessee Williams once noted, "The future is called 'perhaps,' which is the only possible thing to call the future."

At the other end of the scale we find countries, which have low-uncertainty-avoidance need. They more easily accept the uncertainty inherent in life and not as threatened by deviant people and ideas, so they tolerate the unusual. They prize initiative, dislike the structure associated with hierarchy, are more willing to take risks, are more flexible, think that there should be as few rules as possible, and depend not so much on experts as on themselves, generalists, and common sense. As a whole, members of low-uncertainty-avoidance cultures are less tense and more relaxed—traits reflected in the Irish proverb "Life should be a dance, not a race."

Power distance

Another cultural value dimension is power distance, which classifies cultures on a continuum of high- to low-power distance. This dimension deals with the extent to which a society accepts that power in relationships, institutions, and organizations is distributed unequally. Although all cultures have tendencies for both high- and low-power relationships, one orientation seems to dominate.

In some cultures, those who hold power and those who are affected by power are significantly far apart (high-power-distance) in many ways, while in other cultures, the power holders and those affected by the power holders are significantly closer (low-power distance).

People in high-power-distance countries believe that power and authority are facts of life. Both consciously and unconsciously, these cultures teach their members that people are not equal in this world and that everybody has a rightful place, which is clearly marked by countless vertical arrangements. Social hierarchy is prevalent and institutionalizes inequality.

Low-power distance countries hold that inequality in society should be minimized. People in these cultures believe they are close to power and should have access to that power. To them, a hierarchy is an inequality of roles established for convenience. Subordinates consider superiors to be the same kind of people as they are, and superiors perceive their subordinates the same way. People in power often try to look less powerful than they really are.

Masculinity and femininity

Hofstede uses the words masculinity and femininity to refer not to men and women, but rather to the degree to which masculine or feminine traits prevail. Masculinity is the extent to which the dominant values in a society are male oriented and is associated with such behaviors as ambition, differentiated sex roles, achievement, the acquisition of money, and signs of manliness.

Cultures that value femininity as a trait stress caring and nurturing behaviors. A feminine world view maintains that men need not be assertive and that they can assume nurturing roles; it also promotes sexual equality and holds that people and the environment are important. Gender roles in feminine societies are more fluid than in masculine societies. Interdependence and androgynous behavior are the ideal, and people sympathize with the unfortunate.

Ranking of Some Countries and Regions on the Four Dimensions

Country/Region	Individualism	Power distance	Uncertainty avoidance	Masculinity
Argentina	49	49	86	56
Australia	90	36	54	61
Austria	55	11	70	79
Belgium	75	65	94	54
Brazil	38	69	76	49
Canada	80	39	48	52
Chile	23	63	86	28
Colombia	13	67	80	64
Denmark	74	18	23	16
France	71	68	86	43
Germany	67	35	65	66
Great Britain	89	35	35	66
Greece	35	60	112	57
Guatemala	6	95	101	37
Hong Kong, China	25	68	29	57
Indonesia	14	78	48	46
India	48	77	40	56
Iran	41	58	59	43
Ireland	70	28	35	68
Israel	54	13	81	47
Italy	76	50	75	70
Japan	46	54	92	95
ROK	18	60	85	39
Malaysia	26	104	36	50
Mexico	30	81	82	69

Country/Region	Individualism	Power distance	Uncertainty avoidance	Masculinity
Netherlands	80	38	53	14
Norway	69	31	50	8
Pakistan	14	55	70	50
Portugal	27	63	104	31
South Africa	65	49	49	63
Singapore	20	74	8	48
Spain	51	57	86	42
Sweden	71	31	29	5
Switzerland	68	34	58	70
Taiwan, China	17	58	69	45
Thailand	20	64	64	34
Turkey	37	66	85	45
USA	91	40	46	62

Some criticism has been leveled against Hofstede's work. First, since Hofstede's original study, numerous other studies have focused on individualism and collectivism; but the other three dimensions he studied lack systematic investigation. Second, because the people Hofstede surveyed were middle managers in large multinational organizations, most of his findings are work related. Third, many important countries and cultures were not included in Hofstede's study. For example, there were no Arab countries, and Africa was represented by only South Africa.

(Adapted from L. A. Samovar et al.: *Communication between Cultures*, Chapter 3)

Notes

disposition 倾向;特性
paramount 最高的;至上的
precedence 居前,优先
consensus 一致意见
deviant 偏离常规的,不正常的
prevalent 流行的,普遍的
institutionalize 使成惯例
nurturing behavior 养育行为
assertive 坚定自信的
androgynous 男女不分的,男女都适用的

Questions

1. How do you think about Hofstede's value dimensions? Do you have anything to add to his dimensions concerning cultural values?

2. What are the similarities and differences between the Hofstede model and the Kluckhohn-Strodtbeck model? Which model do you think is more powerful in describing and explaining cultural differences?

3. Can you use the Hofstede model to illustrate some differences between the Chinese culture and a foreign one?

Exploration

In nearly every culture, proverbs, communicated in colorful and vivid language, offer important instructions for the members of the culture to follow. They teach people about what a culture deems significant.

In Japan, there is a proverb "the nail that sticks up will be pounded down." Compare the Japanese proverb with an American one, that is, "the squeaky wheel gets the grease." The American proverb implies that a person who stands out and is the most vocal will be rewarded. The Japanese proverb means that no one should stand out or be more important than anyone else.

Do we have a similar proverb in Chinese? If you think we do, what is it?

Then try to find more proverbs and sayings that are still frequently used by people nowadays in our society, and to see what cultural values they transmit.

Cases for Discussion

Case 1

Joe is an Assistant Professor in an American university. Two years ago, he made friends with Hong, a Chinese visiting scholar in another American university when he was in the final year of his Ph. D. program. He began teaching in a university after graduation. Hong, who had been back to China, recommended Joe to her university. Soon, Joe was invited by Hong's university for a five-day visit to give lectures.

Joe was very excited about the trip, as it was his first time in China. Hong and the Chair of her department met him at the airport, then put him up in a nice hotel. They had arranged a big dinner for him for the meeting and made Joe feel very welcome. At the end of the evening, Hong gave him the itinerary for the next few days. Apart from the lectures, all his time would be filled with meals, concerts, shopping, and a one-day trip to a nearby resort, all paid for by the university. Joe had thought he would have time to explore the city and the area, but the itinerary would leave him no free time.

Joe was grateful to Hong and the host department who took great care of him during his visit. At the end of the visit, he insisted on treating Hong and the Department Chair to dinner to thank them. But they said a dinner had been arranged. Joe was very frustrated. He was not very happy at the dinner, and did not show any enthusiasm when the Department Chair said that they hoped Joe would come back for another visit.

When it came time for Joe to leave, he did not know what to say. He knew he should be grateful for everything Hong had done for him, but he had also felt deprived and trapped since he never found the time to do anything by himself. The tight itinerary never allowed him to explore on his own; he felt especially annoyed that all the plans had been made without consulting him. Ironically, as soon as Joe left, Hong was very relieved. She felt Joe's visit had been successful but it had required most of her time to make sure that Joe's visit would be a smooth one. She never knew that Joe, still upset about the tight control placed on his schedule, complained to the person next to him on the plane, "While in China, I sometimes felt like a prisoner!"

Questions

1. Why do you think Joe sometimes felt like a prisoner while he was in China?
2. What do you think is the appropriate way we should treat our foreign friends?

Case 2

Phil Downing, an eager young executive, was involved in the setting up of a branch of his company that was merging with an existing Japanese counterpart. He seemed to get along very well with the executive colleagues assigned to work with him, one of whom had recently been elected chairman of the board when his grandfather retired. Over several weeks' discussion, they had generally laid out some working policies and agreed on strategies that would bring new directions needed for development.

Several days later, as they were going over some details, the young chairman's grandfather happened to drop in. He began to comment on how the company had been formed and had been built up by the traditional practices that the young executives had recently discarded. Phil expected the new chairman to explain some of the new innovative and developmental policies they had both agreed upon. However, the young man said nothing; instead, he just nodded and agreed with his grandfather. Phil was bewildered and frustrated over the days of work he had put into the development of those strategies, and he started to protest. The atmosphere in the room became immediately tense, but no one offered any further argument.

A week later the Japanese company withdrew from the negotiations concerning a relationship with Phil's company.

Questions

1. Why did the young chairman say nothing but just nod and agree with his grandfather?
2. How would you behave if you found yourself in a similar situation?

Case 3

Mr. Zhao and Mr. Qian have been on good terms with each other, though Mr. Zhao lives in China while Mr. Qian became an overseas Chinese working in the United States. The two both have children about the same age. Mr. Qian has two brothers who live in the U.S. and manage their family businesses. And both Mr. Zhao and Mr. Qian have business that seems fairly prosperous.

Two years ago, however, Mr. Qian was bogged down with some difficulties, and in fact, his business was almost on the rocks. But, he had an opportunity to invest in a very promising venture but at the moment did not have enough cash. He realized that this venture would be able to help him nurse his business back, and that his two bothers did not have the large sum he needed. He weighed the situation carefully and then telephoned Mr. Zhao for help. Mr. Zhao gladly lent him the money, and the venture did turn out very profitably for Mr. Qian, who was then able to repay Mr. Zhao with the interest immediately.

Later that year, when Mr. Zhao's daughter was applying for a course in the United States, he called Mr. Qian to help to get his daughter into the college by using his connections. Mr. Qian acquiesced and secured a place for Mr. Zhao's daughter. A year later, Mr. Zhao's nephew was going to the States. He asked Mr. Qian if his brothers could help him and give him a job when he got there. Again, Mr. Qian complied without hesitation.

But when this was known by one of Mr. Qian's American friends, Jackson, he didn't seem to be able to understand all the assistance Mr. Qian had given to Mr. Zhao, though Mr. Qian had told him a lot about the relation between them. Jackson said that Mr. Zhao was asking too much.

Note

bog down with some difficulties 陷入困境

Questions

1. Why do you think Jackson said that Mr. Zhao was asking too much?

2. What differences are there between the Chinese understanding of friendship and the American one?

Readings for Further Study

1
So Near the United States

"Poor Mexico," said Porfirio Diaz, Mexico's last pre-Revolutionary President, "so far from God, so near the United States." In the years since he said these words the nations on both sides of the border have been greatly altered. No one would deny that geographically and commercially Mexico has never been so near the United States. The cultural distance, however, is something else, for in many respects the cultural gaps between these societies are as great as ever.

Insights into contrasting cultural assumptions and styles of communication cannot be gained without an appreciation of the history and geography of the two societies.

North Americans trace their history from the time of the first English settlers. The people already living on the continent possessed no great cities or monuments to rival anything in Europe, and they held little interest for the European colonists so long as they could be displaced and their land cultivated. The North American Indian has remained excluded from the shaping of the dominant culture of the new nations just as he had been excluded from the land. With political independence and the continuous arrival of immigrants, largely from Northern Europe, the nation took shape in a steady westward pattern. The outlook was to the future, to new land and new opportunities. The spirit was of optimism.

When the Spanish soldiers arrived in Mexico in the 16th century they found cities and temples of civilizations that had flourished for thousands of years. In what some have called a holy crusade, the Spanish attempted to destroy the old societies and reconstruct a new order on top. In religion, in language, in marriage, there was a fusion of Indian and European which was totally different from the pattern in the United States. The fusion of European and native American cultures is a source of great pride, not only in Mexico but extending throughout the Latin American republics. This serves in part to give a sense of identification with other Latin Americans and a sense of separateness from those of the Anglo world.

The images which the people on each side of the border hold of the other differ. Mexico's image of the United States was to a great extent shaped in Europe, formed at a time when European writers had little good to say about the Anglo-American world. Even today when Mexicans speak of the ideals of freedom and democracy, their inspiration is more likely to be French than North American. The rivalry between England and Spain, compounded by the religious hostility between Protestants and Roman Catholics, influenced in a comparable way the North American's image of Mexico.

The history of relations between the United States and Mexico has not been one of understanding and cooperation, though many persons on both sides of the border are working toward those ends. Even under the best of conditions and with the best of intentions, Mexicans and North Americans working together sometimes feel confused, irritated, distrustful.

In the North American value system are three central and interrelated assumptions about human beings. These are (1) that people, apart from social and educational influences, are basically the same; (2) that each person should be judged on his or her own individual merits; and (3) that these "merits," including a person's worth and character, are revealed through the person's actions. Values of equality and independence, constitutional rights, laws and social programs arise from these assumptions. Because a person's actions are regarded as so important, it is the comparison of accomplishments—X compared to X's father, or X five years ago compared to X today, or X compared to Y and Z—that provides a chief means of judging or even knowing a person.

In Mexico it is the uniqueness of the individual which is valued, a quality which is assumed to reside within each person and which is not necessarily evident through actions or achievements. That inner quality which represents the dignity of each person must be protected at all costs. Any action or remark that may be interpreted as a slight to the person's dignity is to be regarded as a grave provocation. Also, as every person is part of a larger family grouping, one cannot be regarded as a completely isolated individual...

Where a Mexican will talk about a person's inner qualities in terms of the person's soul or spirit, North Americans are likely to feel uncomfortable using such words to talk about people. They may regard such talk as vague or sentimental, the words seeming to describe something invisible and hence unknowable, or at the very least "too personal."

Even questions about the family of a person one does not know well may discomfit many North Americans, since asking about a person's parents or brothers or sisters may also seem too personal. "I just don't know the person well enough to ask about his family," a North American might say, while the Mexican may see things just the opposite: "If I don't ask about the person's family, how will I really know him?"

The family forms a much less important part of an individual's frame of reference in the United States than is usually the case in Mexico. Neighbors, friends or associates, even some abstract "average American," may be the basis for the comparison needed in evaluating oneself or others. "Keeping up with the Joneses" may be important in New York or Chicago, but keeping up with one's brother-in-law is more important in Mexico City. In the same way, the Mexican depends upon relatives or close friends to help "arrange things" if there is a problem or to provide a loan. While this is by no means rare in the United States, the dominant values in the culture favor institutions which are seen as both efficient and fair.

(Adapted from J. C. Condon: So Near the United States, *The Bridge*)

Notes

crusade 十字军东征，此处指西班牙征服墨西哥
Anglo 盎格鲁的(主要指英国的)
compounded 加剧了的
Protestant 基督教新教徒
Roman Catholic 罗马天主教徒
slight 蔑视
provocation 挑衅
discomfit 使困窘，使狼狈
keeping up with the Joneses 与邻居攀比

Questions

1. Do cultural distance and geographical distance coincide? Does contact between different cultures necessarily increase intercultural understanding? Why or why not?

2. What are the major differences between Mexicans and North Americans in their cultural assumptions about individuals?

2

The Basic Unit of Society: The Individual or the Collective?

When businesses in the United States first began exploring the reasons for Japanese success and ways to market products in Japan, they found surprisingly different attitudes in Japanese organizations. In Japan an individual is a fraction of a unit; the group is the fundamental unit. An often-quoted proverb in Japan is "the nail that sticks up will be pounded down." Any assertion of individualism—valuing the individual over the group—is regarded as a negative threat to the group and will result in punishment by the group.

Individualism in Japan is tantamount to selfishness. It is the opposite of self-denial for the good of the group, which is highly valued in Japan. That means Japanese managers are closely knit to the department they manage, which are also highly cooperative and closely knit. Organizations can count on the loyalty and wholehearted commitment of their employees.

Organizations have their own songs, their own uniforms, and their own ways to build loyalty and groupness.

Individuals in Western cultures make career choices on the basis of personal needs and goals, if a job offers insufficient advancement, for example, or a personality conflict arises with a superior, or the tasks become boring, an ambitious individual likely moves to another job. If lifestyle changes—for instance if a child's schooling or care for an elderly relative becomes a priority—an individual may very well change employers. When the employer wants more overtime from an employee but the employee prefers a job that does not require overtime, the employee may change employers.

In Japan, however, none of these situations is reason for a move. Changing employers is an admission of failure and brings loss of face both to the one who could not cooperate in harmony with the organization and to the organization for **spawning** such an antisocial misfit. In Japan, if personal goals are not met by work, the employee is persuaded to change or defer the goals. When lifestyle changes create new needs, the superior expects to be told and to share the concerns. Child care is typically the responsibility of a wife who stays at home and health insurance is available from all employers, yet employees discuss changes in their personal lives with their superiors. It is not because they may link these changes to a need for more income or housing; it is because the boss is owed the information and is expected to take an interest in the family life of the employee. When the organization demands overtime, employees eagerly respond. In many organizations in Japan, employees come in for overtime work even when they have little actual work to do, just to show their solidarity with other members of their corporate group.

Throughout Asia, in varying degrees, collectivism is celebrated. This is not surprising considering the high value given to relationships in these cultures. What matters is the close-knot interlocked human network, individual recognition is less important, particularly if it means a penalty or some kind of **ostracization**. Harmony among the interdependent group members is the key, and it takes priority above nearly all other values.

In the United States, where individualism is valued, competitiveness is encouraged as a means for determining the best competitor. When individuals compete against one another, inevitably there are many more losers than winners, but the competitiveness principle asserts that as long as you can enter into competition again and again, you too may one day win. In other words, consolation for losing lies in having a chance to compete. The United States has passed legislation for equal opportunity that is probably based in part on the value of having a chance to compete.

The individualist-collectivist priorities mean cultures interpret what obligation means differently. Everyone has had an experience in which someone came to the rescue and offered help just when it was needed. But obligation has rules, determined by different cultural priorities, and that can cause problems in intercultural encounters.

To consider the issue of indebtedness, we'll turn to a situation that generates obligation. Person A must meet a visitor at the airport, but finds the means of transportation relied upon to get to the airport is not available. So Person A asks Person B to provide transportation to the airport. In India, friendship means entering into a willingness to be indebted. In fact, in some languages in India, no word exists for "thanks"; if one is in this relationship, one incurs indebtedness and one is expected to repay the debt owed. No words are necessary. Nor does one hesitate to request a favor of a friend; that's what friendship means.

Compare this with obligation in the United States where someone might preface a request with, "I really hate to ask you, but..." or "I wouldn't dream of asking you, only..." This opening is usually followed by a detailed explanation of why the asker has no alternative but to become indebted. The request finishes with elaborate thanks: "Thanks a million; I'm so grateful." In a culture that values individual achievement, independence, and control over events by personal action, a request that puts someone in another's debt is almost an admission of failure.

People in some cultures are not happy about being indebted, and often try to repay and thus erase the debt as quickly as possible. Perhaps too many obligations make people feel that their personal freedom is threatened and that they have lost some control over choices they could have made. Some independent individuals may go to lengths to avoid putting themselves in someone else's debt and to avoid making others indebted to them. For example, Person A who wants to go to the airport but doesn't have transportation might hire a taxi rather than ask someone to make a special trip. Similarly, rarely are gifts given for no apparent reason; on occasions when they are given for no specific reason, they are made to seem unimportant by a casual giving style. The reason: the giver does not want to make the receiver feel too heavily obligated.

The dominant culture in the United States, with its value of individual responsibility, invented the pot-luck dinner (everyone brings a dish and thus nobody is host and nobody is indebted), and "going dutch" (people who go to a restaurant together or attend other entertainment and pay their own bill). Asians, Europeans and Middle-Easterners are appalled; their values of hospitality and of indebtedness as the mark of a relationship are offended.

In fact, in most cultures of the world significant relationships are those that involve webs of obligation. Relationships of two or more individuals—or groups—can last for decades and even generations. In China, Japan, and other Asian countries, a first act that places someone's family under an obligation leads to a reciprocal act and so on throughout years, and the obligation responsibilities are passed down to succeeding generations. The obligations are the responsibility of everyone in the group, not only the individual who first became indebted. To bring to an end the indebtedness once and for all, to clear and erase the debt, is to end the relationship. This is serious. In fact, ending a relationship is an event of such magnitude that usually every measure will be taken to avoid it.

(Adapted from L. Beamer & I. Varner: *Intercultural Communication in the Global Workplace*, Chapter 4)

Notes

tantamount 无异于，等于
spawn 引发，引起
ostracization 排斥
go to lengths 不顾一切，竭力
reciprocal 互惠的，相应的

Questions

1. What do you think is the meaning of the Japanese proverb "the nail that sticks up will be pounded down"? Do we have a similar saying in Chinese? If you think we do, what is it?

2. What is your view about obligation and indebtedness in relationships? Is it individualistic or collectivistic?

Summary

1. As values are learned, they are not universal, and they tend to differ from culture to culture. By comparing the possible responses to some basic questions, we can get rough pictures of the striking contrasts and differences of values between cultures.

2. Even though the values may be in the process of marked change due to rapid modernization, they have a way of persisting in spite of change.

3. There are many dimensions on which culture may differ. Four value dimensions for comparing cultures identified by Hofstede are: individualism v. collectivism; uncertainty avoidance; power distance; masculinity v. femininity.

4. Intercultural communicators are concerned, chiefly, with the difficulties that can occur when cultural beliefs, values, and attitudes come in conflict and clash with one another.

Chapter 5 Culture and Language

The limits of my language are the limits of my world.

—Ludwig Wittgenstein

Chapter 5 Culture and Language

Preview Questions

1. Is language just a tool for us to use in communication?

2. Have it ever occurred to you that you may have been greatly influenced by the language you use?

3. Is learning a language the same as learning a culture? Why or why not?

Text A

Language and Its Cultural Influence

We begin our preview of language by noting that it is impossible to separate our use of language from our culture. In its most basic sense, language is a set of symbols and the rules for combining those symbols that are used and understood by a large community of people. When we study another language, we soon discover that not only are the symbols (words) and sounds for those symbols different, but so are the rules (phonology, grammar, syntax, and intonation) for using those symbols and sounds.

Word differences are obvious in various languages. In English, we live in a *house*. In Spanish, we live in a *casa*. In Thai, we live in a *ban*. Grammatical structures are unique to each language as well. In English, verb tenses express contrast between past, present, and future acts, but in Vietnamese, the same verb reflects all three and the time of the action is inferred from the context. Syntax, or the word order and structure of sentences, also varies depending on the language. The normal word order for simple sentences in Filipino is the reverse of the word order in English. For example, the English sentence "The teacher died" would be "*Died the teacher*" or "*Namatay ang guro*" in Filipino. In English, the subject is followed by a verb and then an object, but in Korean, the subject is followed by the object and then the verb. So in English we might say, "The cat ate the mouse," but in Korean, "*Cat mouse ate*" would be correct.

These examples indicate that if we want to communicate in another language, it is important for us to know not only the symbols (words) of that language, but also the rules for using those symbols. As you know, language is much more than a symbol and rule system that allows us to communicate with another person—language also shapes the process by which people become introduced to the order of the physical and social environment. Language, therefore, would seem to have a major impact on the way an individual perceives and conceptualizes the world.

Language and its cultural influence are exemplified in the theoretical formulations of the Sapir-Whorf hypothesis, which in essence states that language is a guide to "social reality." This hypothesis implies that language is not simply a means of reporting experience but, more important, it is a way of defining experience. Sapir wrote:

> Human beings do not live in the objective world alone, nor alone in the world of social activity as ordinarily understood, but are very much at the mercy of the particular language which has become the medium of expression for their society... The real world is to a large extent unconsciously built up on the language habits of the group. No two languages are ever sufficiently similar to be considered as presenting the same social reality. The worlds in which different societies live are distinct worlds, not merely the same world with different labels attached.

Here is an excellent example of the Sapir-Whorf concept in practice:

If my language has only one term—bother-in-law—that is applied to my sister's husband, husband's sisters' husbands, I am led by my language to perceive all of these relatives in a similar way. Vocabulary, through what it groups together under one label and what it differentiates with different labels, is one way in which language shapes our perception of the world.

Another instance of how language defines experience can be seen in the Navaho language, which emphasizes the nature and direction of movement. Rather than saying, "One dresses," the Navaho would say, "One moves into clothing." Instead of saying, "One is young," the Navaho would say, "One moves about newly." Language is one aspect of the Navaho culture that coincides with the notion of a universe in motion.

Although complete acceptance of the Sapir-Whorf hypothesis may be controversial, its application to culture and language is clear: language is a reflection of culture, and culture is a reflection of language. We have seen that culture influences language by way of symbols and rules as well as our perceptions of the universe. Equally important is the fact that meaning shifts from culture to culture.

As children, most of us asked our parents, "What does that word mean?" This question reflects the way we view language. It suggests that we tend to look for meaning in words themselves, but we are incorrect if we think that words possess meaning. It is more accurate to say that people possess meaning and that words elicit these meanings. We can have different meanings for the same word. For instance, to one person, the word grass might mean something in front of the house that is green, has to be watered, and must be mowed once a week; to another person, grass may mean something that is rolled in paper and smoked. All people, drawing on their backgrounds, decide what a word means. People have similar meanings only to the extent that they have had or can anticipate similar experiences.

Culture teaches us both the symbol and what the symbol represents. When you are communicating with someone from your own culture, the process of using words to represent your experiences is much easier because within a culture people share many similar experiences. But when communication is between people from distinct cultures, different experiences are involved and the process is more troublesome. Objects, events, experiences, and feelings have the labels or names they do because a community of people arbitrarily decided to so name them. If we extend this notion to the intercultural setting, we can see that diverse cultures can have both different symbols and different responses.

(Adapted from L. A. Samovar et al.: *Communication between Cultures*, Chapter 5)

Notes

Thai 泰国语
Vietnamese 越南语
conceptualize 使形成概念
exemplify 举例说明
E. Sapir 萨丕尔（1884—1939），美国语言学家
B. L. Whorf 沃尔夫（1897—1941），美国语言学家
at the mercy of 受……支配
Navaho(美国西南部印第安人的)纳瓦霍语

Questions

1. What do you think of Sapir-Whorf hypothesis?
2. How do word, meaning and culture interact with each other in communication process?
3. Can you give some examples to show the influence of culture on people's use of language?

Text B

How to Say "Yes" and "No"

In intercultural communication, even simple things such as saying "yes" or "no" are very important, for in different cultures a "yes" may mean different things, and there are different ways of saying "no".

Imagine an American businessman reviewing an important contract with his Japanese counterpart. "We've got to work together," the American says.

"Hai," the Japanese smiles. ("Hai" is the Japanese word for "yes.")

"We're going to try for a 50-50 partnership," the American says.

"Hai."

"We will use American know-how and a Japanese work force."

"Hai."

After this exchange, the American executive might very well assume he has a hard and fast agreement. But nothing could be further from the truth.

When he says "hai," the Japanese businessman is simply telling the man across the table that he hears what he is saying. There is no agreement. The Japanese, after all, are supreme team players, and one businessman would never make an agreement without first consulting other members of his team.

Sometimes, "yes" may mean "no." Look at the following dialogue between an American physician and a recent immigrant from Vietnam:

Physician: "You did not take your medicine?"

Immigrant: "Yes. Yes."

As a matter of fact, what the immigrant means by the first "yes" is "I hear you", and what he means by the second "yes" is "I did not take it." Obviously, these responses will leave the American physician frustrated, and communication between them may break down.

Saying "no" seems to be more complicated.

One of the more interesting observations about "no" is that sometimes "no" may mean "maybe" given the right time and circumstances. This is quite important in interpersonal relations and in politics. Look at the following sex-biased joke:

What's the difference between a lady and a diplomat?

When a diplomat says "yes," he means maybe.

When a diplomat says "maybe," he means no.

When a diplomat says "no," he's no diplomat.

When a lady says "no," she means "maybe."

When a lady says "maybe," she means "yes."

When a lady says "yes," she's no lady at all!

Besides saying "no" directly, there are other ways of expressing "no" across cultures. Some of them are worth listing:

(1) Being silent or showing a lack of enthusiasm. In many cultures in the world, being silent is a way of refusing an offer or an invitation or of giving an answer. But the big problem for a foreigner is that silence may mean many other things such as consent, or contempt, or even defiance.

(2) Offering an alternative. In some cases, in order not to offend or to direct the

conversation away from the request, people may divert attention by suggesting an alternative.

a. —How do you like this book?

—It's good but I prefer...

b. —Mary, can you help with the cooking?

—Susan can do it better.

(3) Postponement (delaying answers). Often in response to a request to perform something or to an invitation, "no" is indicated by postponement.

a. —Can you come over this evening?

—Not today, next time, I'll let you know.

b. How about going to the concert?

It's a great idea, but I don't have time at the moment.

(4) Putting the responsibility on a third party or something over which you have no control.

a. —Will you go to Florida with us for holiday?

—My budget docsn't permit me to go.

b. —Is my new program going to be funded by the local government?

—We'll put it up to the committee, but I can't promise anything.

(5) Avoidance. One way to answer a question or an offer is to avoid responding directly.

—Would you please have some noodles?

—I like rice more.

(6) General acceptance of an offer but giving no details.

For example, in Arabic-speaking countries, the answer in the following dialogue is actually negative:

—Let's have a picnic next Saturday?

—*Inshaallah* (God willing).

But saying *Inshaallah* plus time and details is equivalent to "yes."

(7) Diverting and distracting.

a. —How old are you?

—Why do you ask? How old do you think?

b. —Please close the door.

—Why?

Many of the above-mentioned approaches to saying "no" are found in every culture. However, there are still many cultural differences.

For example, societies differ in how to accept or reject something offered. In France, when offered something, the best refusal is "merci." The translation of this word is "thanks" but it actually means "no, thanks." In the U.S., "thanks" means "yes, thanks." In the U.S., a hostess will offer more food usually only once, but in many parts of the Arab world one mustn't accept food the first or second time it is offered; refusal the third time is definitive. An anecdote was recounted by an Arab speaker's first encounter with some Americans. On his first visit to an

American home, he was served some delicious sandwiches. When the hostess came to offer seconds, he refused. Much to his chagrin, the hostess didn't repeat the offer, for the Americans take a "no" to mean "no", whether it's the first, second, or third time. Thus, the Arab sat there, confronted by some lovely sandwiches which he couldn't eat.

This is also the case with the Chinese. Once some members of a delegation sent to China by a large American corporation complained that the Chinese had asked them three times if they would be willing to modify some proposal, and each time the Americans had said "no" clearly and definitely. The Americans were angry because the Chinese had not taken their word the first time. If these Americans had studied up on cultural differences before coming to China, it would have saved them a lot of perplexity and frustration in their negotiations.

Differences between Japanese and Western ways of doing business, however, often confuse the foreign businessman and make doing business in Japan difficult for foreigners.

The American businessman, for example, wants to start talking business immediately. He wants quick decisions. He does not want to wait. The Japanese, on the other hand, likes to arrive at decisions gradually after giving them a great deal of thought. Another thing foreign businessmen have difficult understanding is when a Japanese means "yes" or "no." This is because of cultural differences between Japanese and Western society which make it difficult for a Japanese to say "no" directly.

In English, it is easy to say "no" to something we do not want to do. But in Japan, it is very difficult to say "no." To refuse an invitation or request with "No", or a similar phrase, is felt to be impolite. It is thought to be selfish and unfriendly. So instead of saying "no" directly, the Japanese have developed many ways to avoid saying "no". These enable them to avoid hurting other people's feelings. However, this often makes communication with the Japanese difficult for foreigners to understand and follow.

Foreign business men in Japan must, therefore, be patient in trying to communicate with the Japanese. They must not be in a hurry. Above all, they must try to understand the Japanese custom of politeness. Once they learn how the Japanese think and behave, they will find doing business with them a lot easier.

Notes

executive 经理,业务主管	defiance 挑战,蔑视
supreme 最优的,极好的	Arabic 阿拉伯语
immigrant 外来移民	divert 转移(注意力)
Vietnam 越南	perplexity 困惑,茫然

Questions

1. Can you find some cases in which 是 in Chinese does not mean "yes" in English?
2. How would you put the following into Chinese?
   1) —Do you like the new school?
      —Yes, I do.
   2) —Please don't say that.
      —Yes, I will.
   3) —I know what he wants.
      —Yes?
      —Money!
   4) —Waiter!
      —Yes, sir.
   5) —Yes?
      —I'd like two tickets, please.
   6) —Everything will be all right soon, yes?
3. Why do people in countries like Japan and China often refuse to say "no" directly?

Exploration

While humor is a universal human characteristic, what is perceived as humorous varies from culture to culture. In the United States, presentations are often started with a joke or cartoon related to the topic to be covered. Most European countries use humor during business meetings. When this same technique is used with many Asian audiences, few are amused. In intercultural communication, even though the intention of humor is to put people at ease and create a more relaxed environment, the risk of offending someone of another culture or of telling a story that no one understands is great. In short, people throughout the world do not all laugh at the same things.

Could you translate the following humorous dialogue into Chinese and have your translations as humorous as the original?

—Why couldn't Cinderella be a good soccer player?

—She lost her shoe, she ran away from the ball, and her coach was a pumpkin.

You must know some jokes in Chinese. Try to translate one or two of them into English. Then ask some English-speaking people to read your translated version and see whether they will be amused or not.

Cases for Discussion

Case 1

Language translation is not only difficult; it can be inept and have extreme consequences.

Near the end of World War II, after Italy and Germany had surrendered, the Allies sent Japan an ultimatum to surrender. Japan's premier announced that his government would *mokusatsu* the surrender ultimatum. *Mokusatsu* was an unfortunate word choice because it could mean both *to consider* and *to take notice of*. The Premier, speaking in Japanese, apparently meant that the government would consider the surrender ultimatum. But, the English language translators in Japan's overseas broadcasting agency used the *to take notice of* meaning of *mokusatsu*.

Consequently, the world heard that Japan had rejected the surrender ultimatum rather than that Japan was considering the ultimatum. This mistranslation led the United States to assume Japan was unwilling to surrender and the atomic bombing of Hiroshima and Nagasaki followed. Quite possibly if the other meaning had been selected in the translation process, the atomic bomb would not have been used in World War II.

Notes

ultimatum 最后通谍

Questions

1. What can we learn from this case?

2. Do you know any other examples of misunderstanding that has resulted from such language translation problems?

Case 2

In intercultural communication, misunderstanding things like intonation may have as tragic consequences as misunderstanding the meanings of the words actually used.

In London's Heathrow Airport, airport staff who ate in the employees' cafeteria complained about rudeness by cafeteria employees from India and Pakistan who had been hired for jobs traditionally held by British women. And the Asian women complained of discrimination. A communication expert was asked to tape talk on the job to see what was going on, and then he had Asian and British employees listen to the tape together.

When a customer coming through the cafeteria line requested meat, the server had to find out if he wanted gravy on it. The British women asked, "Gravy?" The Asian women also said "Gravy." But instead of rising, their intonation fell at the end. During the workshop session, the Asian women said they couldn't see why they were getting negative reactions, since they were saying the same thing as the British women. But the British women pointed out that although they were saying the same word, they weren't saying the same thing. "Gravy?"—with question intonation—means "Would you like gravy?" The same word spoken with falling intonation seems to mean, "This is gravy. Take it or leave it."

Notes

Heathrow Airport 希思罗机场 gravy 肉汁，肉卤

Questions

1. British novelist E. M. Forster put it in his well-known novel *A Passage to India*, "A pause in the wrong place, an intonation misunderstood, and a whole conversation went awry." What do you think of it?

2. Have you ever had any similar experiences in your communication with others?

Case 3

The following are just taken from one of Mao Zedong's poems. Compare the Chinese original with the two English versions given below.

我失骄杨君失柳，
杨柳轻飏直上重霄九。(《蝶恋花·答李淑一》)

Version 1

I lost my proud Poplar and you your Willow,
Poplar and Willow soar into the Ninth Heaven.

Version 2

I've lost proud Yang and you've lost Liu,

Their souls fly up into the blue.

Questions

1. Do you know the meanings of 杨柳 here? What do they refer to? How should they be translated into English?

2. What do you think of the two English versions? Could you offer a better one?

Readings for Further Study

1

Language, Thought, and Culture

It is commonly observed that the manner in which an idea or "fact" is stated affects the way we conceptualize the idea. Words shape our lives. The advertising world is a prime example of the use of language to shape, persuade, and dissuade. "Weasel words" tend to glorify very ordinary products into those that are "sparkling" or "refreshing." In the case of food that has been sapped of most of its nutrients by the manufacturing process, we are told that these products are now "enriched" and "fortified." A foreigner in the United States once remarked that in the United States there are no "small" eggs, only "medium," "large," "extra-large," and "jumbo."

Verbal labels can shape the way we store events for later recall. In a classic study, subjects were briefly exposed to figures like those in the following:

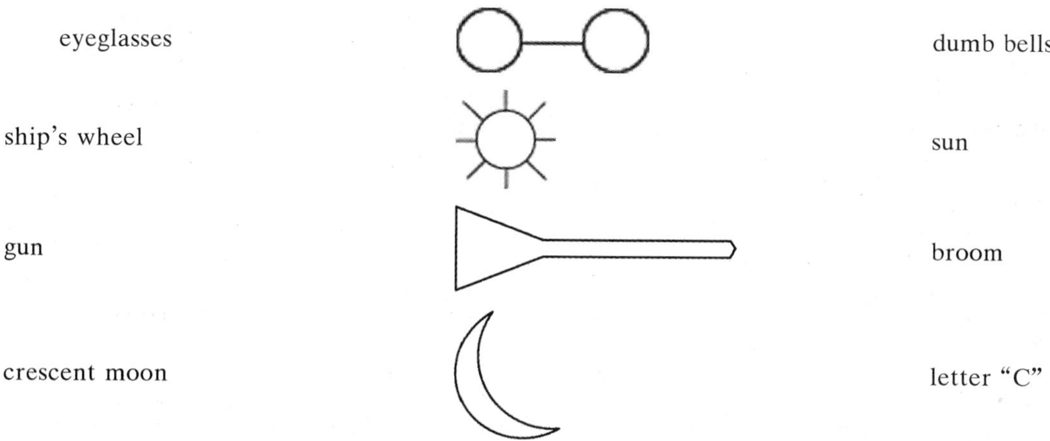

Later when the subjects were asked to reproduce them, the reproductions were influenced by the labels assigned to the figures. For example, the first drawing tended to be reproduced as something like this:

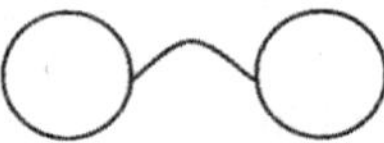

if the subject had seen the "eyeglasses" label, and on the other hand like this:

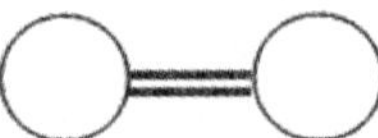

if the subject had seen the "dumbbells" label.

Words are not the only linguistic category affecting thought. The way a sentence is structured will affect nuances of meaning. It has been discovered that subtle differences in the structure of questions can affect the answer a person gives. For example, upon viewing a film of an automobile accident, subjects were asked questions like "Did you see *the* broken headlight?" in some cases, and in other cases "Did you see *a* broken headlight?" Questions using *the* tended to produce more false recognition of events. That is, the presence of the definite article led subjects to believe that there *was* a broken headlight, whether they saw it or not. Similar results were found for questions like "Did you see some people watching the accident?" vs. "Did you see any people watching the accident" or even for questions containing a presupposition: "How fast was the car going when it hit the stop sign?" (presupposing both the existence of a stop sign and that the car hit a stop sign, whether the subject actually saw it or not).

Culture is really an integral part of the interaction between language and thought. Cultural patterns, customs, and ways of life are expressed in language; culture-specific world views are reflected in language. Cultures have different ways of dividing the color spectrum, for example, illustrating differing world views on what color is and how to identify color. It has been noted that the Shona of Zimbawee and the Bassa of Liberia have fewer color categories than speakers of European languages and they break up the spectrum at different points, as is shown below.

Color Categories in Three Cultures

English

Purple	Blue	Green	Yellow	Orange	Red

Shona

Cipsuka	Citema	Cicena	Cipsuka

Bassa

Hui	Ziza

Of course, the Shona or Bassa are able to perceive and describe other colors, in the same way that an English speaker might describe a "dark bluish green," but the labels which the language provides tend to shape the person's overall cognitive organization of color and to cause varying degrees of color discrimination. Eskimo tribes commonly have as many as seven different words for snow to distinguish among different types of snow (falling snow, snow on the ground, fluffy snow, wet snow, etc.), while certain African cultures in the equatorial forests of Zaire have no word at all for snow.

But even more to the point than such geographically conditioned aspects of language are examples from the Hopi language. Hopi does not use verbs in the same way that English does. For example, in English we might say "he is running," but in Hopi we would have to choose from a number of much more precise verbal ideas, depending upon the knowledge of the speaker and the validity of the statement. A different form of the verb expresses: "I know that he is running at this very moment," "I know that he is running at this moment even though I cannot see him," "I remember that I saw him running and I presume he is still running," or "I am told that he is running."

A question emerges from such observations. Does language *reflect* a cultural world view or does language actually *shape* the world view? Wilhelm von Humboldt claimed that language shaped a person's *Weltanschauung*. Today many scholars have little concern about a debate over whether a language shapes thought or thought shapes language. They are more concerned, and rightly so, with the fact that language and culture interact, that world views among cultures differ, and that the language used to express that world view may be relative and specific to that view.

(Adapted from H. D. Brown: Learning a Second Culture, in *Culture Bound*)

Notes

weasel words 含糊的语词
sapped 耗尽
jumbo 特大的
subjects 受试者
Shona of Zimbawee 津巴布韦的马绍纳人
Bassa of Liberia 利比里亚的巴萨人
equatorial 赤道地区的
Zaire 扎伊尔
Wilhelm von Humboldt 洪堡特(1767—1835),德国哲学家
Weltanschauung (德语)对世界的看法

Questions

1. Can you explain with examples in our life how the use of language in advertisement influence or change people's attitude toward different products?

2. How does the structure of a question exert subtle influence on people's answers?

3. Do you believe that the language we use shapes our thought? Why or why not?

2
Achieving Equivalence in Translation

The translation of one language into another is far more complex than most people believe. Most people assume that text in one language can be accurately translated into another language, so long as the translator uses a good bilingual dictionary. Unfortunately, languages are not this simple, and direct translations in many cases are difficult if not impossible because (1) words have more than one meaning; (2) many words are culture-bound and have no direct translations, and (3) cultural orientations can render a direct translation into nonsensical results; and (4) a culture may not have the background and understanding to translate experiences specific to other cultures.

Problems often arise in translation when we hope to achieve equivalence between languages.

Lexical equivalence

One of the goals of translation is to convey the meaning of the original language, but dictionary translations rarely reflect common language usage in a culture. Translators also need to deal with nuances and with words that have no equivalents in other language. Eskimo languages have many different words to refer to snow. Were you to translate on a word-for-word basis, you would translate all those different words into the one English word "snow." Much of the meaning of the more specific and more descriptive words—for example, qualities of slushiness or hardness or newness—would be lost in your translation. As another example, there is no equivalent to the English color word *blue* in Russian—the words *goluboj* and *sinij* (usually translated as "light blue" and "dark blue," respectively), refer to what are in Russia distinct colors, not different shades of the same color, as their translation into English might suggest. Consider the problem of the Russian translator of an English-language novel in which there appears the phrase "a blue dress." How should it be translated?

Idiomatic equivalence

Idiomatic expressions are culture-bound; they do not translate well. Consider this example of an Italian idiom translated into English: "*Giovanni sta memando il cane per l'aia*." Translated literally, this is "John is leading his dog around the threshing floor." A better translation, with greater correspondence of meaning, is "John is beating around the bush." Coming up with the second translation thus requires that the translator be familiar with American idioms. It is easy to think of many idioms in common use in English that can be misunderstood: "break a leg," "eat one's words," "hold your horses," "kick the bucket," "raining cats and dogs." This is one of the reasons why foreign languages are difficult for non-native people to learn.

Grammatical-syntactical equivalence

Difficulties may also arise when there are no equivalent grammatical or syntactical features. In the Filipino language, there is no equivalent of the English verb "to be." No relative pronouns in Korean are comparable to the English "who," "which," "that," or "what." In Japanese, there is no parallel for the distinctions made in English between modifiers of nouns that are "countable" and "uncountable" ones. As a result, Japanese translations may render statements like "much shoes" or "many patience."

Experiential equivalence

If an object or experience does not exist in one culture, it is difficult to translate words referring to it into the language of that culture when no word may exist for them. The meanings that cultures have for words are based on shared experiences. When we lack experiential equivalents, we lack the words in our vocabulary to represent those experiences. For instance, when the vocabulary of a tribe in a mountainous jungle region has words for rivers and streams but not oceans, how do you translate the notion of an ocean?

Translations frequently produce misunderstanding or incomprehension because of differences in orientation. For instance, the Quechua language of Peru uses past and future orientations that are the opposite of those used in the English language. Quechua visualizes the past as being in front of or ahead of a person because it can be seen, and it visualizes the future as being behind one because it cannot be seen. Americans instead speak of the past being behind them and the future being ahead. If this difference in orientation were not known or were ignored, translations about time, the past, and the future could be incomprehensible.

Conceptual equivalence

Abstract concepts may not exist in the same fashion in different languages. For example, people in the United States have unique meaning for the word "freedom," that meaning is not universally shared. Speakers of other languages may say they are free and are correct in their culture, but the freedom they refer to is not equivalent to what you experience as freedom in the United States. Difficulty in translation lies in matching concepts. Some concepts are culture-specific and others culture-general. By definition, it is impossible to translate perfectly a culture-specific concept. So different, for instance, are Spanish cultural experiences from English ones that many words cannot be translated directly. Strong affection is expressed in English with the verb *to love*. In Spanish, there are two verbs, *te amo* and *te quiero*. *Te amo* refers to nurturing love, as between a parent and a child or between two adults. *Te quieto* translates literally as *I want you*, which connotes ownership, a concept not present in the English expression *I love you*. Commonly used to express love between two adults, *te quieto* falls somewhere between the English statements *I love you* and *I like you*.

(Based on L. A. Samovar et al.: *Communication between Cultures*, Chapter 5)

Notes

nonsensical 无意义的	beat around the bush 旁敲侧击
nuance 细微差别	visualize 想象

Questions

1. What problems in translation are people likely to encounter?
2. Why are direct translations difficult in some cases? What can we do about it?

Summary

1. It is impossible to separate our use of language from our culture. Language reflects our cultural priorities and values, and culture influences the way we use language.

2. Language is a guide to "social reality," indicating that language is not simply a means of reporting experience but rather a way of defining experience.

3. Culture teaches us both the symbols (words) we use to communicate and what the symbols mean. Symbols and the rules for using the symbols vary from culture to culture.

4. The differences between languages are much more than mere obstacles to communication; they often reflect basic differences in the "world view" of the various people and in what they understand about their life and environments.

Chapter 6 Culture and Verbal Communication

Words have frightening power.

—Colin Cherry

Chapter 6 Culture and Verbal Communication

Preview Questions

1. Do you think you can always talk about anything you know and in any manner you prefer? Why or why not?

2. After years of learning English, do you still have any difficulty talking with English-speaking people? If you do, what is the difficulty?

Text A

Verbal Patterns

Have you noticed how often Americans use the expression "thank you"? A customer, after paying $100 for a meal in a restaurant, says "thank you" to the person who hands him the bill. In response to "I like the color of your car," an American might answer "thank you". In both of these cases no great favor or compliment was extended, yet "thank you" was the automatic response.

When you listen to people speak a foreign language that you understand, have you noticed that the native speakers of that language use words and phrases in a manner different from what you are used to? In American English, for example, people say "thank you" frequently. A word for "thank you" exists in almost every language, but how and when it is used is not always the same. In your language, do you thank people for trivial as well as important or unusual favors? For Americans, this expression is used as a polite response to different kinds of favors and compliments, and is often automatic (e.g., "Thanks for calling" to someone on the phone or "Thank you" to a teller in a bank).

In language there are tacit rules of speaking that, unlike rules of grammar or spelling, are not usually studied in a formal manner. These unspoken "rules" exist in every language but differ significantly from culture to culture. Acquiring a second language demands more than learning new words and another system of grammar. It involves developing sensitivity to aspects of language that are usually not taught in language textbooks. Some important rules include permissible degrees or directness in speech and forms of politeness used in daily conversation.

Compared with other languages, American English strongly emphasizes directness in verbal interaction. Many expressions exemplify this tendency: "Don't beat around the bush," "Let's get down to business," and "Get to the point" all indicate impatience with avoiding issues. If a son hesitates telling his father that he received a bad grade in school, his father might respond angrily with, "Out with it!" or "Speak up!"

Directness is also seen when information is requested from strangers or from people who are not well known to you. For example, when passing a professor's office a student may say, "Excuse me, I'd like to ask you a couple of questions." Her professor may respond, "Sure, go right ahead. What's the problem?" In this interaction, the student stated her purpose and the professor responded immediately.

Offers and responses to offers provide another example of directness in verbal interaction. At a dinner party it would not be unusual to hear the following conservation:

HOST: Would you like some more dessert?

GUEST: No, thank you. It's delicious, but I've really had enough.

HOST: OK, why don't we leave the table and sit in the living room?

In this conversation between two Americans, the host does not repeat the offer more than once. While, for example, in parts of the Middle East a host is expected to offer food several times, a host in the United States may occasionally offer food twice but usually not more than that. If guests are hungry, they need to say directly, "Yes, I'd like some more, thank you." If they are hungry but say, "No, thank you," out of politeness, they may remain hungry for the rest of the evening. A host will assume that a guest's refusal is honest and direct.

Of course, there are limits to the degree of directness a person is allowed to express, especially with people of higher status. A male student was surprised at the reaction of his female teacher when he said, "What has happened to you? You look like you gained a lot of weight!" When the teacher replied, "That's none of your business," he answered in an embarrassed tone, "I was just being honest." In this case, his honesty and directness were inappropriate and unappreciated because of the teacher-student relationship.

Many rules governing speech patterns are learned in childhood and people grow up thinking that everyone has the same rules for speaking. People unconsciously expect others to use the same modes of expression as they do. For instance, not all languages use silence and interruptions in the same way. Have you observed the ways people from different cultures use silence? Have you noticed that some people interrupt conversations more than other people? All cultures do not have the same rules governing these areas of communication.

Many Americans interpret silence in a conversation to mean disapproval, disagreement, or unsuccessful communication. They often try to fill silence by saying something even if they have nothing to say! On the other hand, Americans don't appreciate a person who dominates a conversation. Knowing when to take turns in conversation in another language can sometimes cause difficulty. Should you wait until someone has finished a sentence before contributing to a discussion, or can you break into the middle of someone's sentence? Interrupting someone who is speaking is considered rude in the United States. Even children are taught **explicitly** not to interrupt.

Individuals in every culture have similar basic needs but express them differently. In daily life we all initiate conversation, use formal and informal speech, give praise, express disagreement, seek information, and extend invitations. Some of the verbal patterns we use are influenced by our culture. Whereas directness in speech is common in the United States, indirectness is the rule in parts of the Far East. Thus people from both of these parts of the world would probably express criticism of others differently. The different modes of expression represent variations on the same theme. Each language reflects and creates cultural attitudes; each has a unique way of expressing human need.

(Adapted from D. R. Levine & M. B. Adelman: *Beyond Language*, Chapter 2)

Notes

tacit 心照不宣的　　explicitly 明晰地，直截了当地

Questions

1. What else should you pay attention to in acquiring a new language in addition to its grammar, pronunciation and spelling?
2. What differences can you find between Americans and Chinese in verbal communication?
3. What does silence usually indicate in our culture?

Text B

Direct and Indirect Verbal Styles

The tone of voice, the speaker's intention, and the verbal content reflect our way of speaking, our verbal style, which in turn reflects our cultural and personal values and sentiments.

Verbal style frames "how" a message should be interpreted. The direct-indirect verbal interaction dimension can be thought of as **straddling** a **continuum**. Individuals in all cultures use the gradations of all these verbal styles, depending on role identities, interaction goals, and situations. However, in individualistic cultures, people tend to encounter more situations that emphasize the **preferential** use of direct talk, person-oriented verbal interaction, verbal self-enhancement, and talkativeness. In contrast, in collectivistic cultures, people tend to encounter more situations that emphasize the preferential use of indirect talk, status-oriented verbal interaction, verbal **self-effacement**, and silence.

The direct and indirect styles differ in the extent to which communicators reveal their intentions through their tone of voice and the straightforwardness of their content message. In the direct verbal style, statements clearly reveal the speaker's intentions and are enunciated in a forthright tone of voice. In the indirect verbal style, on the other hand, verbal statements tend to camouflage the speaker's actual intentions and are carried out with more nuanced tone of voice. For example, the overall U. S, American verbal style often calls for clear and direct communication. Phrases such as "say what you mean," "don't beat around the bush," and "get to the point" are some examples. The direct verbal style of the larger U.S. culture is reflective of its low-context communication character.

By the way of comparison, Chinese tend to beat around the bush. They are not forthright enough, so that Westerners often perceive them as insincere and untrustworthy. For example, in a verbal request situation, U.S. Americans tend to use a straightforward form of request whereas Chinese tend to ask for a favor in a more roundabout and implicit way. This can be demonstrated by the following pair of contrastive "airport ride request" scenes between two U.S. Americans and two Chinese:

Scene 1

A1: We're going to New Orleans this weekend.

A2: What fun! I wish we were going with you. How long are you going to be there? [If she wants a ride, she will ask.]

A1: Three days. By the way, we may need a ride to the airport. Do you think you can take us?

A2: Sure. What time?

A1: 10: 30 p.m. this coming Saturday.

Scene 2

C1: We're going to New Orleans this weekend.

C2: What fun! I wish we were going with you. How long are you going to be there?

C1: Three days. [I hope she'll offer me a ride to the airport.]

C2: [She may want me to give her a ride.] Do you need a ride to the airport? I'll take you.

C1: Are you sure it's not too much trouble?

C2: It's no trouble at all.

Here we see that in the Chinese culture such requests for help are likely to be implied rather than stated explicitly and directly. Indirect requests can help both parties to save face and uphold harmonious interaction. When the hearer detects a request during a conversation with the speaker, the hearer can choose to either grant or deny the request. If the hearer decides to deny it, he or she usually does not respond to it or subtly changes the topic of conversation. Consequently, the speaker discerns the cues from the hearer and drops the request. An implicit understanding generally exists between a speaker and a hearer in Chinese culture that is essential to maintain relational harmony at all costs in everyday social interaction.

Intercultural misunderstanding therefore becomes highly probable when Chinese and U.S. Americans communicate with each other. They each adhere to their habitual verbal styles and carry out their cultural scripts to inform them of what to expect in the interaction. Let us look at Scene 3 of the"airport ride request" dialogue, this time between a Chinese speaker and a U.S. American hearer.

Scene 3

C: We're going to New Orleans this weekend.

A: What fun! I wish we were going with you. How long are you going to be there?

C: Three days. [I hope she'll offer me a ride to the airport.]

A: [If she wants a ride, she'll ask me.] Have a great time.

C: [If she had wanted to give me a ride, she would have offered it. I'd better ask somebody else.] Thanks. I'll see you when I get back.

Thus we see that while the U.S. American verbal model rewards direct assertions and opinions, the Chinese model emphasizes indirect verbal style to cultivate relational harmony and implicit interpersonal understanding.

(Adapted from S. Ting-Toomey: *Communication across Cultures*, Chapter 4)

Notes

straddle 跨越
continuum 差异序列连续体
preferential 优先的
self-enhancement 凸显自我
self-effacement 隐匿自我
straightforwardness 坦率，易懂
enunciate 阐述
forthright 直截了当的
camouflage 隐蔽
nuanced 有细微差异的
beat around the bush 转弯抹角
untrustworthy 不可靠的，不值得信任的
roundabout 迂回的，间接的
assertion 断言，认定
cultivate 建立，形成

Questions

1. How does style reflect our cultural and personal values and sentiments?

2. Are Chinese always more indirect than Americans? If not, can you give some counter examples?

3. Which style, direct or indirect, do you think is more polite than the other?

Exploration

In our everyday life there are many situations where people tend to use indirect ways to express themselves. For instance, they do not often say "no" directly to others but express this meaning in some other ways.

Think of how you would behave in the following situations:

1. When you are offered a drink the taste of which you find very unpleasant.
2. When your friends ask if you will go to a picnic with them and you do not feel like going.
3. When you are asked by a younger student about the meaning of an English word that you do not know.
4. When you are asked whether you agree with a professor's idea about learning English that you do not quite appreciate.
5. When you find yourself in class unable to answer the question the teacher asks you.
6. When someone asks for your finished homework to copy and you do not like to comply.
7. When you are asked by your parents about your problems in your studies and you do not want to tell them.
8. When you are asked by your boss to work overtime at the weekend and you do not really like to.

Then try to find out what are the possible ways people can use in expressing the negative, unfavorable, or unpleasant meanings of "no" in our society.

Cases for Discussion

Case 1

In an attempt to locate an outlet for its products in Europe, a large U.S. manufacturer sent one of its promising young executives to Frankfurt to make a presentation to a reputable German **distributor**. The U.S. company had considerable confidence in the choice of this particular junior executive because the man not only spoke fluent German but also knew a good deal of German culture.

When the American entered the conference room where he would be making his presentation, he did all the right things. He shook hands firmly, greeted everyone with a friendly *guten tag*, and bowed his head slightly as is customary in Germany. Drawing on his experience as a past president of the Toastmasters Club in his hometown, the U.S. executive started his presentation with a few humorous anecdotes to set a relaxed mood. At the end of his presentation, however, he sensed that his talk had not gone well. In fact, the presentation was not well received, for the German company chose not to distribute the U.S. company's products.

Notes

distributor 经销商　　*guten tag*（德语）你好

Questions

1. What was wrong? Which of the following may have been the factors contributing to the failure of the presentation?

a. The American did not make a careful preparation for his presentation.

b. The American did not know extensively enough about his company's products.

c. Starting his presentation with several jokes made the Germans think that he was not very serious about the business.

d. The Germans considered the American executive too young for such an important job.

e. The Germans did not like the American, a foreigner, speaking their language with great fluency.

2. What can we learn from the story?

Case 2

The following are two letters, one in Chinese and the other in English. Compare them to see if there is similarity in their verbal patterns.

A

尊敬的节目主持人：

我作为贵台英语教学节目和《你喜欢的歌》节目的忠实听众已有好几年的历史了。我认为贵台的这两个节目办得非常好。

请让我做个自我介绍：我是一名中学生，今年十八岁。我的家乡是一个边疆小城，文化活动办得也不错。由于我喜欢学习英语，所以比较关注这方面的电台节目。但是因为中央人民广播电台的英语节目比较深奥，不适合我学习，所以我一直从贵台的英语节目里得到听力、会话能力训练。这种训练使我受益匪浅。随着课程难度一步步地提高，我深感没有一本教材，学习会遇到很多困难。因为这个，我抽出时间给贵台写这封信，希望能得到一本贵台英语节目的教材。教材的费用请来信告知。

另外，我希望得到贵台印制的年历，并祝你们的节目办得更加有趣。

B

Dear Professor X,

How are you? Please pardon me for bothering you while you are so busy. But there is one thing on which I need our help.

I am a lover of English, but for a long time I have not been able to study English systemically. Now I am staying at home on sick leave and it occurred to me that I should take it up seriously. I went to the Foreign Language Book Store in our provincial capital and had a look. I found the English textbook which you edited suits my level. But the store had no tapes. Could you please tell me where I can get the tapes through mail order and how much I need to pay? Besides, the textbook has only two volumes. Is there supplementary material to accompany them? Can I get both the books and the tapes through mail order?

I am almost thirty years old, but learned English only at secondary school. I like it very much and it will be useful for future work. So I want to begin from the beginning and I wonder if the book is right for me.

I look forward to hearing from you.

Questions

1. What do you think of the two letters above? What do they have in common though they are written in different languages?

2. When you are making a request in English, will you do it in the Chinese way or not?

Case 3

A Turkish male graduate student in the United States lived in a residence hall where he shared a room with an American. One day his roommate went into the bathroom and completely shaved his head. The Turkish student discovered this fact when he visited the bathroom and saw the hair everywhere. He returned to his room and said to his roommate, "You've shaved your head." The American replied, "Yeah, I did."

The Turkish student waited a little, then said, "I discovered you'd shaved your head when I went into the bathroom and saw the hair." "Yeah," the American confirmed.

The Turk was at a loss. He believed he had communicated in the strongest possible language his wish that the American would clean up the mess he'd made in the bathroom.

Later he discussed the surprising episode with Turkish friends, who told him, "Listen, with Americans you actually have to say 'Clean up the bathroom'!" The Turkish student believed his message had been very clear.

Notes

episode 插曲；一段经历

Questions

1. Why did the Turkish student just said "You've shaved your head" when he wanted the American to clean up the mess he'd made in the bathroom?

2. Why didn't the American student clean up the bathroom as the Turkish student wished?

Readings for Further Study

1
Communication Is Culturally Relative

What is it that can be culturally relative in communication? The answer is, just about everything—all the aspects of what to say and how to say it.

When to talk

To start on the most general level, the question of when to talk is culturally relative. I had an opportunity to see the extent to which this is true when I recently co-edited a collection of papers on the topic of silence. Moreover, cultures differ with respect to what is perceived as silence and when it is deemed appropriate.

People experience silence when they think there could or should be talk. If two people are sitting together, one may think there's a silence when the other does not. Athabaskan Indians consider it inappropriate to talk to strangers, and that this has an odd effect when an Athabaskan meets a non-Athabaskan, white or black. One wants to get to know the other by talking, and the other feels it is inappropriate to talk until they know each other.

The result of this kind of difference that non-Athabaskans conclude that Indians are sullen, uncooperative, even stupid, because they don't talk in situations where the non-Athabaskans expect them to talk (hence they have nothing to say or refuse to say what's on their minds). And on the other side, Athabaskan Indians have negative stereotypes of non-Athabaskans as ridiculously garrulous and also hypocritical because they act as if they're your friends when they're not.

Such mutual negative stereotypes are found in country after country. Those who expect more talk stereotype the more silent group as uncooperative and stupid. Those who use less talk think of the more talkative group as pushy, hypocritical, and untrustworthy. The same pattern is also seen in the United States in the mutual negative stereotypes of New Yorkers and non-New Yorkers.

What to say

Once a speaker decides to talk, what is it appropriate to say? Can one ask questions, and what can one ask about? Australian Aborigines never ask the question "Why?" Alaskan Athabaskans rarely ask questions. For these and other speakers, questions are regarded as too powerful to use, because they demand a response.

A universal way of communicating is telling stories. But when are they told? How many can be told? What can they be about? What can the point be, and how is the point communicated? Often stories may seem obviously appropriate when they pop out of our mouths, but may not seem appropriate to those whose ears they pop into—especially if the speaker and hearer have different cultural backgrounds. For example, when and how and about what can jokes be told? When is it appropriate to use irony and sarcasm, and how are they signaled? When can advice or information be solicited or offered—and how? How and when are compliments given and taken?

A personal experience in Greece made me aware of the cultural convention involved in exchanging compliments, which I, in my naive pre-linguist state, had assumed to be evidence of personality. I was invited to join a dinner party at the home of a man who was an excellent cook. He had prepared an elaborate dinner, including many small individually-prepared delicacies. During dinner, I complimented the food, "These are delicious." My host agreed, "Yes they are delicious." I praised, "It must have taken hours to prepare." "Oh, yes," he agreed."These take many hours to prepare." Taking for granted that a host should not compliment his or her own cooking and should minimize his or her effort, I decided that this host was egotistical.

When leaving the dinner party, I said, "Thank you for the wonderful meal".And the host retorted, "What, those little nothings?" with a dismissing wave of his hand in the direction of the table and a self-deprecating grimace on his face. I was surprised again, and even felt hurt, as if he were implying I had been making too big a deal about the effort involved in preparing the meal. I expected him to accept the compliment this time, saying something like, "The pleasure was mine; come again."

So I saw that we differed not about whether compliments should be accepted or deflected, but rather which compliments should be accepted and which deflected—and how. What I had interpreted as a personality characteristic was a cultural convention.

Pacing and pausing

The next level of cross-cultural difference is that of the conversational control mechanisms of pacing and pausing. How fast does one speak, and how long does one wait following another speaker's utterance, before concluding the other has no more to say? Differences in expectations about these matters can bring a conversation to an end.

If two people who are talking have even slightly different expectations about how long to wait between turns, then the person who expects a slightly shorter pause will take a turn first—filling and thus curtailing the pause that the other is waiting for. I had a British friend who I thought never had anything to say (which was becoming rather annoying) until I learned that she was waiting for a pause to take her turn—a pause of a length that never occurred around me, because before it did, I perceived an uncomfortable silence which I kindly headed off by talking.

Even being married is no proof against mutual misinterpretation. These kinds of slightly different habits explain misunderstandings that have plagued many people their entire married lives. Slightly slower partners accuse faster ones of not giving them a chance to talk and not being interested in what they have to say. Slightly faster partners accuse slower ones of not talking to them and not saying what's on their minds.

Listenership

Another level of processing in conversation that is automatic and taken for granted is showing listenership. Oneway is through gaze. It has been found that white participants in counseling interviews maintained eye gaze when listening and frequently broke their gaze when speaking. Blacks did the opposite. They maintained steady eye contact when speaking and frequently broke their gaze when listening.

This meant that when a white speaker talked to a black listener, s/he got the feeling that the listener wasn't paying attention because the expected sign of attention—steady gaze—wasn't there. And when the white speaker sent a small signal asking for confirmation of comprehension, the black listener often missed it because s/he was looking away. So the speaker said the same thing again, in simpler terms—talking down. When the white was the listener, the black speaker's steady gaze seemed overbearing.

If one's speaking habits create a strange reaction in a listener, one rarely realizes that the strange behavior is a reaction to one's own way of talking. One thinks, instead, that the other has strange speaking habits—or is a strange person.

Indirectness

Communication in any culture is a matter of indirectness. Only a part of meaning resides in the words spoken; the largest part is communicated by hints, assumptions, and audience filling-in from context and prior experience. Yet how to be indirect is culturally relative.

Americans as a group tend to ignore or even rail against indirectness. We believe that words should say what they mean and people should be accountable only for what they say in words. We tend to forget the importance of the interpersonal level of interaction and think that in some (if not most or even all) instances, only the "content" counts.

This is the value associated with "getting-down to brass tacks" and "sticking to facts"—values taken for granted in American business and education, and perhaps more generally by American men. But it gets American businessmen in trouble when they try to skip the small talk and get right down to business with Japanese, Arab, or Mediterranean counterparts, for whom elaborate "small talk" is big and essential, furnishing the foundation for any business dealings.

Communication is, by its very nature, culturally relative. Ways of communicating meaning in talk are learned in the speech community, that is by talking to people with whom one identifies socially. As social networks are always local, not global, people in different communities have different ways of using linguistic means to communicative ends, and their ways of talking, like other cultural patterns, define them as a community. This illustrates Edward Hall's assertion that culture is communication. To the extent that no two people have exactly the same communicative background, to that extent, all communication is cross-cultural, and understanding cross-cultural communication is a means to understanding language at the same time that it is a means to understanding and, one hopes, improving problems and tasks facing the world and the people in it, including the task of teaching and learning new languages.

(Adapted from D. Tannen: The Pragmatics of Cross-Cultural Communication, in *Applied Linguistics*, Vol.5, No.3)

Notes

Athabaskan Indian (北美)阿撒巴斯卡印第安人
garrulous 非常啰唆的，喋喋不休的
stereotype 成见，刻板印象
Australian Aborigine 澳大利亚土著居民
solicit 征求
egotistical 自负的
grimace 怪相，鬼脸
deflect 偏转；不接受
curtail 截短，缩短
talk down 以居高临下的口气说话
overbearing 傲慢的
accountable 负有责任的

Questions

1. Is talking more or less a cultural matter as well as a personal preference?

2. How should we behave when we are listening to others? Are there any cultural or sub-cultural differences you have ever noticed in your experiences of communication?

3. What does "getting down to brass tacks" mean? Do people always have the same idea about what are important facts and what are not?

2
The Impact of Confucianism on Communication

Confucianism's primary concern with social relationships has strongly influenced communication patterns in East Asia. In general, it has strengthened patterns that help to build and maintain proper human relationships.

Process vs. outcome oriented communication

Since the main function of communication under Confucian philosophy is to initiate, develop, and maintain social relationships, there is a strong emphasis on the kind of communication that promotes such relationships. For instance, it is very important in East Asia to engage in small talk before initiating business and to communicate personalized information, especially information that would help place each person in the proper context.

In contrast, when the main function of communication is to actualize autonomy and self-fulfillment, as in North America, the outcome of the communication is more important than the process. Tangible outcomes in terms of friends gained, opponents defeated, and self-fulfillment achieved become the primary function of communication.

Differentiated vs. less differentiated linguistic codes

East Asian languages are very complex and are differentiated according to social status, the degree of intimacy, age, sex, and the level of formality. There are also extensive and elaborate honorific linguistic systems in East Asian languages. These differentiations result from Confucian ethical rules that place the highest value on proper human relationships.

One of the main differences between English, Japanese, and Korean is the levels of speech. In both Korean and Japanese, there are two axes of distinction: the axis of address and the axis of reference. The axis of address is divided into plain, polite, and honorific while the axis of reference is divided into humble and neutral. An honorific form is used to refer to the receiver's action, while a humble form is used to refer to the sender's action—the reverse would not be appropriate.

In Korean or Japanese, pronouns, verbs, and nouns all have different levels. Thus, in English "to eat" is "to eat" regardless of the person addressed. In the Korean language, however, there are three different ways of saying "to eat": *mul-da* (plain), *du-shin-da* (polite), and *chap-soo-shin-da* (honorific). Different levels of a verb are often accompanied by different levels of a noun: rice may be *bap* (plain), *shik-sa* (polite), or *jin-ji* (honorific).

Indirect vs. direct communication

Most cultures have both direct and indirect modes of communication. Even though the indirect mode of communication seems to be universal, however, the degree to which it is elaborated varies from culture to culture.

The Confucian legacy of consideration for others and concern for proper human relationships has led to the development of communication patterns that preserve one another's face. Indirect communication helps to prevent the embarrassment of rejection by the other person or disagreement among partners, leaving the relationship and each other's face intact. It has been suggested that "defending face" is one of the main factors influencing Japanese behavior. There are a number of ways for defending face, such as asking someone else to transmit the message, talking to a third person in the presence of the hearer, and conveying one's message as being from someone else, which are all indirect forms of communication.

It has also been suggested that there is a significant difference in the level of indirectness between North American and East Asian communication patterns. An American might say "The door is open" as an indirect way of asking the hearer to shut the door, while in Japan, instead of saying "The door is open," one often says "It is somewhat cold today." This is even more indirect, because no words refer to the door.

Receiver vs. sender centeredness

North American communication very often centers on the sender, and until recently the linear, one-way model from sender to receiver was the prevailing model of communication. Much emphasis has been placed on how senders can formulate better messages, improve source credibility, polish their delivery skills, and so forth. In contrast, the emphasis in East Asia has always been on listening and interpretation.

Infinite interpretation has been identified as one of the main principles of Chinese communication. The process presumes that the emphasis is on the receiver and listening rather than the sender of speech making. In Japan, instead of the speaker's having to tell or ask for what he or she wants specifically, others guess and accommodate his or her needs, sparing him or her embarrassment in case the verbally expressed request cannot be met. In such cases, the burden of communication falls not on the message sender but on the message receiver. A person who "hears one and understands ten" is regarded as an intelligent communicator. One of the common puzzles expressed by foreign students from East Asia is why they are constantly being asked what they want when they are visiting in American homes. In their own countries, the host or hostess is supposed to know what is needed and serve accordingly. The difference occurs because in North America it is important to provide individual freedom of choice.

With the emphasis on indirect communication, the receiver's sensitivity and ability to capture the under-the-surface meaning and to understand implicit meaning becomes critical. In North America, an effort has been made to improve the effectiveness of senders through such formal training as debate and public speech, whereas in East Asia, the effort has been on improving the receiver's sensitivity.

The East Asian emphasis on social relationships and the North American emphasis on individualism produce very different patterns of interpersonal relationships and communication. The conclusions drawn in this paper are not absolute, however. Each culture contains both orientations to some degree.

The North America and the East Asian Orientations to Communication Patterns

East Asian Orientations	North American Orientations
Process orientation Communication is perceived as a process of infinite interpretation	Outcome orientation Communication is perceived as the transference of messages
Differentiated linguistic codes Different linguistics codes are used depending upon persons involved and situations	Less differentiated linguistic codes Linguistic codes are not as extensively differentiated as East Asia
Indirect communication emphasis The use of indirect communication is prevalent and accepted as normative	Direct communication emphasis Direct communication is a norm despite the extensive use of indirect communication
Receiver centered Meaning is in the interpretation Emphasis is on listening, sensitivity, and removal of preconception	Sender centered Meaning is in the messages created by the sender Emphasis is on how to formulate the best messages, how to improve source credibility and delivery skills

(Adapted from J. O. Yum: Confucianism and Interpersonal Relationships and Communication Patterns in East Asia, in *Communication Monographs*, Vol.55, No.4)

Notes

actualize 实现,使发生
elaborate 详尽的,复杂的
honorific 表示敬意的,敬语的
reference 指代,指称
legacy 遗产
intact 未受损的,未触动的
source credibility 信息来源的可信度
polish 改进
accommodate 迎合,满足

Questions

1. Why are the East Asians and Americans so different in the way they communicate?

2. What problems may arise in communication between East Asians and North Americans?

3. Which of the East Asian orientations to communication patterns are still very strong in our life in China today? And which are not? Supply examples to support your observation.

Summary

1. Tacit rules of speaking differ significantly from culture to culture. These rules include permissible degrees or directness in speech and forms of politeness used in daily conversation. These unspoken "rules" exist in every language but differ significantly from culture to culture.

2. The importance of verbal communication appears to be universally acknowledged, but cultures differ in the importance they place on words, talk and context.

3. Our communication with people who speak in a different way from us can easily lead to misunderstandings or inaccurate predictions if we assume their way of speaking is the same as ours.

4. Communication is, by its nature, culturally relative, such as when to say, what to say, how to say it, and how much to say about it.

Chapter 7 Culture and Nonverbal Communication

There's language in her eye, her cheek, her lip. Nay, her foot speaks.

—William Shakespeare

Chapter 7 Culture and Nonverbal Communication

Preview Questions

1. Apart from verbal language, what other means of communication do you know?

2. How do you use the nonverbal means of communication in everyday life?

3. Have you ever noticed some differences between us Chinese and people from other countries in nonverbal behavior?

Text A

The Silent Language

Language studies traditionally have emphasized verbal and written language, but recently have begun to consider communication that takes place without words. In some types of communication people express more nonverbally than verbally. If you ask an obviously depressed person, "What's wrong?", and he answers, "Nothing, I'm fine," you probably won't believe him. When an angry person says, "Let's forget this subject, I don't want to talk about it any more!" you know that he hasn't stopped communicating. His silence and withdrawal continue to convey emotional meaning.

One study done in the United States showed that in the communication of attitudes, 93 percent of the message was transmitted by the tone of the voice and by facial expressions, whereas only 7 percent of the speaker's attitude was transmitted by words. Apparently, we express our emotions and attitudes more nonverbally than verbally.

Nonverbal communication expresses meaning or feeling without words. Universal emotions, such as happiness, fear, and sadness, are expressed in a similar nonverbal way throughout the world. There are, however, nonverbal differences across cultures that may be a source of confusion for foreigners. For example, feelings of friendship exist everywhere but their expression varies. It may be acceptable in some countries for men to embrace each other and for women to hold hands; in other countries these displays of affection may be shocking.

What is acceptable in one culture may be completely unacceptable in another. One culture may determine that snapping fingers to call a waiter is appropriate; another may consider this gesture rude. We are often not aware of how gestures, facial expressions, eye contact, and the use of space affect communication. In order to correctly interpret another culture's style of communication, it is necessary to study the "silent language" of that culture.

Gestures

Gestures refer to specific body movements that carry meaning. Hands can form shapes that convey many meanings: "That's expensive," "Come here," "Go away," and "it's OK" can be expressed nonverbally using only hands. The gestures for these phrases may differ among languages. As children we imitate and learn these nonverbal movements and often use them to accompany or replace words. When traveling to another country, foreign visitors soon learn that not all gestures are universal.

The "OK" gesture in the American culture is a symbol for money in Japan. The same gesture is obscene in some Latin American countries.

Facial expressions

Facial expressions carry meaning determined by contexts and relationships. For instance, the smile, which is typically an expression of pleasure, has many functions. A woman's smile at a policeman who is about to give her a ticket does not carry the same meaning as the smile she gives to a young child. A smile may show affection, convey politeness, or disguise true feelings. Pain is conveyed by a grimace, which also signifies disgust or disapproval. Surprise, shock, or disbelief can be shown by raising the eyebrows. A wink given to a friend may mean "You and I have a secret" or "I'm just kidding." Between a man and a woman, a wink can be flirtatious. Our faces easily reveal emotions and attitudes.

The degree of facial expressiveness also varies among individuals and cultures. The fact that members of one culture do not express their emotions as openly as members of another does not mean they do not experience emotions. Rather, there are cultural restraints on the amount of nonverbal expressiveness permitted. Given individual differences, it is difficult to make generalizations about a cultural style of communication. Americans express themselves facially in varying degrees. People from certain ethnic backgrounds in the United States may use their hands, bodies, and faces more than other Americans. There are no fixed rules, although it is considered negative or suspicious to have a "deadpan" expression or a "poker face." Some people can be "read like a book"; others are difficult to read.

Eye contact

Eye Contact is important because insufficient or excessive eye contact may create communication barriers. It is important in relationships because it serves to show intimacy, attention, and influence. As with facial expressions, there are no specific rules governing eye behavior except that it is considered rude to stare, especially at strangers. It is, however, common for two strangers to walk toward each other, make eye contact, smile and perhaps even say "Hi." The strangers may immediately look away and forget that they even had any contact. This type of glance does not mean much; it is simply a way of acknowledging another person's presence. In a conversation too little eye contact may be seen negatively because it conveys lack of interest, inattention, or even mistrust. The relationship between mistrust and lack of eye contact is stated directly in the expression, "Never trust a person who can't look you in the eye."

Touch

Just as our words and gestures are messages carrying our internal thoughts and feelings, so touch, too, conveys messages. The meaning we assign to being touched, and our reasons for touching others, help us gain insight into the communication encounter.

Studies on touching have uncovered some interesting insights. For example, the meaning inferred from a touch is influenced by a number of factors. First is the state we are in at the time of the touch. Second, our personal past history helps define the contact. Third, our perceived relationship with the toucher will influence the meaning we attach to the touch. Finally, the location of the touch (arm, leg, breast), the relative pressure of the touch (firm handshake, soft kiss), the duration of the touch (momentary, prolonged), the relative temperature of the skin, whether the touch was active or passive (purposeful touching or accidental brushing), and the situation (two people alone or a crowded room), are all conditions that affect the meaning of the message.

There is widespread agreement about a number of generalizations regarding touching and nontouching cultures. The English, British-Americans, and the Germans, for instance, are cultures that employ very little touching in public. In contrast, Hispanic-Americans and peoples of Eastern European Jewish descent represent cultures with a great deal of tactile experiences. The Italian, French, and Arab cultures also are highly tactile people.

Culture does not always determine the messages that our body movements convey. Contexts, personalities, and relationships also influence them. Therefore, no two people in any one society have the same nonverbal behavior. However, like verbal language, nonverbal communication cannot be completely separated from culture. Whether we emphasize differences or similarities, the "silent language" is much louder than it first appears.

(Adapted from D. R. Levine & M. B. Adelman: *Beyond Language*, Chapter 3)

Notes

snapping fingers 手指弹出响声

obscene 下流的;令人厌恶的

grimace 怪相,鬼脸

flirtatious 调情的,轻佻的

Hispanic-American 拉美裔的美国人

tactile 触觉的

Questions

1. Why is nonverbal communication inseparable from culture?
2. How do we Chinese express emotions and attitudes nonverbally? Give some examples.

3. How do people coordinate their verbal and nonverbal behavior in communication process?

Text B

Some Nonverbal Behaviors in Different Cultures

It should be obvious by now that the study of nonverbal behavior is an important component to the study of intercultural communication. Much of our difficulty with people in other countries stems from the fact that so little is known about nonverbal communication. Formal training in the language, history, government, and customs of another nation is only the first step in a comprehensive program. Of equal importance is an introduction to the nonverbal language which exists in every country of the world and among the various groups within each country.

The importance of nonverbal communication, and its significance to the study of intercultural communication, is made even more apparent if you recall that culture is invisible, omnipresent, and learned. Nonverbal communication has these same qualities. Individuals are aware of little of their own nonverbal behavior, which is enacted mindlessly, spontaneously, and unconsciously. Much of our nonverbal behavior, like culture, tends to be elusive, spontaneous, and frequently beyond our awareness.

Another parallel between culture and nonverbal behavior is that both need to be learned. Although much of outward behavior is innate (such as smiling, moving, touching, eye contact), cultures formulate display rules that dictate when, how, and with what consequences nonverbal expressions will be exhibited. Put in slightly different terms, we are born with the capacity to cry, yet what makes us cry and who is allowed to see us cry need to be learned as part of our cultural "education."

We remind you that culture is all-persuasive, multidimensional, and boundless; it is everywhere and in everything. The same is also true of nonverbal behavior. Our clothes and jewelry, the countless expressions we can reflect with our face, the hundreds of movements we can make with our bodies, where and how we touch people, our gaze and eye contact, vocal behaviors such as laughter, and our use of time, space, and silence are just some of the behaviors in which we engage that serve as messages.

General appearance and dress

In intercultural communication, appearance and objects are important because the standards we apply and the judgments we make are subject to cultural interpretations. In the United States, people tend to value the appearance of tall, slender women. In Japan, diminutive females are deemed the most attractive.

Clothing—how much, how little, and what kind—is also a reflection of a culture's value orientation. For example, modesty is highly valued among Arabs. Muslim girls usually wear scarves to cover their heads, and in most instances, "girls are not allowed to participate in swimming classes because of the prohibitions against exposing their bodies."

We all know from personal experience that even the color of someone's skin can influence how we perceive and communicate with him or her. This information often dictates eye contact, our use of space, topic selection, and even the amount of time we spend with the other person.

Posture

Posture and sitting habits offer insight into a culture's deep structure. In many Asian cultures, the bow is much more than a greeting. It signifies the culture's concern with status and rank. In Japan, for example, low posture is an indicator of respect. Although it appears simple to the outsider, the bowing ritual is actually rather complicated. The person who occupies the lower station begins the bow, and his or her bow must be deeper than the other person's. The superior, on the other hand, determines when the bowing is to end. When the participants are of equal rank, they begin the bow in the same manner and end at the same time.

In the United States, where being casual and friendly is valued, people often fall into chairs or slouch when they stand. In many countries, such as Germany and Sweden, where lifestyles tend to be more formal, slouching is considered a sign of rudeness and poor manners. In Turkey, putting one's hands in one's pockets is a sign of disrespect.

The manner in which we sit also can communicate a message. In Ghana and in Turkey, sitting with one's legs crossed is extremely offensive. People in Thailand believe that because the bottoms of the feet are the lowest part of the body, they should never be pointed in the direction of another person. In fact, for the Thai, the feet take on so much significance that people avoid stomping with them.

Paralanguage

When the German poet Klopstock wrote "The tones of human voices are mightier than strings or brass to move the soul," he knew that sounds we generate often communicate more than the words that they produce.

Paralanguage involves the linguistic elements of speech, that is, how something is said and not the actual meaning of the spoken words. Most classifications divide paralanguage into three kinds of vocalizations: (1) vocal characterizers (laughing, crying, yelling, moaning, whining, belching, yawning); (2) vocal qualifiers (volume, pitch, rhythm, tempo, resonance, tone); and (3) vocal segregates ("un-huh," "shh," "uh," "oooh," "mmmh," "humm"). It is extraordinary how many inferences about content and character we can make just from the sounds people produce. For example, paralanguage cues assist us in drawing conclusions about an individual's emotional state, socioeconomic status, height, weight, age, intelligence, race, regional background, and educational level.

As with all other aspects of our nonverbal behavior, culture influences our use of and response to paralanguage. We only have to look at differences in the use of volume to see this. Arabs speak very loudly because loudness for them connotes strength and sincerity, while softness communicates weakness and deviousness. For Israelis, increased volume reflects strong beliefs toward the issue under discussion. The Germans conduct their business with a commanding tone that projects authority and self-confidence. On the other end of the continuum, there are cultures that have a very different view toward loud and firm voices. For Thai people, a loud voice is perceived as being impolite. In Japan, raising one's voice often implies a lack of self-control. For them, a gentle and soft voice reflects good manners and helps maintain social harmony—two important values in Japanese culture. When interacting with Americans, people from cultures that speak softly often believe that Americans are angry or upset because of their relatively loud speech.

(Adapted from L. A. Samovar: *Communication between Cultures*, Chapter 6)

Notes

omnipresent 无所不在的
diminutive 娇小的
slouch 懒散地坐或站
Turkey 土耳其
Ghana 加纳
Thailand 泰国
stomp 跺脚
strings or brass 弦乐器或铜管乐器
paralanguage 辅助语言,副语言
deviousness 旁敲侧击,迂回
Israeli 以色列人

Questions

1. Why is nonverbal communication important to intercultural communication?
2. Can you illustrate how nonverbal communication reveal basic cultural trait?
3. Can you generalize the features of the use of nonverbal language in China?

Exploration

Do you think what a person wears will influence your communication with him or her? Many of us like to feel that we are not generally influenced by what a person wears; we prefer to think that we judge a person by what he or she actually is.

But think for a moment for how often our first judgments are based on the manner in which a person is dressed. More important, those initial messages usually influence the perception of everything else that follows. But in fact we do draw conclusions about other people based on the way they dress. Our choice of clothing always communicates a message, and we often use it and other body adornment (e.g. make up, jewelry, hairstyle) to create a particular image of ourselves.

In this aspect, culture has a powerful influence upon us. By dressing ourselves in the culturally appropriate way, we are sending messages about us not just as individuals, but also as a member of a particular cultural group.

Do you think the way we are dressed is very important in intercultural communication? How would you dress yourself when you communicate with foreigners?

Cases for Discussion

Case 1

Linda was a young Puerto Rican girl studying in a New York City high school. She was once suspected of smoking with a group of troublemakers and was punished with them by the principal. She was thought so because when she was interviewed by the principal, she avoided meeting his eyes and only stared down at the floor, hence being regarded as sly and dishonest. Her mother insisted that she was a good girl while the principal firmly believed that she was not. This led to a demonstration of Puerto Rican parents at the school the next morning. It was when John Flores, a Spanish literature teacher at the school, explained some basic facts of Puerto Rican culture to the principal that he realized that he might have misunderstood the girl. And later he found that Linda was indeed a gentle and sweet girl.

Notes

Puerto Rican 波多黎各(人)的

Questions

1. How could the principal have so clearly misinterpreted Linda's behavior?
2. What kind of role did Flores play in solving the problem?

Case 2

Selma had only recently arrived in Indonesia from the United States as a part of a student exchange program and she was delighted in living in such a foreign country. Upon her arrival, she forgot her fatigue from the journey and began to explore new things and experience the local culture. Very soon, her love for the local culture was increased and she had made quite a few friends with the local students.

One day, she was asked to attend a birthday party and she was delighted, for she was curious to know what an Indonesian birthday party was like. When she arrived at the party she was amazed at the new things: the food was different, the drinks were different, and the birthday greeting was different, too. But to her surprise, she was the only one that dressed in typically Western clothes. Although she had no strong reason to become uneasy, her uneasy feeling prevailed as the party was going on. Trying to make herself feel better, she went to the foot table and began to help herself. But, upon leaving the table, she tripped on the leg of a chair and spilled her drink on the floor. Immediately, one of the girls nearby stooped down to begin mopping up the spill and everyone else in the room began laughing out aloud. Selma, uncertain what to do next, quietly moved out of her way with her head lowered in shame. She was so down that she tried hard to avoid more trouble. She was obviously embarrassed.

Selma was embarrassed because she thought others were laughing at her. In her eyes the others' laughing upon her awkward behavior was a kind of insult and humiliation. But if she had known a little about Indonesian culture on the meaning of laughing, she wouldn't have had such a bad time.

Interestingly, for Indonesians, laughing has a special function on some tense social occasions. People laugh to release the tension, embarrassment or difficult situations. They laugh to express their concern about you, their intention to put you at ease or to help you come out of the embarrassment. In Indonesia, people laugh even when they talk about the death or disasters of their friends or relatives. They laugh just to help their friends get rid of sorrow or such bad emotions. But to Americans, laughing on such an occasion is surely an insulting response, humiliating and negative.

Questions

1. What function(s) does laughing serve in similar situations in China?

2. What should we do to help ourselves or other people out of embarrassment caused by cultural differences in laughing?

Case 3

Wang Ping, a Chinese university lecturer, was teaching in a Mexican university. He had made some friends with professors and students there. One day he went to a party where the atmosphere became less and less inhibited. Wang Ping noticed that men and women touched each other a lot more than he was used to. At the end of the party, most people hugged each other good-bye. One woman came to hug Wang Ping, but he stiffened as she attempted to give him a hug. He had never hugged any women except his wife in his life. Other women noticed this, and no one else tried to hug him.

However, Wang Ping felt left out when people hugged each other but not him. He found himself in a very awkward situation: he did not want to be hugged, neither did he want to be left out. He did not know what he wanted or how to resolve his conflicting emotions.

Questions

1. Are you accustomed to being hugged by other people? Do you like it?
2. If you were in the place of Wang Ping, what would you do?

Readings for Further Study

1
Black Walk and Japanese Bow

Nonverbal patterns are a learned form of communication which are patterned within a culture, and they convey particular messages.

The "Black walk," as it is called, communicates certain nonverbal messages. Young Black males have their own way of walking. Observing young Black males walking down ghetto streets, one can't help noticing that they are, indeed, in Thoreau's words "marching to the tune of a different drummer." The "different drummer" is a different culture; the nonverbal message of their walk is similar to the nonverbal message of young White males, but not quite the same.

The young White males' walk is usually brisk, and they walk on the balls of their feet with strides of presumed authority. Both arms swing while they walk. The nonverbal messages is: "I am a strong man, possessing all the qualities of masculinity, and I stride through the world with masculine authority."

The young Black males' walk is different. First of all, it's much slower—it's more of a stroll. The head is sometimes slightly elevated and casually tipped to the side. Only one arm swings at the side with the hand slightly cupped. The other arm hangs limply to the side or it is tucked in the pocket. The gait is slow, casual and rhythmic. The gait is almost like a walking dance, with all parts of the body moving in rhythmic harmony. It is referred to as "walking that walk."

The walk of young Black males communicates the same nonverbal message as that of young White males. In addition, the Black walk communicates that the young Black male is beautiful. Finally, the Black walk communicates that the walker is "cool"; in other words, he is not upset or bothered by the cares of the world and is, in fact, somewhat disdainful and insolent towards the world.

The Black walk is used for mobility (as any walk is) and to arrive at a destination. Sometimes, however, one gets the feeling that where the young Black male is going is not as important as how he gets there. There is a great deal of "styling" in the walk. The means are more important than the end.

One of the most important nonverbal communications in hierarchy-conscious Japan is the bow (*o-jigi*). Its first task is to establish a certain condition of communication. As has been pointed out, bowing is the beginning of human relations in Japan. Furthermore, it enhances and augments many civilities mentioned during a conversation between people and can finally be used to end the interaction.

However, bowing is usually a far more intricate procedure in Japan because it may involve several repeats, and the angle at which the trunk of human body moves downward from the vertical position is of great importance. In Japan, mutual bowing is largely determined by rank: the social inferior bows more deeply and the superior decides when to stop bowing. Where the relative social standing is not clear-cut, these decisions may be difficult for both. Here an especially close watch must be kept on the other person to estimate depth and duration of the other's bow. Frequently one tries to be the more polite one, and this can result in a "bowing contest." When bowing deeply, one should bend slightly to one's right so as to avoid hitting the other's head with one's own.

That bowing has become a largely automatic movement is evidenced by the fact that many Japanese can be seen to bow repeatedly to invisible partners at the other end of a telephone line.

The handshake, however, is very much a Western import, and the dilemma whether to bow or to shake hands with Westerners can be rather great, especially if a cosmopolitan Japanese meets a foreigner in love with Japanese customs. One compromise often seen is to shake hands while bowing at the same time—a procedure fraught with the danger of knocking heads together, apart from looking extremely funny. This is very common among Japanese male immigrants in the U. S.

(Based on K. R. Johnson: Black Kinesics & N. Morsbach: Aspects of Nonverbal Communication in Japan)

Notes

ghetto 贫民窟

H. D. Thoreau 梭罗(1817—1862),美国散文作家

swing 摇摆

gait 步态

augument 增加

civilities 礼貌,客气

intricate 错综复杂的

Questions

1. How is black males' walk different from white males' walk? What is the difference in the messages they are intended to send?

2. An American journalist once said that "after three days in Japan, the spinal column becomes extraordinarily flexible." What does that suggest? How important is it for one in the Japanese society to learn to bow appropriately?

3. Is bowing in Japan just a behavior of politeness? Does it function the same as handshaking or embracing in other cultures? If not, what are the differences?

2

Functions of Nonverbal Behavior in Communication

Arab men often greet by kissing on both cheeks. In Japan, men greet by bowing, and in the United States, people shake hands. In Thailand, to signal another person to come near, one moves the fingers back and forth with the palm down. In the United States, people beckon someone to come by holding the palm up and moving the fingers toward our body. The Tongans sit down in the presence of superiors; in the West, we stand up. Crossing one's legs in the United States is often a sign of being relaxed; in People's Republic of Korea, it is social taboo. In Japan, gifts are usually exchanged with both hands. Muslims consider the left hand unclean and do not eat or pass objects with it. Buddha maintained that great wisdom arrived during moments of silence. In the United States, people talk to arrive at the truth.

To appreciate the importance of nonverbal communication to human interaction, reflect for a moment on the countless times in a single day that you send and receive nonverbal messages when in the presence of other people.

Consciously and unconsciously, intentionally and unintentionally, we make important judgments and decisions concerning the internal states of others—states they often express without words. For example, we evaluate the quality of our relationships according to interpretations of these nonverbal messages. From tone of voice, to the distance between us and our partners, to the amount of touching in which we engage, we can gather clues to the closeness of our relationships.

Nonverbal communication is significant in human interaction because it is usually responsible for first impressions. Think for a moment for how often your first judgments are based on the color of a person's skin or the manner in which he or she is dressed. More important, those initial messages usually influence the perception of everything else that follows.

Nonverbal communication has value in human interaction because many of our nonverbal actions are not easily controlled consciously. This means that they are relatively free of distortions and deception. It is difficult to control a blushing face when we are embarrassed or a clenched jaw when we are angry.

Our nonverbal behavior has many uses and functions in communication. Let us examine five of them:

Repeating

In the United States, people often use nonverbal messages to repeat a point they are trying to make. We might hold up our hand in the gesture that signifies a person to stop at the same time we actually use the word "stop". Or we might point in a certain direction after we have just said, "The new library is south of that building." The gestures and words have a similar meaning and reinforce one another.

Complementing

Closely related to repeating is complementing. Although messages that repeat can stand alone, complementing generally adds more information to messages. For example, you can tell someone that you are pleased with his or her performance, but this message takes on extra meaning if you pat the person on the shoulder at the same time. Physical contact places another layer of meaning on what is being said. Many writers in area of nonverbal communication refer to this as a type of accenting because it accents the idea the speaker is trying to make. You can see how an apology becomes more forceful if your face, as well as your words, is saying, "I'm sorry."

Substituting

We use substitution in nonverbal communication when we perform some action instead of speaking. If you see a very special friend, you are apt to enlarge the size of your smile and throw open your arms to greet him or her, which is a substitute for all the words it would take to convey the same feeling. If a group of people is boisterous, you might place your index finger to your lips as an alternative to saying, "Please calm down so that I can speak."

Regulating

We often regulate and manage communication by using some form of nonverbal behavior: we nod our head in agreement to indicate to our communication partner that we agree and that he or she should continue talking; or we remain silent for a moment and let the silence send the message that we are ready to begin our speech. Or we have direct eye contact with someone to let him or her know the channels are open. In short, our nonverbal behavior helps us control the situation.

Contradicting

On some occasions, our nonverbal actions send signals opposite from the literal meanings contained in our verbal messages. You tell someone you are relaxed and at ease, yet your voice quivers and your hands shake. It also is a contradictory message when you inform your partner that you are glad to see him or her, but at the same time you are sulking and breaking eye contact. Because people rely mostly on nonverbal messages when they receive conflicting data, we need to be aware of the dangers inherent in sending opposing messages.

In this important area of study, we need to recognize that there are some potential problems. One of them is related to individual differences. Simply stated, not all people engage in the same actions. We might, for example, note that many Native American children avoid direct eye contact as a sign of respect; yet because of individual differences, there may well be some exceptions to this assertion. We should note that we are more than our culture.

Another one is the problem of forgetting that nonverbal behaviors seldom occur in isolation. Individual messages, in reality, are but part of the total communication context. We usually send many nonverbal cues simultaneously, and these cues are normally linked to both our verbal messages and the setting in which we find ourselves.

(Adapted from L. A. Samovar et al.: *Communication between Cultures*, Chapter 6)

Notes

Tongan (南太平洋岛国)汤加人

boisterous 狂暴的,汹涌的

accent 强调

Questions

1. What are the differences between communications with and without nonverbal means? Which do you think is more effective in achieving our goals?

2. Besides those mentioned in the reading, what other functions does our nonverbal behavior sometimes serve?

Summary

1. Nonverbal means for communication, which is considered as "silent language," expresses meanings or feelings without using words. People tend to express their emotions and attitudes more nonverbally than verbally.

2. Some nonverbal differences exist across cultures and they may greatly influence intercultural communication. What is acceptable in one culture may be completely unacceptable in another.

3. The nonverbal communication behaviors involve people's gestures, facial expressions, eye contact, posture, touch, general appearance and dress, etc. However, the same nonverbal action can be perceived and understood differently in different cultures.

4. Nonverbal behavior plays a very important role in communication, and it has some basic functions: to repeat, complement, substitute for a verbal action, regulate, and contradict a communication event.

Chapter 8 Time and Culture

Time is human; nature knows only change.

—Anonymous

Chapter 8 Time and Culture

Preview Questions

1. How do you usually view time?

2. Do you think there is always a proper time for doing certain things (e.g. having classes, making a telephone call, going out on a date, etc.)?

3. Do you agree that time is everything in our life?

Text A

The Heartbeat of Culture

"If a man does not keep pace with his companions, perhaps it is because he hears a different drummer." This thought by Thoreau strikes a chord in so many people that it has become part of our language. We use the phrase "the beat of a different drummer" to explain any pace of life unlike our own. Such colorful vagueness reveals how informal our rules of time really are. The world over, children simply "pick up" their society's time concepts as they mature. No dictionary clearly defines the meaning of "early" or "late" for them or for strangers.

I learned this firsthand, a few years ago, and the resulting culture shock led me halfway around the world to find answers. It seemed clear that time "talks." But what is it telling us?

My journey started shortly after I accepted an appointment as visiting professor of psychology at the federal university in Niteroi, Brazil, a mid-sized city across the bay from Rio de Janeiro. As I left home for my first day of class, I asked someone the time. It was 9: 05 a.m., which allowed me time to relax and look around the campus before my 10 o'clock lecture. After what I judged to be half an hour, I glanced at a clock I was passing. It said 10: 20! In panic, I broke for the classroom, followed by gentle calls of "*Hola*, professor" and "*Tudo bem*, professor?" from unhurried students, many of whom, I later realized, were my own. I arrived breathless to find an empty room.

Frantically, I asked a passerby the time. "9:45" was the answer. No, that couldn't be. I asked someone else. "9:55." Another said, "Exactly 9:43." The clock in a nearby office read 3: 15. I had learned my first lesson about Brazilians: their timepieces are consistently inaccurate. And nobody minds.

My class was scheduled from 10 until noon. Many students came late, some very late. Several arrived after 10: 30. A few showed up closer to 11. Two came after that. All the latecomers wore the relaxed smiles that I came, later, to enjoy. Each one said hello, and although a few apologized briefly, none seemed terribly concerned about lateness. They assumed that I understood.

The idea of Brazilians arriving late was not a great shock. I had heard about "manha," the Portuguese equivalent of "manana" in Spanish. The real surprise came at noon that first day, when the end of class arrived.

Back home in California, I never need to look at a clock to know when the class hour is ending. The shuffling of books is accompanied by strained expressions that say plaintively, "I'm starving... I've got to go to the bathroom.... I'm going to suffocate if you keep us one more second." (The pain usually becomes unbearable at two minutes to the hour in undergraduate classes and five minutes before the close of graduate classes.)

When noon arrived in my first Brazilian class, only a few students left immediately. Others slowly drifted out during the next 15 minutes, and some continued asking me questions long after that. Several remaining students kicked off their shoes at 12: 30.

I could not, in all honesty, attribute their lingering to my superb teaching style. I had just spent two hours lecturing on statistics in halting Portuguese. Apparently, for many of my students, staying late was simply of no more importance than arriving late in the first place.

Problems with time present a major stumbling block to Americans abroad. Many Americans working in other countries have said that their greatest difficulties with the local people, after language problems, were the general pace of life and the punctuality of others. Formal "clock time" may be a standard on which the world agrees, but "social time," the heartbeat of society, is something else again.

How a country paces its social life is a mystery to most outsiders, one that we're just beginning to unravel. Twenty-six years ago, anthropologist Edward Hall noted that informal patterns of time "are seldom, if ever, made explicit. They exist in the air around us. They are either familiar and comfortable, or unfamiliar and wrong." When we realize we are out of step, we often blame the people around us to make ourselves feel better.

Appreciating cultural differences in time sense becomes increasingly important as modern communications put more and more people in daily contact. If we are to avoid misreading issues that involve time perceptions, we need to understand better our own cultural biases and those of others.

According to historian Will Durant, "No man in a hurry is quite civilized." What do our time judgments say about our attitude toward life? How can a North American, coming from a land of digital precision, relate to a North African who may consider a clock "the devil's mill"?

As you envision tomorrow's international society, do you wonder who will set the pace? Americans or the Japanese? In both countries, speed is frequently confused with progress. Perhaps looking carefully at the different paces of life around the world will help us distinguish more accurately between the two qualities. Clues are everywhere but sometimes hard to distinguish. You have to listen carefully to hear the beat of even your own drummer.

(Adapted from R. Levine & E. Wolff: Social Time—The Heartbeat of Culture, in *One World, Many Culture*)

Notes

Niteroi(巴西东南部港口城市)尼泰罗伊	suffocate 窒息
Rio de Janeiro(巴西城市) 里约热内卢	statistics 统计学;统计资料
Hola(葡萄牙语)你好(Hello)	halting 结结巴巴的
Tudo bem(葡萄牙语)你好吗?(How are you?)	unravel 解开;澄清

Questions

1. Is time everything in our life?

2. What do you think of being punctual? How do the Westerners define punctuality with measures of time?

3. Do you agree that "a person who is consistently late is probably more successful than one who is consistently on time"? Why or why not?

Text B

Cultural Conceptions of Time

When Shakespeare wrote "The inaudible and noiseless foot of Time," he was putting into words what we all know but often overlook. Although we cannot hold or see time, we respond to it as if it had command over our lives. Because time is such a personal phenomenon, all of us perceive and treat it in a manner that expresses our character. A culture's use of time can also provide valuable clues to how members of that culture value and respond to time. In America, we hear people saying, "Time is money" and "He who hesitates is lost." All Chinese know the Confucian proverb "Think three times before you act." Reflect for a moment on how differently each of these cultures perceives time. A culture's conception of time can be examined from three different perspectives: (1) informal time; (2) perceptions of past, present, and future; and (3) monochronic and polychronic classifications.

Informal time

Most of the rules for informal time, such as pace and tardiness, are not explicitly taught.

Like most of culture, these rules usually function below the level of consciousness. How late is "late"? This varies greatly. In Britain and America, one may be 5 minutes late for a business appointment, but not 15 and certainly not 30 minutes late, which is perfectly normal in Arab countries. On the other hand, in Britain it is correct to be 5-15 minutes late for an invitation to dinner. An Italian might arrive 2 hours late, an Ethiopian after, and a Javanese not at all—he had accepted only to prevent his host from losing face.

In the United States, people have all learned that the boss can arrive late for a meeting without anyone raising an eyebrow; if the secretary is late, he or she may receive a reprimand in the form of a stern glance. A rock star or a doctor can keep people waiting for long periods of time, but the warm-up band and the nurse had better be on time. In Latin America, one is expected to arrive late to appointments as a sign of respect. This same tardiness would be perceived as rudeness in Germany.

We can ascertain a culture's attitude toward time by examining the pace at which members of that culture perform specific acts and respond to certain events. Americans, because of the pace of life in the United States, always seem to be in a hurry for them, there is always one more thing to do. Conveniences—from fast-food restaurants, one-stop gas stations, and microwave ovens—help get things done quickly. Other cultures see time differently and hence live life at a pace different from that of most people in the United States. The Japanese, Arab, and Chinese cultures, for example, treat time in ways that often appear at cross-purposes with American goals.

For example, when negotiating with the Japanese, Americans like to get right down to business. They were socialized to believe that "time is money." They can accept about 15 minutes of "small talk" about the weather, their trip, and baseball, but more than that becomes unreasonable. The Japanese, on the other hand, want to get to know their business counterparts. They feel that the best way to do this is to have long conversations with Americans about a wide variety of topics. The Japanese are comfortable with hours and hours, and even days and days, of conversation.

Past, present, and future

How a culture perceives and uses the concepts of past, present, and future has already been discussed. Now let us review some of those findings so that you can see how time and behavior are linked.

Past-orientated cultures such as the British place much emphasis on tradition and are often perceived as resisting change. A statement one often hears in England when people ask about the monarchy is "We have always done it this way." The Chinese, with their tradition of ancestor worship and strong pride in their culture's persistence for thousands of years, are another culture that uses the past as a guide to how to live in the present. As a Chinese proverb advises, "Consider the past and you will know the present." Native Americans also value tradition and look to the past for guidance when confronting new situations.

Filipinos and Latin Americans are present oriented and emphasize living in the moment. These cultures tend to be more impulsive and spontaneous than others and have a casual, relaxed lifestyle. Cultures with a strong Islamic tradition, because they believe that future events belong to Allah also tend to perceive the present as a place where past, present, and future come together. They have little desire to chart events that they believe are out of their control.

The third orientation, which puts great faith in the future, is the one most Americans have. As a people, Americans are constantly planning for the future. Many of them can hardly wait to finish what they are doing so that they can move on to something else. Having an eye to the future often produces a very low tolerance for extensions and postponements. What they want, they want now, so they can dispose of this moment and move on to the next.

Monochronic (M-time) and polychronic (P-time)

Anthropologist Hall advanced another classification of time as a form of communication. Hall proposed that cultures organize time in one of two ways: either monochronic (M-time) or polychronic (P-time). Although he did not intend these as either/or categories, they do represent two distinct approaches to time.

M-time is characteristic of people from Germany, Austria, Switzerland, and America. As the word *monocbronic* implies, this approach sees time as lineal, segmented, and manageable. Time is something people must not waste; they must be doing something or they feel guilty. They behave as if time were tangible: they talk of "saving time," "losing time," or "killing time." The time clock records the hours they must work, the school bell moves them from class to class, and the calendar marks important days and events in their lives. Appointments and schedules are very important to members of monochronic cultures.

People from cultures on P-time live their lives quite differently. P-time cultures, for example, deal with time holistically. They can interact with more than one person or do more than one thing at a time. They also take great stock in the activity that is occurring at the moment and emphasize people more than schedules. They do mot perceive appointments as iron-clad commitments and therefore often break them. For P-time cultures, time is less tangible; hence, feelings of wasted time are not as prevalent as in M-time cultures. This leads, of course, to a lifestyle that is more spontaneous and unstructured.

Within the United States, there are co-cultures that use time differently from the dominant culture. Mexican Americans frequently speak of "Chicano time" when their timing varies from that of the dominant culture. The Polynesian culture of Hawaii has "Hawaiian time," a concept of time that is very relaxed and reflects the informal lifestyle of the Native Hawaiian people. And among Samoans, there is a time perspective referred to as "coconut time," which is derived from the notion that it is not necessary to pick coconuts because they will fall when the time is right. African Americans often use what is referred to as "BPT" (Black People's Time) or "hang-loose time." This concept, which has its roots in the P-time cultures of Africa, maintains that priority belongs to what is happening at that instant.

Monochronic People	Polychronic People
Do one thing at a time	Do many things at once
Concentrate on the job	Are easily distracted and subject to interruptions
Take time commitments (deadlines, schedules) seriously	Consider time commitments an objective to be achieved, if possible
Are committed to the job	Are committed to people and human relationships
Adhere to plans	Change plans often and easily
Are concerned about not disturbing others; follow rules of privacy	Are more concerned with people close to them (family, friends, close business associates) than with privacy
Show great respect for private property; seldom borrow or lend	Borrow and lend things often and easily
Emphasize promptness	Base promptness on the relationship
Are accustomed to short-term relationships	Have strong tendency to build lifetime relationships

(Adapted from L. A. Samovar: *Communication between Cultures*, Chapter 6)

Notes

tardiness 迟缓，拖拉
Ethiopian 埃塞俄比亚人
Javanese（印度尼西亚）爪哇人
reprimand 斥责
ascertain 弄清
spontaneous 本能的，自然的
Allah 安拉，真主
segmented 切分开的
take great stock in 非常看重
iron-clad 取消不了的
Chicano 墨西哥裔美国人的
Polynesian（中太平洋岛群）波利尼西亚的
Samoan（南太平洋的）萨摩亚群岛人
priority 优先，重点

Questions

1. Some say that time is money while others say that time is life. What do you think of the two sayings? Are they very different from each other?

2. Are you mainly past-oriented, present-oriented or future-oriented?

3. Are we Chinese still very polychronic? Why or why not?

Exploration

Darwin seemed to believe that "a man who wastes one hour of time has not discovered the meaning of life," but according to Will Durant, "no man in a hurry is quite civilized." How should we understand these seemingly conflicting views on time?

Do you usually move faster or slower than most of those people around you in your life? Have you had any problems with people whose pace of life seems to be different from yours? If you have, how have you dealt with the problems?

In today's society, the pace of life seems to be faster and faster. There has already been a lot of evidence to suggest that the fast pace of modern life is affecting our well-being in various ways. It is obvious that the higher rate of heart disease, hypertension, ulcers, suicide, alcoholism, divorce and other psychological and physical problems can, to some extent, be related to the faster pace of life. What can we do about it? We can at least try to discover what is the appropriate pace of life for ourselves and do our best to keep with it.

Discuss with your class members what effects this sense of time may have on intercultural communication.

Cases for Discussion

Case 1

Americans' understanding of time is typical of Western cultures in general and industrialized societies in particular. Americans view time as a commodity, as a "thing" that can be saved, spent, or wasted. They budget their time as they budget their money. And they like to "spend" time wisely by keeping busy. The following story humorously describes the daily life of one American student. The story is told from the point of view of his foreign roommate.

Robert Rushmore tells me to use time wisely, but I think he abuses time. He crams a thousand activities into what he calls "just a second." The busier the better—that's Robert's motto. He moves fast, he eats fast, he talks fast, he even got married and divorced fast.

From the moment my roommate wakes up, he tries to beat the clock. The alarm buzzes; he jumps up, washes quickly, snatches a piece of toast, gulps down a cup of coffee, and crams for his classes. He has a special watch with a built-in alarm so he can time his arrival to class three minutes before it begins. He uses these three fleeting minutes to proofread his homework or to continue reading the morning paper.

Once when I borrowed his notes I found that 50 percent of the words were abbreviated. He even abbreviates his name when he writes personal notes. Once the bank called and told him that "signatures" were not allowed on his checks.

What's really strange is although Robert doesn't have very much money, he prefers to call people long distance rather than write letters. However, he does send manufactured greeting cards and get-well cards for special occasions. At Christmas time all his friends got a xeroletter.

Robert is a lot of fun, but the way he uses time is exhausting. Last week we decided to double-date. I thought we'd have a quiet dinner at home and enjoy an evening of conversation. Robert offered to make the meal: quickie spaghetti, precooked French bread, and instant pudding. We spent only forty-five minutes for dinner and then hurried to catch an 8 p.m. movie. Afterwards we went dancing. By 2 a.m. I was dragging my feet.

Sometimes I wonder if Robert ever tries to slow down his pace. He says that he would like to stop the world and get off but for that he doesn't have time. I don't know if that is true... only time will tell.

Notes

abbreviated 缩写，缩略

double-date 赴两对男女一同参加的约会

xeroletter 复印信件

Questions

1. How do you like the way Robert uses his time? Why does he use his time that way?
2. What is your sense of time? Are you often in haste?

Case 2

Visiting a friend can be full of fun and enjoyment, but sometimes you need to be very considerate not to wear out your welcome. Read the following case and think over the questions after it.

Magid was an Arabian working in a company in the U.S.A. One Sunday morning he was home and didn't have much to do. He thought of his good friend, Jock, an American, who he used to study with. They had not seen each other for a long time though they lived in the same city. And he had told Jock that he would come and visit him long before. Now this Sunday morning seemed like a wonderful time for him to fulfill his visit. Without informing Jock of his visit, Magid went to Jock's house and rang the door bell.

At the same time, Jock, after a whole busy week, was just looking forward to spending his Sunday reading and relaxing himself. Just as he started to read in his most comfortable chair, the doorbell rang. He opened the door and to his surprise, it was Magid who was standing at the door. He didn't look completely happy to see Magid. Then, after a few seconds, he smiled and said, "Hi, Magid, come on in." They drank coffee and chatted about their life after their separation. Magid stayed about four hours and he decided to leave. Jock walked Magid to the door. They said goodbye to each other and Jock thanked Magid for coming. After they left each other, both of them felt a little uncomfortable.

Questions

1. What feelings do you think Jock had when he saw Magid again? Why did both of them feel a little uncomfortable?
2. What do you think Magid should have done before he actually visited Jock?

Case 3

Katherine came to Beijing in 1998 and found a job as an English teacher in a foreign language institute. Soon after her classes began, she found that her students showed no interest in her teaching and quite a few of them avoided attending her class. She was feeling quite upset and depressed so she decided to ask the Director, Prof. Wang, for help.

One day, she came to the Director and told him that she would like to talk to him about her problem. The Director looked at his timetable and asked if they could meet at ten o'clock on Thursday morning and she agreed. On Thursday, she arrived at the Director's office at the exact time of their appointment when she found that Prof. Wang was talking with another teacher in Chinese. Seeing that she had come, Prof. Wang smiled to gesture a seat and asked her to sit down. She got herself seated, and the professor excused himself and carried on the talk with the teacher.

About five minutes later, Prof. Wang concluded his talk and made a profound apology before he began to talk with Katherine. The Director showed great concern and asked her what the problem was. Just as she was specifying her problem, another Chinese teacher came in, with a form that apparently needed signature of the Director. The Director smiled an apology to Katherine again and turned to talk with that teacher, also in Chinese. Katherine became impatient, wondering why their talk should be interrupted since they had already made an appointment. She was so upset and got choked by their talking in Chinese in front of her that she became quite angry. Although their talk continued, she was apparently unhappy about what had happened.

Questions

1. How can you explain the Director's behavior to Katherine?
2. According to Katherine, what kind of rules did the Director violate in their communication?

Readings for Further Study

1
Patterning of Time in Different Cultures

In his book *The Silent Language*, anthropologist Edward Hall theorizes that perceptions of time and space are different in different cultures and that these perceptions are culturally patterned. Hall called these dimensions of culture "out of awareness," because people are not conscious of having learned them. It may well be true that most important aspects of culture, such as our perceptions of our physical environment or our food tastes, are learned "out of awareness." And certainly our perceptions of time and space are among the most deeply instilled of our cultural values.

For example, members of modern, industrialized Western societies are conditioned to view time, space, and matter in Newtonian terms. Sir Isaac Newton, the seventeenth-century English scientist, transformed mathematics and science to such an extent that even though we may not be able to list or explain his discoveries, we are influenced by them. Newton formulated several laws of motion that are basic to the Westerner's understanding of the universe. His first law of motion states that every body in the universe continues at rest or in uniform motion in a straight line unless it is compelled to change that state by other forces acting upon it. This notion also underlies the concept of time in Western culture, and to Westerners it appears that it should be an intuitive concept of time shared by all people everywhere. But as anthropologists have demonstrated through their studies of other cultures, these Newtonian "laws" are not universal. They are instilled by a specific culture, thought system, and language.

In fact, "telling time" is a strictly human invention. All cultures have some system of measuring duration, or keeping time, but in Western industrial societies we keep track of time in what seems to other peoples almost an obsessive fashion. We view time as motion on a space, a kind of linear progression measured by the clock and the calendar. Our sense of time leads us to imagine it as a ribbon marked off into equal blank spaces, suggesting that each of these spaces can be filled with an entry. This perception contributes to our sense of history and the keeping of records, which are typical aspects of Western cultures. We are fascinated by sequencing, dating, charting, and measuring pieces of time. We calculate not only the seasons but also the years, months, weeks, days, hours, minutes, seconds, and even thousandths of seconds. We find it useful to divide the past into named periods such as "the Renaissance" or "the classical age." And our linguistic treatment of time has guided many other aspects of our lives. For example, literature is taught in schools by being divided into periods—or framed time slots—rather than by being treated in a thematic fashion that cuts across time boundaries.

Although our perceptions of time seem natural to us, we must not assume that other cultures operate on the same time system. For instance, why should we assume that a Hopi raised in the Hopi culture would have the same intuitions about time as that we have? In Hopi history, if records had been written, we would find a different set of cultural and environmental influences working together. The Hopi people are a peaceful agricultural society. Their agriculture is successful only by the greatest perseverance. Extensive preparations are needed to ensure crop growth. Thus the Hopi value persistence and repetition in activity. They have a sense of the cumulative value of numerous, small, repeated movements, for to them such movements are not wasted but are stored up to make changes in later events. The Hopi do not speak, as we do in English, of a "new day" or "another day" coming every twenty-four hours; among the Hopi, the return of the day is like the return of a person, a little older but with all the characteristics of yesterday. This Hopi conception, with its emphasis on the repetitive aspect of time rather than its onward flow, may be clearly seen in their ritual dances for rain and good crops, in which the basic step is a short, quick stamping of the foot repeated thousands of times, hour after hour.

Of course, the American conception of time is significantly different from that of the Hopi. Americans' understanding of time is typical of Western cultures in general and industrialized societies in particular. Americans view time as a commodity, as a "thing" that can be saved, spent, or wasted. We budget our time as we budget our money. We even say, "Time is money." We are concerned in America with being "on time"; we don't like to "waste" time by waiting for someone who is late or by repeating information; and we like to "spend" time wisely by keeping busy. These statements all sound natural to a North American. In fact, we think, how could it be otherwise? It is difficult for us not to be irritated by the apparent carelessness about time in other cultures.

Americans have a sense of time that is oriented toward the future, not an infinitely extending future, but the **foreseeable** future. We look back at the past only to measure how far we have come in the present, and we look at the present as a stepping stone to foreseeable future accomplishments. We **project** ourselves into the future by producing calendars, programs, schedules, and budgets for upcoming periods of time. Other cultures do not share such a future orientation.

Just as other cultures' concepts of time may irritate Americans when we come up against them in our activities, so our concept of time may evoke amusement or even **disdain** from people in other cultures. For example, many foreigners must have been puzzled by an article in *The New York Times* business section that described a man who defined himself as a "time consultant." This expert suggested that one way to use time more efficiently was to program the subconscious to consider a plan of action for the following day while falling asleep. In this way, he said, one's sleeping time would be well spent, not wasted. Such a notion is considered perfectly rational in the American business community. But in an agricultural community where one cannot control the elements governing crop growth, or in a nonindustrialized nation, where the speed of a walking animal or a human hand controls production, such a perception of time would be valueless. With these different, culturally patterned views of time that exist all over the world, it is no wonder that some American business people come into conflict with businesspeople form other cultures, where sociability is more important than using every minute of one's time for business.

(Adapted from J. Y. Gregg: *Communication and Cultures*, Chapter 5)

Notes

theorize 建立理论，使理论化
instilled 被灌输
Newtonian 牛顿学说的
obsessive 着迷的
ribbon 缎带，丝带
thematic 主题的，专题的
foreseeable 可预见的
project 设想(自己)处于……
disdain 蔑视

Questions

1. How should we understand the statement that the Newtonian "laws" are not universal?
2. How can different views of time cause conflicts among people from different cultures?

2

People of the Future

The inhabitants of the earth are divided not only by race, nation, religion or ideology, but also, in a sense, by their position in time. Examining the present populations of the globe, we find a tiny group who still live, hunting and food-foraging, as men did millennia ago. Others, the vast majority of mankind, depend not on bear-hunting or berry-picking, but on agriculture. They live, in many respects, as their ancestors did centuries ago. These two groups taken together compose perhaps 70 percent of all living human beings. They are the people of the past.

By contrast, somewhat more than 25 percent of the earth's population can be found in the industrialized societies. They lead modern lives. They are products of the first half of the twentieth century, molded by mechanization and mass education, brought up with lingering memories of their own country's agricultural past. They are, in effect, the people of the present.

The remaining two or three percent of the world's population, however, are no longer people of either the past or present. For within the main centers of technological and cultural change, in Santa Monica, California and Cambridge, Massachusetts, in New York and London and Tokyo, are millions of men and women who can already be said to be living the way of life of the future. They live today as millions more will live tomorrow.

What makes them different from the rest of mankind? Certainly, they are richer, better educated, more mobile than the majority of the human race. But what specifically marks the people of the future is the fact that they are already caught up in a new, stepped-up pace of life. They "live faster" than the people around them.

Some people are deeply attracted to this highly accelerated pace of life—going far out of their way to bring it about and feeling anxious, tense or uncomfortable when the pace slows. They want desperately to be "where the action is." (Indeed, some hardly care what the action is, so long as it occurs at a suitably rapid clip.) A person living in Mississippi reports: "People who are used to a speeded-up urban life—can't take it for long in the rural South. That's why people are always driving somewhere for no particular reason."

But if some people thrive on the new, rapid pace, others are fiercely repelled by it. To engage at all with the emergent super-industrial society means to engage with a faster moving world than ever before. They prefer to disengage, to idle at their own speed.

Much otherwise incomprehensible conflict—between parents and children, between husbands and wives—can be traced to differential responses to the acceleration of the pace of life. The same is true of clashes between cultures.

Each culture has its own characteristic pace. F. M. Esfandiary, the Iranian novelist and essayist, tells of a collision between two different pacing systems when German engineers in the pre-World War II period were helping to construct a railroad in his country. Iranians and Middle Easterners generally take a far more relaxed attitude toward time than Americans or Western Europeans. When Iranian work crews consistently showed up for work ten minutes late, the Germans, themselves super-punctual and always in a hurry, fired them in droves. Iranian engineers had a difficult time persuading them that by Middle Eastern standards the workers were being heroically punctual, and that if the firings continued there would soon be no one left to do the work but women and children.

This indifference to time can be maddening to those who are fast-paced and clock-conscious. Thus Italians from Milan or Turin, the industrial cities of the North, look down upon the relatively slow-paced Sicilians, whose lives are still geared to the slower rhythms of agriculture. Swedes from Stockholm or Göteborg feel the same way about Laplanders. Americans speak with derision of Mexicans for whom *manana* is soon enough. In the United States itself, Northerners regard Southerners as slow-moving, and middle-class Blacks condemn working-class Blacks just up from the South for operating on "C. P. T."—Colored People's Time. In contrast, by comparison with almost anyone else, white Americans and Canadians are regarded as hustling, fast-moving go-getters.

Precisely this issue is symbolized by the angry outcry that has greeted the recent introduction of American-style drugstores in Paris. To many Frenchmen, their existence is infuriating evidence of a sinister "cultural imperialism" on the part of the United States. It is hard for Americans to understand so passionate a response to a perfectly innocent soda fountain. What explains it is the fact that at Le Drugstore the thirsty Frenchman gulps a hasty milkshake instead of lingering for an hour or two over an aperitif at an outdoor bistro. It is worth noticing that as the new technology has spread in recent years, some 30,000 bistros have padlocked their doors for good, victims in the words of *Time* magazine of a "short-order culture." Indeed, it may well be that the widespread European dislike for *Time* itself, is not entirely political, but stems unconsciously from the connotation of its title. Time, with is brevity and breathless style, exports more than the American way of life. It embodies and exports the American pace of life.

(Adapted from A. Toffler: *Future Shock*)

Notes

ideology 意识形态
food-foraging 食物采集
millennia 数千年
mechanization 机械化
Sanato Monica(美国加利福尼亚州西南部城市)圣莫尼卡
Cambridge(美国马萨诸塞州东部城市)剑桥
stepped-up 加快的
go far out of their way 想尽一切办法
incomprehensible 不能理解的,难懂的
Iranian 伊朗人
in droves 成群,大批
Milan(意大利城市)米兰
Turin(意大利城市)都灵
Sicilian 西西里人
Stockholm(瑞典首都)斯德哥尔摩
Göteborg(瑞典西南部港市)哥德堡
Laplander(挪威、瑞典、芬兰等国北部和俄罗斯的科拉半岛的)拉普兰人
derision 嘲笑
manana(西班牙语)明天
connotation 隐含之意

Questions

1. Are you people of past, present, or future?

2. Do you have any problem with your parents or any other elderly people in pace of life? If you do, what is it?

3. Do you agree that faster is better? Why or why not?

Summary

1. Formal "clock time" may be a standard on which the world agrees, but "social time," the heartbeat of society, is something more complex.

2. Appreciating cultural differences in time sense becomes increasingly important as modern communications put more and more people in daily contact. If we are to avoid misreading issues that involve time perceptions, we need to understand better our own cultural biases and those of others.

3. Each culture perceives time differently. Although our perceptions of time seem natural to us, we must not assume that other cultures operate on the same time system.

4. A culture's conception of time can be examined from three different perspectives: informal time; perceptions of past, present and future; monochromic and polychronic classifications.

Chapter 9 Space and Culture

Physical concepts are free creations of the human mind, and are not, however it may seem, uniquely determined by the external world.

—Albert Einstein

Chapter 9 Space and Culture

Preview Questions

1. When you speak to a person, what do you think is the proper distance between you and your listener?

2. How is space used in your home? Does everybody have a special place all to himself or herself?

3. Do you think the environment in which you grew up has some effect on you? If you do, what effect is it?

Text A

The Language of Space

The language of space is powerful. How close can we get to people? How distant should we be? Most of us never think about space; we intuitively know what the right distance is. Our use of space in communication is an excellent illustration that culture is learned and not inborn, though our parents may have given us some verbal instruction on space, we have learned most of our behavior by observation. We simply do what is "right."

Arabs learn the same way, and so do Japanese, Mexicans, Russians, and members of all other cultures. The problem is that the acceptable use of space varies widely among cultures. What feels right for us may be totally offensive to someone else. Space in many ways becomes an extension of us, and we feel uncomfortable with people who play by different rules.

Private space

Our private space is sacred, and we feel violated if someone invades that personal bubble. In the United States that bubble is about the length of an arm and we talk about arms-length relationships, meaning that we keep someone at a distance and don't allow them into our personal sphere. That bubble is a little bit smaller in France but larger in the Netherlands and Germany. It is even larger in Japan but much smaller in Latin countries and the Middle East. The size of the private space is also influenced by social status, gender, age, and level of authority, further complicating the interpretation of space in communication.

Northern Europeans cherish their privacy and arrange their dwellings accordingly. Property boundaries are carefully marked, and everyone ensures that they are not violated. Fences and hedges separate gardens. Traditionally, a German house had a fence around the front yard with a gate that was closed and in many cases locked. Over the past years, the front gate was increasingly left open, and today if frequently has been removed altogether. As more and more Germans acquire automobiles, dealing with the gate became inconvenient.

In Germany, elaborate laws detail rules on the use of garden. Fences must be on the property line, and their height is regulated. In a country that is crowded and where sun is cherished, the fence must be low enough so as not to hinder the growth of vegetables in the neighbor's garden. Trees must be planted at a prescribed distance from the lot line so they don't shade the neighbor's property. Germans send a strong signal that they don't have a predisposition toward privacy.

In the German house itself, the emphasis on privacy also becomes obvious. For example, all rooms have doors with locks, and the doors are closed and often locked. It would be inconsiderate to enter someone's room without first knocking on the doors and waiting for the invitation to come in. In the common areas, one may enter without knocking, but the doors are still closed. As more and more houses have central heat, the doors to the common living area tend to remain open, but bedroom and bathroom doors are always closed.

In contrast to Germany, houses in the United States may have fences or hedges surrounding the backyard, but the front yards are wide open and inviting. Doors tend to be open, an open invitation to come in. If someone wants to be alone, then the door may be closed.

In Japan, privacy is defined altogether differently from the United States and Germany. Japan is a crowded country, and space is costly; therefore, houses and apartments are smaller. Walls and doors are thin, traditionally made of wood and parchment paper. Sound carries easily. Yet, within this crowdedness, the Japanese are able to create their privacy sphere. The private bubble and the personal space are more a creation of the mind than an actual existence. Americans connect privacy with physical space, whereas the Japanese connect privacy with mental space.

Middle Eastern and Latin cultures also reflect their attitudes toward privacy and personal space in the way they arrange their houses. A house in the Middle East traditionally has few or no windows to the street; all windows open into an inner courtyard. The family is protected from the outside world by walling itself off in a realm of privacy. Within the house, however, personal space for the individual is often limited; family togetherness is emphasized. To remove oneself physically and insist on one's own space is not acceptable and is not easily tolerated. Individuals are first and foremost part of a family, and the living arrangement emphasizes that concept. Within the family space, men's and women's areas are also separated in Islamic homes. In many ways men and women dwell in the same compound, but they live separate lives in separate quarters.

Public space

The way people arrange and use public spaces also reflects cultural attitudes toward space and privacy. Business people from the United States going to Japan or China often comment how crowded the cities are and that there just is not enough breathing space. That may be true by U.S. standards, but the Japanese and Chinese may interpret the conditions differently. Two people from different cultures may look at the same space, yet they may come to different conclusions as the following examples illustrate.

Numerous articles have illustrated the prime example of crowdedness in Japan: rush hour on the subway in Tokyo. They usually show a picture of a person whose job is to push people into the train so that the doors can close. When looking at these pictures, one wonders how the throngs of people fit with the cultural emphasis on personal distance and private space. How do the Japanese cope with that? Many Japanese do not like the crowded conditions, and increasingly people are moving from Tokyo back to their hometowns to have more space.

Most Japanese have found a way of coping with the overcrowded public space of the subway system. In this environment, filled with people pushing and shoving one another, the Japanese riders each becomes an island. Each is alone as long as he does not acknowledge any of the other people; the others do not really exist in his space. As pointed out earlier, space becomes a psychological phenomenon. The Chinese deal with the crowded public space in a similar fashion.

People from the United States carry their idea of individuality over into public spaces. They consider it their right to walk and play in the grass in the park. After all, it is their park; their taxes paid for it. Government buildings in the United States are open to the public. Anyone can go into the Capitol in Washington or the various state capitols. In no other country is the residence of the president open to the public. In the United States, right to access is considered important. In contrast, ordinary citizens are not allowed entry into the new Shanghai City Hall. It is where the mayor and vice mayors, as well as all the key officials for the city, work. Ordinary people have no business there, and are turned away by security officers.

The Germans organize their public spaces like their private lives. *Alles muβ* seine Ordung haben (*everything must have its order*). *Order is an* overriding concern, and detailed provisions are made to guarantee that order. Germans tend not to have problems with this control because they grew up with an emphasis on order. As a result, parks tend to be clean and neat; the grass is not trampled down. This order is achieved through the use of numerous sigh; *Betreten des Rasens verboten* (It is forbidden to step on the grass) is typical and strictly enforced.

Germans tend to be very aggressive in crowds. The British queue (line up) at the bus, in stores, and at theaters. Theater-goers in London, for example, follow strict unwritten rules on queuing to get tickets; it is expected that everyone follow the unwritten honor system. Germans, in contrast, form throngs and push and shove without any order at all, and they are surprised at the voluntary order of the British.

As conditions in big cities become more crowded, traditional etiquette and rules of acceptable verbal and nonverbal communication behavior may face major challenges. The pushing and shoving on Japanese subways, as pointed out earlier, does not fit the traditional value of personal distance and harmony.

Behavior in public spaces is carried over into offices and business practices. One cannot separate general cultural behavior from business behavior. The two go together. How we approach people and how we deal with space and issues of privacy have deep cultural roots. We may not agree with or like what others do. That is not the issue; the point is that we must understand what the others are doing and why they are doing it.

(Adapted from L. Beamer & I. Varner: *Intercultural Communication in the Global Workplace*, Chapter 6)

Notes

predisposition 倾向,癖性 | overriding 最重要的
parchment 羊皮纸 | etiquette 礼节,礼仪

Questions

1. How do you understand it when the author says that space in many ways has become an extension of us?

2. What problems may arise in communication because of cultural differences in the use of private space?

3. How does the way people arrange and use public spaces reflect their cultural attitudes? Please give some examples.

Text B

How Space Is Used

Winston Churchill once said, "We shape our buildings and they shape us."

When we travel abroad we are immediately impressed by the many ways buildings, homes, and cities are designed. The division and organization of space lend character and uniqueness to villages, towns and cities. Yet, architectural differences may also cause confusion or discomfort for the traveler. In the following example, a group of Americans living in a country in South America reacted emotionally to the architectural differences they observed.

The Latin house is often built around a patio that is next to the sidewalk but hidden from outsiders behind a wall. It is not easy to describe the degree to which small architectural differences such as this affect outsiders. American technicians living in Latin America used to complain that they felt "left out" of things, that they were "shut off." Others kept wondering what was going on "behind those walls."

The separation of space inside homes may also vary from culture to culture. In most American homes the layout of rooms reveals the separateness and labeling of space according to function—bedroom, living room, dining room, playroom, and so on. This system is in sharp contrast to other cultures where one room in a house may serve several functions. In Japan, homes with sliding walls can change a large room into two small rooms so that a living room can also serve as a bedroom.

When a home or a city's design is influenced by another culture, the "naive" architecture can be lost or disguised. For example, a French architect was asked to design the capital city of Punjab in India. He decided to plan the city with centralized shopping centers which required public transportation and movement away from the village centers. Eventually the Indians stopped meeting each other socially in their small neighborhoods. Apparently, the introduction of a non-Indian style of architecture affected some of the cultural and social patterns of those living in the city.

Architectural design influences how privacy is achieved as well as how social contact is made in public places. The concept of privacy is not unique to a particular culture but what it means is culturally determined. For example, it is said that there is no Japanese word for privacy. Yet one cannot say that the concept of privacy does not exist among the Japanese but only that it is very different from the Western conception. Similarly, there is no word in the Russian language that means exactly the same as the English word "privacy."

People in the United States tend to achieve privacy by physically separating themselves from others. The expression "good fences make good neighbors" indicates a preference for privacy from neighbors' homes. If a family can afford it, each child has his or her own bedroom. When privacy is needed, family members may lock their bedroom doors.

When the American want to be alone, they go into a room and shut the door—they depend on architectural features for screening... The English, on the other hand, lacking rooms of their own since childhood, never developed the practice of using space as a refuge from others.

In some cultures when individuals desire privacy, it is acceptable for them simply to withdraw into themselves. That is, they do not need to remove themselves physically from a group in order to achieve privacy.

Young American children learn the rule "knock before you enter" which teaches them to respect others' privacy. Parents, too, often follow this rule before entering their children's rooms. When a bedroom door is closed it may be a sign to others saying, "I need privacy," "I'm angry," or "Do not disturb... I'm busy." For Americans, the physical division of space and the use of architectural features permit a sense of privacy.

The way space is used to enable the individual to achieve privacy, to build homes or to design cities is culturally influenced. Dr. Hall summarizes the relationship between individuals and their physical surroundings in the following words:

Man and his extensions constitute one interrelated system. It is a mistake to act as though man were one thing and his house or his cities or his language were something else.

(Adapted from D. R. Levine & M. B. Adelman: *Beyond Language*, Chapter 8)

Notes

patio(西班牙语)院子　　Punjab(印度)旁遮普

Questions

1. How are people influenced by the environment they have created?
2. What do people of different cultures do to achieve privacy when they are with others?
3. In what ways are individuals and the physical surroundings interrelated?

Exploration

We all know that the earth is the only home of us human beings and we have no other in the universe. Yet we do not feel at home in it unless we have made some alternation on it. For instance, we have applied physical force to clear bushes and trees and converted wild nature into orderly fields and houses. All such alternation is the work of culture. In a sense, we can say that culture has been built into our environment, into our landscape, into our cities and houses. By looking at the environment alternated to some extent by people living in it, we will discover some of the important features of their culture.

Since China is a very large country, it is difficult to decide what is the common feature in Chinese houses. In different parts of the country, houses may be differently designed to be suitable for the local environment. However there may still be something common in the traditional houses. For instance, the so-called "*siheyuan*," a kind of quadrangle, compound with houses around a square courtyard seems to be found across the country, especially in the northern areas.

What are the basic values of the Chinese culture that may be reflected in the way space is used in our life?

Cases for Discussion

Case 1

In the following story, an American tells us how he and his son discovered the Latin use of space.

My son Michael and I have come to Latin America to study Spanish at a language institute. We are living with a local family in a middle-class home.

In a typical day in our new home, at least six to ten visitors drop in usually unannounced. Among these are relatives and friends of all family members. I am astounded by the sheer amount of socializing in this house from midday through late at night.

The phone rings incessantly. It is found in the TV room, which is something like a small den just off the large main living room (which no one uses because it is too formal). While five or more people are crammed the small space watching TV, Michael or one of the family members sits on the phone for hours chatting with friends.

In this house, we have found that our personal space is smaller than it ever was in North America. People stand very close when talking with us, and we know it is impolite to back away. Everyone is very friendly and physical, even though we are foreigners and they don't know us well yet.

We are starting to do things the Latin way ourselves. We now use very warm, physical greetings, often kissing and hugging the people in the house. We talk loudly and shout from room to room to get messages across, just like our hosts do. We are not surprised if someone walks into one of our rooms to sit down and have a personal chat, or if someone "borrows" one of our rooms to have a private talk with someone else. Like our hosts, we freely lend things and ask for what we need. The distance of the U.S. has evaporated, even though there is still some formality in addressing older people.

We find the same situation about space at the institute. There is a lot of background noise (city traffic, airplanes flying overhead, four thousand students studying in one building) to intrude on our territory. People stand very close to each other and talk loudly during coffee breaks, which take place in the hallways even if classes are going on inside some of the classrooms right next to the hall. Girls often hold hands, and boys sometimes put arms around each other's shoulders as they walk. Students consider their social life as important as their learning. To us, the new experience in small personal space is pleasant and friendly—most of the time.

Note

evaporate 蒸发；消失

Questions

1. Why was the American astounded by the amount of socializing in the house? How would you feel if you experienced the same thing?

2. Why do you think the American and his son started to do things the Latin way after staying there for some time?

Case 2

Nairobi, like many African cities since the 1960s, has experienced enormous population growth. A major problem facing urban planners in Kenya over the past several decades has been that of providing adequate and affordable housing for the rapidly growing number of urban residents. During the 1970s, the city council of Nairobi attempted to solve this problem by building low-cost houses. However, the response of the African people to these new, clean, and spacious housing units was somewhat less than enthusiastic.

The architectural design of these public housing units—comprising a living room, a dining room, a kitchen, a bathroom, and two bedrooms—was indistinguishable from the design of units one might find in Detroit, Boston, or Los Angeles. Like those built in the United States, the apartments built in Nairobi had the kitchen located next to the dining room, with no more than an open portal separating the two rooms. While this design feature works well in the United States, it violates a basic cultural value in East Africa—i.e., that the preparation of food is considered to be an unclean activity. The idea of serving food to one's guests in a room that has a full view of the kitchen is considered rude, offensive. To place a doorless kitchen next to the dining room would be as inappropriate in East Africa as it would be to place a doorless bathroom next to the dining room in American society. Thus, it is important that architects, wherever they may practice, take into consideration the cultural features of the people for whom they are designing buildings.

Notes

Nairobi 内罗毕(肯尼亚首都)　　indistinguishable 难以区分的

Kenya 肯尼亚

Questions

1. Why were the African people not much enthusiastic about the "new, clean, and spacious" housing?

2. Can you find in our society today some cases in which architects or city planners have not taken local cultures into consideration in the work they do?

Case 3

During his stay in Japan, Boon, an American student, found that with the exception of a few one- and two-room apartments every house he ever visited in Japan was designed to incorporate three common elements: *tatami*, *fusuma* (sliding screens made of paper and light wood) and *sboji* (a type of even simpler sliding screen). In the houses of rich people the *tatami* might last longer, the *fusuma* decorations might be more costly, but the basic concept was the same. The interior design of all houses being much the same, it was not surprising to find certain similarities in the behavior and attitudes of the people who lived in them.

The most striking feature of the Japanese house was lack of privacy; the lack of individual, inviolable space. In winter, when the *fusuma* were kept closed, any sound above a whisper was clearly audible on the other side, and of course in summer they were usually removed altogether. It is impossible to live under such conditions for very long without a common household identity emerging which naturally takes precedence over individual wishes.

There was no such thing as the individual's private room, no bedroom, dining- or sitting-room as such, since in the traditional Japanese house there was no furniture determining that a room should be reserved for any particular function. A person slept in a room, for example, without thinking of it as a bedroom or as his room. In the morning his bedding would be rolled up and stored away in a cupboard; a small table known as the *kotatsu*, which could also be plugged into the mains to provide heating, was moved back into the center of the room and here the family ate, drank, worked and relaxed for the rest of the day.

Although it was becoming standard practice in modern Japan for children to have their own rooms, many middle-aged and nearly all older Japanese still lived in this way. They regarded themselves as "one flesh," their property as common to all; the *uchi* (household, home) was constituted according to a principle of indivisibility. The system of moveable screen meant that the rooms could be used by all the family and for all purposes: walls were built round the *uchi*, not inside it.

Notes

inviolable 不可侵犯的

Questions

1. What do you think are the most important characteristics of a Japanese house?
2. Can you relate certain aspects of the Japanese culture to the interior design of their houses?

Readings for Further Study

1
Home in Various Cultures

Home is one of the places where we can discover some basic cultural differences, for that is just where we begin to be shaped and molded into members of our culture.

Middle- and upper-class people in the U.S., and in much of North America, are very proud of their large homes (large by comparison with houses in Europe and elsewhere). Their homes are their castles. They want to show visitors around these homes, where there are often individual rooms for each of the children. This "showing off" is a practice considered highly unusual in most other parts of the world. In this practice, U.S. desire for privacy competes with the U.S. need for flaunting its possessions.

In traditional, authoritarian homes in the U.S., doors to all the rooms have locks, but people are not allowed to use them; the only door that one can lock is the bathroom door. Locking any other door raises suspicion that something is wrong. The kitchen is the place for negotiation between the mother and the children. The parents' bedroom is mostly off-limits. However, in a more relaxed, less traditional home, there is more social activity and openness. Visitors are plentiful. They are told to "make themselves at home," which translates into fixing their own drinks, sitting where they want, doing what they want, and perhaps even helping cook dinner or set the table. This "freedom" (or increased responsibility) can be disconcerting to foreigners, who are not used to being treated like one of the family when invited initially as a guest.

The German concept of self requires a wide area of privacy, which is often formal and regimented. Doors, hedges, fences: these physical features of a German home reflect an emphasis on privacy, which is pervasive throughout German life. In German houses, doors are firmly shut between rooms to suggest the need for personal space and individual privacy. The ideal German house has an entrance hall that leads visitors into the house without showing specific rooms and spoiling the family's privacy. It is an honor to be invited into a German home; this does not frequently happen to foreigners, who are usually viewed with suspicion. Pieces of furniture are heavy and placed far apart, so that personal space is maintained during conversation. Formal interactions—not relaxed, happy-go-lucky conversations—are common. Heavy drapes prevent prying eyes from the outside from seeing in.

Germany is similar to many other northern European countries, including Scandinavian countries and England. In these countries, people living next to each other are not necessarily expected to interact unless they have already met socially. "Dropping in" is simply not an option; you are considered very rude if you do not call in advance to arrange a visit in countries like England, Belgium, Luxembourg, Finland, Norway, and Denmark. Even in Austria, where there is a customary visiting hour at 3: 00 p.m., you still must call in advance. Only in certain countries (Sweden is an example) can you drop in unannounced—and this can occur just in the countryside or at summer homes, never in the city. In most of these northern European countries, don't expect the grand tour of the host's home. Unlike the informality and openness found in the United States, northern European privacy dictates that you will not get to see most of the rooms of the house.

Mediterranean countries are alike in that they do not call for much personal space, yet they are different in their need for privacy.

French people do not particularly like foreigners as a whole and are elitist, proud, and somewhat sensitive. Never drop in unannounced to a home in France, no matter how well you think you know the hosts. If you are invited to a home in France, there will be no tour of the house. French people do not want guests wandering everywhere inside the house or outside it. Guests are usually received in the living room, with the doors to the other rooms closed. Thus, though personal space for individuals is often very minimal, the French maximize privacy in their homes. French people—like Germans—can live next to neighbors for years and still have no relationship with them at all. Living near people is no reason to strike up a friendship. The French do not want overnight guests making loud noises or bathing late at night, because they are concerned about what the neighbors think, even if they do not know the neighbors! As in less traditional homes in the U.S., it is good for guests in a French home to volunteer to help with the dishes or with preparing a meal, even if the offer is refused.

In Italy, the next-door neighbor of France, things are different. You can drop in anytime without calling first, except for the resting hours of 2: 00 to 4: 00 p.m.. Many Italian families are much more comfortable with drop-in guests than French families are. Privacy and formality are not as important to Italians as to the French. Italians are **legendary** for their warmth and friendliness.

Spanish people, despite their lack of need for personal space, demand their domestic privacy. They are not as carefree about visitors as Italians. Spaniards prefer that you call ahead to make sure it is convenient to visit. Normal visiting hours are 4: 00 to 6: 00 p.m. It is not good to visit immediately after lunch, when many people are resting. An invitation to a Spanish home is very special. Spanish people rarely invite foreigners to their homes until they know them well. They think carefully before inviting people and are very formal when they offer the invitation.

Physical closeness (lack of personal space) is the norm in Latin American countries, just as it is in Mediterranean countries. People in most Latin American countries feel comfortable if guests drop in without warning. In fact, the more guests the better, some people feel! Guests are greeted warmly, often with hugs and kisses. Do not be surprised if you are asked to stay for a full meal even if you have just come by for a chat.

Many middle-class and upper-class Latin American homes have maids, so the hosts do not expect (or want) the guests to take the plates off the table after dinner or to offer to help do dishes or cook; thus, the kitchen area is not a popular place for guests. The dining room is one of the favorite spots, because it's where people communicate easily and well. Latin Americans are happy enough showing you around if you demonstrate an interest, but they do not feel any great **compulsion** to do so (as many people in the U.S. often do).

The Latin house is often built around a *patio* that is next to the sidewalk but hidden from outsiders behind a wall. It is not easy to describe the degree to which small architectural differences such as this affect outsiders. American technicians living in Latin America used to complain that they felt "left out" of things, that they were "shut off." Others kept wondering what was going on "behind those walls."

The separation of space inside homes may also vary from culture to culture. In most American homes the layout of rooms reveals the separateness and labeling of space according to function—bedroom, living room, dining room, playroom, and so on. This system is in sharp contrast to other cultures where one room in a house may serve several functions. In Japan, homes with sliding walls can change a large room into two small rooms so that a living room can also serve as a bedroom.

In most homes of the Middle Eastern countries the **salon** is usually the room farthest away from all others, and the closest to the door leading to the outside. Actually, in older buildings, a door leading to the outside opens directly into the salon or guest room on one end and another door opens to the inside of the home. In such a layout the guest knocks at the door and is either led into the salon through the home or asked to please wait until the other door leading immediately to the salon is opened for him. This behavior reflects two of the most important cultural values of the area. The first is the concern with the concept of faces, facades, and appearances. The guest is exposed only to the most shining, formal, and stylized part of the home and gets to meet only the members whom the family intends for him to meet. On the other hand, relationships in the Middle East reflect great concern with guest-host relationships. The host is expected to welcome guests and provide hospitality. He should keep the image of an open house. Thus, in receiving the guest in the most distinguished part of the home and in having him meet only the members of the family dressed for the occasion, the guest is honored and the family status is reflected.

As contacts increase and a friendship develops, a guest comes to be accepted by the family and is received in the family room or what is commonly referred to in the Middle East as the sitting room. However, between the time a guest is received in the salon and the time he is accepted as "one of us," certain changes take place in the guest's relationship to the family. When the guest is allowed to meet the members of the opposite sex in the host's family, and how long the guest can stay on a visit depends on the values and lifestyle of the family. For example, it is not unusual in the Middle East for two men to have known each other for a number of years without either of them having met the female members of the other's family, even though they may know a lot about each other's life.

Notes

flaunt 夸耀,夸示
authoritarian 独裁的,专制的
off-limits 禁止进入的
disconcerting 让人困窘的;让人无所适从的
regimented 严格管制的
pervasive 遍布的
drape 帷帘
pry 窥探
Luxembourg 卢森堡
elitist 自以为杰出的
legendary 著名的,传奇的
compulsion 强制;不可抗拒的冲动
salon 客厅,接待室

Questions

1. What differences are there between Mediterranean countries in their need for privacy?

2. Why did American technicians living in Latin America complain that they felt "left out" of things and that they were "shut off"?

3. What differences can you find between the traditional Chinese home environment and the contemporary one?

2
Cultures Built into the Landscape

Human beings build not only to provide shelter but also to provide structures for ordering relationships and activities. Our cultures are built into the layout of cities, villages and farmland, and in the design of buildings. These physical forms both reflect and are reflected in social patterns and in the languages we speak.

Most of the cities and towns of the United States are arranged in a **grid** pattern of right-angled stress. A map of New York City shows that the streets running east and west are numbered in sequence. Thirty-fourth Street (famous for its large department stores) is south of Forty-second Street (famous for its movie theaters). The north-south streets are also numbered in sequence but are called avenues. Fifth Avenue with its fashionable shops is east of Seventh Avenue, home of the fashion industry. On the southern tip of Manhattan Island, streets do not follow this pattern but continue to reveal the decisions made by the earliest Western settlers. Here we find the origin of the one street that breaks the overall pattern, **Broadway**. It runs **diagonally** across the grid, causing trouble for taxi drivers, visitors and residents who have come to expect that they can easily find and point on the logical grid of the city.

The naming and numbering system varies from city to city, but the basic grid pattern is the same. Some small towns name their streets after trees and name them in **alphabetical order**, so that Maple Street follows Locust Street and comes before Oak Street and Pine Street. With a pattern like this it is difficult to get lost, because the address of any building locates it in a specific place on the grid. This is a pattern that provides easy access even to strangers and is low context in that the visitor does not need to rely on a knowledgeable insider to find his way. My brother's address is 46040 125th Street East in a small city in southern California. In fact he does not live in a city at all, but far out in the desert. The grid pattern has been extended endlessly into the desert, so anyone can find him. Just follow the grid east to the intersection of 46th Street and 125th Street and there he is.

The same pattern can be seen in the interstate highway system that covers the country with a grid of regularly numbered highways. The odd numbered roads run north and south and the even numbered roads run east and west. Highway 95 will take you from **Maine** to **Florida** and Highway 3 will take you north or south along the West Coast.

The large farms of the Midwest are arranged in a similar way. After the War of Independence the United States acquired large **tracts** of unsettled land from England and promptly divided them into regularly shaped states, counties, townships, and farms. Notice that the boundaries of many states are straight lines. Each farm is a regular **rectangle** and one plot in each township and a larger tract in each state were set aside to meet the educational needs of the area. This pattern encouraged settlers to move west, because the grid provided a path for them to follow. It ordered and civilized the wilderness.

You can find the same pattern in the characteristic American suburban sprawl. People who rise in social class and income move out from the city into newer and newer and more expensive housing areas far from the city. Older areas in the inner city are taken over by new arrivals. They live there until their fortunes improve at which time they follow the grid out to more desirable housing on the outskirts.

This pattern does not have a fixed center. Any point on the grid can become important depending on what is located there. It can just as easily disappear into obscurity if economic development or public taste favors another location. New cities grow up at the intersections of the interstate highway system while the centers of older towns die from neglect. I am often asked questions like, "What is the best university in the US?" or "What is the greatest city in the US?" I can only answer that there are many good universities and that I appreciate various cities for their particular characteristics. I am the product of a grid culture. I am not looking for the center. Like other Americans I want to know what opportunities I will find as I move out across the grid. Any corner can become a center.

The grid pattern has many advantages, but for a wonderful holiday trip, I would choose to go to France. Once I traveled there with friends. We started in Paris and then rented a car and went out to the edges of the country. We traveled around the periphery stopping in local areas, each one delighting us with its own flavor, its own wines and cheeses, its own unique style of cooking. Traveling by car is fairly easy but quite different from moving across the American grid. In France we had to look for signs to the city center. We followed those signs, found the center, and oriented ourselves from there. In the star patten, important things are at the center and everything else radiates out from the center. In France, all major roads lead to Paris and most mileage signs tell you how far you are from Paris. Since we were moving around the edge of the country, we had to travel by minor roads. The treasures we found were the treasures typical of the forgotten corners of a society where the center sets the standard. If you look at a map of France that shows the highway system, the radiating star is clearly visible. The star pattern is also visible in the social and political life of the country.

In France, people live in towns and villages where the church and town hall are at the center. In a French office, the leader's office is at the center, and you can tell how important anyone in the organization is by how far his or her office is from the leader's office. It is unthinkable that the city of Paris would suffer from neglect or decay. French leaders follow the tradition of remodeling a section of the city or building a new monument to ensure that the city is as wondrous in the future as it was in the past. The most important buildings, events and organizations are in the center of Paris and the poorer, less important people live in the suburbs.

France is known for its highly centralized government and educational system. It is said that school children all over the country study the same lesson on the same day. Decisions about the curriculum and even specific lessons are made in Paris and communicated through a system of sub-centers until they reach the smallest school in the most remote area. In contrast, the American governmental and educational systems are decentralized with local units having much independent authority and responsibility.

(Adapted from L. Davis: *Doing Culture*, Chapter 9)

Notes

grid 格栅；坐标方格	sprawl 蔓生，诞生
Broadway 百老汇大街	obscurity 湮没无闻
diagonally 对角线地；斜地	periphery 周边，外围地区
alphabetical order 按字母顺序	radiate 辐射
Maine（美国）缅因州	wondrous 奇妙的
Florida（美国）佛罗里达州	centralized 中央集权的
tract 大片土地，地带	decentralized 权力分散或下放的
rectangle 矩形，长方形	

Questions

1. How do you find the layout of the city where you are living now? Is it similar to the American pattern or the French one?

2. In what ways does the layout of Chinese cities reflect the Chinese social structure and cultural values?

Summary

1. Each person has around him or her an invisible bubble of space which expands and contracts depending on a number of things: the relationship to the people nearby, the person's emotional state, cultural background, and the activity being performed.

2. The way space is used to enable the individual to achieve privacy, to build homes or to design cities is culturally different. Cultures differ in their perception and use of personal space, seating, and furniture arrangement.

3. Human beings build not only to provide shelter but also to provide structures for ordering relationships and activities. Our cultures are built into the layout of cities, villages and farmland, and in the design of buildings. These physical forms both reflect and are reflected in social patterns and in the languages we speak.

4. How we approach people and how we deal with space and issues of privacy have deep cultural roots. We may not agree with or like what others do, but we must understand what the others are doing and why they are doing it.

Chapter 10 Generation Gap in Communication

The most immutable barrier in nature is between one man's thought and another's.

—William James

Chapter 10 Generation Gap in Communication

Preview Questions

1. Do you know what generation gap is?
2. Is there a generation gap between you and people much older or younger than you?
3. Have you ever tried to understand your parents as they are?

Text A

The Struggle to Be an All-American Girl

It's still there, the Chinese school on Yale Street where my brother and I used to go. Despite the new coat of paint and the high wire fence, the school I knew ten years ago remains remarkably the same.

Every day at 5 p.m., instead of playing with our fourth- and fifth-grade friends or going out to the empty lot to hunt ghosts and animal bones, my brother and I had to go to Chinese school. No amount of kicking, screaming, or pleading could dissuade my mother, who was solidly determined to have us learn the language of our heritage.

Forcibly, she walked us the seven long, hilly blocks from our home to school, placing our defiant faces before the stern principal. My only memory of him is that he swayed on his heels like a palm tree, and he always clasped his impatient twitching hands behind his back. I recognized him as a repressed crazy child killer, and knew that if we ever saw his hand we'd be in big trouble.

We all sat in little chairs in an empty hall. The room smelt like Chinese medicine, an imported faraway mustiness. Like ancient mothballs or dirty closets. I hated that smell. I favored crisp new scents. Like the soft French perfume that my American teacher wore in public school.

Although the emphasis at the school was mainly language-speaking, reading, writing—the lessons always began with an exercise in politeness. With the entrance of the teacher, the best student would tap a bell and everyone would get up, kowtow, and chant, "Sing san ho," the phonetic for "How are you, teacher?"

Being ten years old, I had better things to learn than ideographs copied painstakingly in lines that ran right to left from the tip of a moc but, a real ink pen that had to be held in an awkward way if blotches were to be avoided. After all, I could do the multiplication tables, name the satellites of Mars, and write reports on *Little Women* and *Black Beauty*. Nancy Drew, my favorite book heroine, never spoke Chinese.

The language was a source of embarrassment. More times than not, I had tried to disassociate myself from nagging loud voice that followed me wherever I wandered in the nearby American supermarket outside Chinatown. The voice belonged to my grandmother, a fragile woman in her seventies who could outshout the best of the street vendors. Her humor was vulgar, her Chinese rhythmless, patternless. It was quick, it was loud, it was unbeautiful. It was not like the quiet, pleasant romance of French or the gentle refinement of the American South. Chinese sounded dull and unimaginative.

In Chinatown, the comings and goings of hundreds of Chinese on their daily tasks sounded chaotic and frenzied. I did not want to be thought of as mad, as talking gibberish. When I spoke English, people nodded at me, smiled sweetly, said encouraging words. Even the people in my culture would say that I'd do well in life. "My, doesn't she move her lips fast," they would say, meaning that I'd be able to keep up with the world outside Chinatown.

My brother was even more fanatical than I about speaking English. He was especially hard on my mother, criticizing her, often cruelly, for her pidgin speech. "It's not 'What it is,' Mom," he'd say in exasperation. "It's 'What *is* it, what *is* it, what *is* it!'" Sometimes Mom might leave out an occasional "the" or "a," or perhaps a verb of being. He would stop her in mid-sentence: "Say it again, Mom. Say it right." When he tripped over his own tongue, he'd blame it on her: "See, Mom, it's all your fault. You set a bad example."

What made my mother extremely angry was when my brother cornered her on her consonants, especially "r." My father had played a cruel joke on Mom by assigning her an American name that her tongue wouldn't allow her to say. No matter how hard she tried, "Ruth" always ended up like "Luth" or "Roof."

After two years of writing with a *moc but* and reciting words with multiples of meanings, I finally was granted a cultural divorce. I was permitted to stop Chinese school. I thought of myself as multicultural. I preferred tacos to egg rolls; I enjoyed Cinco de Mayo more than Chinese New Year.

At last, I was one of you; I wasn't one of them.

Sadly, I still am.

(Adapted from E. Wong: The Struggle to Be an All-American Girl, in *Crossing Cultures*)

Notes

heritage 遗产,传统
twitch 抽搐
repressed 抑制的,忍住的
mustiness 陈腐,发霉
mothball 樟脑丸
closet 壁橱,衣橱
crisp 清新的
chant 齐声说(唱)
ideograph 表意文字
moc but(音译) 毛笔
blotch 斑点;污渍
multiplication table 乘法表
nagging 唠唠叨叨的
chaotic 混乱的
frenzied 狂乱的
gibberish 快而费解的话;胡说八道
fanatical 狂热的
pidgin 不纯粹的语言;混杂语言
exasperation 恼怒,愤怒
trip over 失足,失言
taco(墨西哥人的)肉末玉米饼卷
Cinco de Mayo 五月五日墨西哥全国性节日

Questions

1. Why was the Chinese language "a source of embarrassment" to the author? What were her feelings about speaking English?

2. At the end of the article the author writes "I finally was granted a cultural divorce." What does the sentence mean? Can we divorce ourselves from our cultures?

3. In the sentence "At last, I was one of you; I wasn't one of them," what do the words "you" and "them" refer to respectively?

Text B

World War II and Generation Gap

Since the 1960s it has been part of the common vocabulary, at least of Americans, to speak of a generation gap. This gap is most clearly perceived to have opened up between those Americans born after World War II, the Baby Boom generation, and those born before that time.

In other words, among contemporary Americans there is a strong belief that the experience of having been born into American culture at a particular time and in a particular place is taken as giving one membership in a particular group. It is widely felt that communication between people born after World War II and those born before that time is a form of intercultural communication.

The most important life event for the Depression/War generation is, of course, the Great Depression, beginning in 1929 and running through the end of World War II. This is the world into which they were born. It is significant to see that the parents of these children were actually living under very precarious social and economic conditions. First the Depression had crushed their expectations by eliminating their savings if they had any, their jobs, and their faith in the American political process.

At the same time, the chaos and terror of World War II, while it did not devastate the continent of America the way it did with that of Europe, left these babies in many cases without fathers. Many of this generation remember the sad, long evenings waiting for news of beloved fathers and brothers and sons. It was a time in which it was hard to maintain that one's success in life would come as an inheritance from the older generation. It is not surprising, then, to see in this generation the development of the belief that if one was going to succeed, one was going to have to go it alone.

In many ways this Depression/War generation is the transitional one in America. The authority of the older generation was no longer simply assumed, and yet there is nothing in this generation of the open self-expression of the Baby Boom generation. Depression/War generation individualism is very much the go-it-alone independence of the self-made man who does not identify with either those who went before or those who came after.

This might also be called the news generation. Perhaps it was because of the strong influence of World War II, but this generation was the first to grow up with the constant sound of radio news in its ears. What is important, however, is the time sense projected by both news and sports broadcasts. This is a much shorter time sense than that of earlier, literate media. Therefore, this generation tends toward a much more compressed sense of time than any preceding generation of Americans.

The post-war boom babies were born into a world of abundance. They were, in fact, part of that abundance. Paradoxically, because of the rapid post-war economic expansion they were born into an increasingly rich country, yet at the same time, because there are so many of them, their share of that richness has never been guaranteed. From shortages of diapers in their infancy and a shortage of school in their childhood they have gone on to experience shortages in the job market and to fear shortages of social security benefits when they reach old age.

It is probably more significant for the Boom babies, however, that they were born into a period in which the historical sense of time had been fractured. The understanding of the past was blocked by an older generation who wanted to put the period of the Depression and World War II quickly behind them. At the same time, this generation was born under the shadow of the Cold War and the potential of total world destruction. They are really the first generation of

Americans to be born into a world in which humankind had finally reached the possibility of complete technological destruction of the earth. As a result, many who belong to this generation invested even less thought in the future than in the past.

The babies of the Baby Boom were brought up in a social environment which was radically different from that of the preceding generations. No longer is the parent in control. It is the child who decides, while the parent waits patiently for this decision to be made. The mandate to extend equality to all has now been extended to infancy. No American will be assumed to have the right to make judgements about what is right for another, not even the parents of a child.

If asked to name the most important world event in their lives, most members of this generation would name the war in Vietnam. This generation assumed that it was their right to decide whether or not they would do things, and their decisions were largely based on the extent to which the things they did would bring them enjoyment or at least encourage self-expression. But the war in Vietnam allowed for them neither enjoyment nor self-expression. In their view, that war was the product of a generation with which they had nothing in common, and they quite naturally opposed it fervently.

Could there have been an anti-war movement in the United States without recorded music and without television? Could there have been a civil rights movement without them? Perhaps, but it is very difficult to imagine "the sixties" without either of these media. The development of the electronic media in the period following World War II was the cause of the communicative style of the Baby Boom generation. What is important to observe is that it is widely believed among that generation that they are the products of music and television. The strongest aspect of this belief is the distrust of linear argumentation and historical or traditional precedent. What is crucial to this generation is to keep moving, to continue to exercise new options, to avoid any form of even apparent permanence or stagnation. Television of course, may not be the cause of this phenomenon, but it is an appropriate medium for its expression.

It is believed that all of the American generations share an emphasis on individualism, but this individualism will be expressed in different ways. For older generations the emphasis will be on the independence of Americans from outside, particularly European, influence. For the Baby Boom generation American, the emphasis will be on independence from tradition, the past, and the excessive influence of given human relationships such as those of the family or the community.

(Adapted from R. Scollon & S. W. Scollon: *Intercultural Communication: A Discourse Approach*, Chapter 10)

Notes

the Great Depression 大萧条	diaper 尿布
precarious 不稳定的，靠不住的	fracture 断裂；破坏
devastate 破坏，蹂躏	fervently 热情地；强烈地
inheritance 继承，遗产	linear argumentation 直线推论
transitional 过渡的；转变的	precedent 先例，惯例
abundance 丰裕，富足	stagnation 停滞，不动
paradoxically 看似矛盾地	

Questions

1. Why is communication between different generations felt to be a form of intercultural communication?

2. What have made the Americans born after World War II differ greatly from those born before it?

3. If people in today's world are generationally different from each other, how can we justify our use of concepts such as American culture and Chinese culture in discussing intercultural communication?

Exploration

In a sense, generation gap is a modern phenomenon, for the environment in which people of a different generation live tends to be different as time changes faster in a modern society than in a traditional one. What are the social changes and developments that have made younger generation today different from older generations?

Young people all over the world nowadays may have much in common and find it easier to communicate with one another than with the older people who share the same roof with them in the same family.

Communication between parents and teenagers tends to be difficult. Have you ever been involved in conflict with your parents? Why do you think conflicts between children (especially teenagers) and their parents seem to be common in our life? What differences can we find between them in the way they communicate? And how do the differences contribute to the problems and difficulties in their communication with one another?

What ways can you suggest to improve communication and achieve understanding between different generations?

Cases for Discussion

Case 1

Meida, a student from India, has been invited to her American friend Carol's home for dinner. She is sitting at the table and enjoying the dinner and conversation with Carol's parents, Dr. Turner and Mrs. Turner. During the dinner the phone rings and Carol's younger brother answers it.

Carol's brother: Carol. It's Bill.

Mrs. Turner: (*surprised*) Bill? I thought you weren't seeing him any more. Carol.

(Without replying, Carol leaves the room to answer the phone. When she returns, she silently continues her dinner.)

Dr. Turner: Carol, was it Bill?

Carol: Yes.

Dr. Turner: Are you still seeing him even though we told you we didn't approve?

Carol: (*angrily*) Do I have to tell you everything? Listen, Dad, I know Bill doesn't have a college education but he is working for his brother in a construction company. He's trying to earn enough money to return to school. You always say that you respect hark-working people. Why shouldn't I see him any more?

Dr. Turner: (*softly but seriously*) I hope you're not serious about Bill, Carol. He promised to stay in college but he dropped out twice. Do you want to marry someone whose personality you'll have to change?

Mrs. Turner: Carol. Bill is different from us. We're only saying this because we love you. Bill just isn't your kind.

Carol: (*furious*) What do you mean, "my kind"? He's a human being! Just because he comes from a family that has less money than we do? What kind of democracy do you believe in? Everyone is supposed to be equal. He and his family are just as good as we are. (*By now, Carol is shouting loudly.*)

(Meida is feeling embarrassed and stares at her plate)

Carol's brother: Come on, Mom and Dad. Bill's a nice guy.

Carol: Just because his parents are farmers who work with their hands and you are professors who work with your heads. What difference does that make?

Mrs. Turner: Carol, we're very disappointed in you. After all, we know what is best for you.

(Suddenly Carol gets up, takes Meida's arm, and pulls her to the door.)

Carol: Come on, Meida. Let's go to my room and study.

(Carol and Meida quickly walk out. Meida tries to say to Carol's parents that she is sorry but Carol pulls Meida away.)

Questions

1. What are the problems between Carol and her parents?
2. Could a similar incident occur in your family? Why or why not?
3. How can a conflict like this be resolved?

Case 2

The following conversation is taken from a scene in the novel Joy Luck Club. It is a novel about four Chinese mothers, who left China for San Francisco in 1949, and their daughters. Despite their skin color, the younger generation was actually American natives with little knowledge about China. Although they loved their mothers, they could not bear their mother's too much care and even struggle against their mothers for independence and egalitarian relationship.

Daughter: Mom, would you please make an appointment beforehand next time if you want to come to my house?

Mother: What? How can you say to me in this way? I'm your mother. I heard yesterday you went to see a psychological doctor. I came here just want to know what happened to you.

(*Embarrassing silence*)

Questions

1. What does "appointment" mean in English? Do you think it is necessary to make an appointment for a casual meeting between a mother and a daughter? Why or why not?
2. What would you do then if you were the daughter? Or if you were the mother?

Case 3

While people of different generations might use the same words, the meanings by which they are interpreted are often radically different. The following is just a case in point.

In an engineering office two of the junior engineers, both members of the Baby Boom generation, came up with the idea for a project which they thought would significantly improve one of their production processes. They went to their supervisor, a member of the Depression/War generation, told him briefly about the project, and asked whether or not he would be willing to support it. His answer was, "That sounds like a great idea. Go right ahead and I'll give you my full support."

The engineers began their work and were enjoying the project, but they noticed after a while that their supervisor had never again made mention of it. He had not stopped by their office to ask into its progress, and he had not mentioned it when they had run across him at the exercise club from time to time. They became discouraged and ultimately abandoned the idea.

This corporation during this period of time was employing a consulting company to assist them with rethinking and developing a new corporate culture. At one of the discussion sessions with junior staff, a point was raised about supervisory staff. These two engineers argued that the biggest problem they experienced was that creativity was that they received "no support" from above when they tried to initiate new projects. They felt that the system was "too hierarchical" and that they were being forced into simply accepting and carrying out management concepts.

Ironically, in discussions with management these same consultants heard a very different story. The particular supervisor in question pointed out that two engineers had come to him with what he thought was a really creative concept and, even though he had given them complete freedom to pursue the project, they had just dropped it for no reason whatsoever.

In this communication between the two generations, the crucial word is "support." From the point of view of the members of the younger generation, "support" means to show an interest, to come around from time to time and ask how things are going, to mention to others that these people are doing something interesting. They took for granted that the organization would give them the resources to do the actual work. From the point of view of the supervisor, as a member of the older generation, "support" means to leave you entirely free and independent, to refrain from meddling, to stay away until the younger engineers can prove they did the job entirely on their own.

Questions

1. Have you had any similar experiences communicating with people of older generations?
2. What should we do to avoid such misunderstandings in communication?

Readings for Further Study

1

Living Generations of Americans

Every generation is a "melting pot" of different kinds of people, yet every generation is united in an "age location" in history. Fads, fashion, and politics reflect specific attitudes about each generation's interpretation on life. Many generations have been labeled with a name reflecting their attitudes and actions. In the United States, living generations of Americans are often recognized in the following way—

G.I. Generation born in 1901 to 1924

Members of the G.I. Generation are high achievers, fearless but not reckless, patriotic, idealistic, and morally conscientious. This generation produced America's first astronauts, Nobel laureates, legendary movie stars, and political leaders. Many members have been labelled heroes for their outstanding accomplishments. The initials "G.I." stand for general issue or government issue. Throughout the G.I. life cycle, the federal government has directed and supported its members with new programs and departments. The G.I. Generation learned early on in life how to be a good team player putting their trust in government, authority and community. A generation of "doers and believers," many achieved a higher standard of living and education than their parents. G.I.s are survivors of the great depression—easily made happy with a good job, mild future, and a little house for family.

Silent Generation born in 1925 to 1942

Members of the Silent Generation are considered cautious, unadventurous, unimaginative, withdrawn, and silent. The Silents felt they were a generation without a cause. Remembering World War II from their childhood, many Silents were looking for a cause.

The vast majority of this generation wanted job security offered by big corporations. Only two percent took the risk to be self-employed. Born mostly during an era of depression and war, the Silent Generation knew hardship and knew how to struggle through tough times. The Silent Generation was the earliest marrying group in American history. Men married at an average age of 23 and women at 20. Ninety four percent of women became mothers and stayed at home raising an average of 3.3 children. And there was also the start of the "divorce epidemic" as men and women born between 1930s and 1940s were rushing to get divorces.

Parents of this generation were strict with their children. Youth felt pressure to conform from the adults than from peers. Housing developments increased and many of the Silent Generation moved to the suburbs. Affordable standardized housing became available. Cars were no longer a luxury but a necessity for transportation from the suburbs.

Suburban life encouraged conformity. Houses were similar and homeowners were all about the same age earning the same income. Many males shared the same background of wartime experiences and schooling. Most items were purchased on credit. Instead of saving, Americans were spending in full confidence that good times would continue.

Boomer Generation born in 1943 to 1960

The Boom Generation developed under parent's care dedicated to nurturing their children to success. Most families had stay-at-home moms whose primary purpose was to devote themselves to their children's well-being whether that be social, economic, or spiritual.

Parents at the time relied heavily on the guidelines set by and advice from the leading pediatrician of the time, Dr. Benjamin Spock. Dr. Spock published a baby care book that became a "Second Bible" in U.S. family homes. This helped set up a democratic environment in which parents believed their children would flourish.

Boomers seemed to develop personalities that mixed high self-esteem with self-indulgence. Since Boomers thought their parents' world was in need of a major overhaul and because they were taught to think critically by questioning everything, they saw their role in society as not to obey its rules but rather to justify, purify, and force change wherever they believed it was necessary. They would make themselves heard by lighting social and political fuses that caused dramatic changes.

13ER Generation born in 1961 to 1981

Generation "X" or the "13 ER" appear shocking to others on the outside and unknown on the inside. Older generations classify this generation as irresponsible, reckless, uneducated, and violent—the generation only concerned about me. "13 ERs" find this criticism both overblown and very unfair. This generation observed parents and other adults not in control of their own lives or their country. It was a country totally out of control, with actions and impacts ranging from the Vietnam War to nuclear power accidents, e.g. Three Mile Island; while on the home front, families broke apart by skyrocketing divorces creating an unprecedented number of single parent households. The surge of mothers into the workplace created latchkey kids left alone to fend for themselves.

This is a generation of children without a childhood. "13 ERs" are survivors of what the adult world have left behind. Forced to grow up fast and overloaded with information, this generation finds it hard to understand what is truth, to tell right from wrong, or how to achieve success in their lives. "13 ERs" are confronted with drug addiction, AIDS, sexual freedom, uncontrollable violence, educational requirements, and environmental and world problems created by past generations. This is the odd generation, born on "Friday the Thirteenth," or the generation "cross-out" with a capital "X."

Although this generation is a very busy group, at times they are also very lonely. Most households have parents working full-time jobs trying to make ends meet while also trying to give their kids the best of life, especially materially, yet at the same time leaving many of the "13ERs" to fend for themselves. With limited face-to-face interaction between each other, families try to meet at meals but many times just pass each other in house hallways between social events, sports practices, health gyms, and jobs. On some days the only communication between family members and "13ERs" is done only by portable telephone, beepers or email. Since "13ERs" have a wide variety of entertainment at their fingertips with TV, video games, computers, and music CDs, this generation seems to best express their feeling through music groups, Internet communication, and with what they wear.

Millennial Generation born since 1982

This is the generation where the "Class of 2000" is born. This new generation is being treated as precious. Politicians and parents are taking an interest in improving conditions today that allows this generation to grow up in a nurturing environment. Parents are making a jointed effort to tell children to stay away from drugs, alcohol, profanity, improper TV, unchaperoned gatherings, aggressive behavior, beware of AIDS, and avoid teen pregnancy. Politicians are taking an interest in the quality education, media affects on children, and the war on drug so this generation is not a "Lost Generation." Sex education calls for abstinence rather than a neutral approach. This is the generation of hope, hope to correct the errors of their parents.

Notes

reckless 鲁莽的
idealistic 理想主义的
conscientious 有良心的;认真的
laureate 获奖者
legendary 传奇的
initial 首字母
withdrawn 孤独的,性格内向的
epidemic 流行
conformity 顺从;墨守成规
pediatrician 儿科专家
self-esteem 自尊
self-indulgence 自我放纵
overhaul 大修;彻底革新
fuse 导火索
overblown 夸大其词
Three Mile Island 三哩岛
skyrocket 突升,猛涨
latchkey kid 挂钥匙的儿童
fend for themselves 照料他们自己
make ends meet 收支相抵
profanity 使用亵渎语言或行为
unchaperoned gathering 无成人陪伴的青少年聚会
abstinence 节制,禁欲

Questions

1. Why are those generations of Americans different from each other?
2. Do you think there exists a generation gap between you and your parents?
3. What should we do when we are confronted with generational differences in communication?

2
A Very Lucky Daughter

My parents seemed so small and out of place in America. But on a trip to China I saw their true stature.

When I was younger, I would try to imagine my parents growing up in China. But I could only envision them in the black-and-white of their faded childhood pictures. Their childhood stories didn't match the people I knew. I couldn't picture my domestic mom, unsure of her halting English, studying international economics at a university in China. I laughed at the image of my stern father, an electrical engineer, chasing after chickens in his Chinese village.

My parents moved to the United States for better lives when they were young adults. They did not step onto Chinese soil for more than 50 years. Then their friends arranged a trip to China. And they asked me to join them on the six-city tour.

There were plenty of reasons not to go. I'd recently graduated from college and was **itching** to move from North Carolina to Washington, D.C., and start my new job. And yet something inside—I could not explain what—urged me to go.

When the plane jerked to a stop in Shanghai, our first destination, all of those reasons I decided to go **materialized** in the expressions on my parents' faces. My mom folded and unfolded her hands impatiently in her lap. I was surprised and slightly scared to see my dad's eyes **glimmering** with emotion. He slipped his hand, soft and spotted with age, in mine.

"Last time I was here," he said, "my parents going from north to south. So much bombing. A lot of people starving," He leaned close. "You very lucky, Sharon." When I would **whine** as a child, my dad's response was inevitable: "Some people not lucky as you."

But I never cared about being lucky. I just wanted to be like the other American kids.

My parents, however, intended me to become a model Chinese American. Starting when I was six, they would drag me away from Saturday cartoons to a Chinese church. I would **squirm** in my seat while a teacher recited Chinese vocabulary. I dutifully recited my *bo po mo fo*s—the ABCs of speaking **Mandarin**. But in my head, I rearranged the chalk marks that made up the characters into pictures of houses and trees.

When I turned nine, I declared I wasn't going to Chinese school anymore. "This **stinks**," I yelled. "None of my friends have to go to extra school. Why do I have to go?"

"Because you Chinese," my mom replied coolly.

"Then I don't want to be Chinese," I shouted back. "It's not fair. I just want to be normal. Why can't you and Dad be like everybody else's parents? I wish I were somebody else's kid."

I waited for my mom to shout, but she just stared at me with tired eyes. "If you don't want to go, don't have to," she said, turning away.

Now when I remember my behavior. I want to **lecture** who I was then: don't yell at your parents because they're different, because that is who they are. Listen when they teach you Chinese, because that is who you are.

I grew up in the early 1980s. In elementary school, I was one of the two Asians in my grade. For the most part, I fit in with my peers. My friends and I wore the same brand of jeans and dyed our hair into the same messes.

But there were daily reminders that I was different. The pork dumplings in my lunch. My reflection in the bathroom mirror. Where did I belong?

I remember facing this question on an elementary-school **standardized test**. The directions said to fill in race. The four choices made a neat row of circles: "White," "Black," "American

Indian," and "Other." I glanced at my best friend, Sara, darkening the "White" bubble.

I contemplated my options. I wasn't black or American Indian. I didn't consider myself "Other." Weren't Sara and I the same? I filled in the "White" bubble.

After the test, the teacher shuffled through the answer sheets. "Sharon," she said. "You've filled in 'White' for your race. You should have filled in 'Other.'"

Heat reddened my cheeks. "I know," I said. How could I forget?

Though my parents had lived in the United States for decades, they still led a Chinese life at home. They spoke to each other in Chinese and read a Chinese paper. Chinese food covered our dinner table. Breakfast consisted of watery rice with pickled vegetables and meat, or fried eggs with soy sauce. At dinner I would douse my rice with ketchup and remind my parents that Sara's family ate hamburgers. I envied my friends' relationships with their parents. My friends didn't have to worry that their parents would embarrass them with questions like "Is this good price?" and "What's this meaning?"

My friends' parents chatted easily with each other and our teachers. Their parents understood dating, and what it was like to grow up with the pressures of drinking, drugs and sex. My parents discussed only my grades, career and prospective salary.

My mom speaks English like I speak Chinese: slowly and punctuated by ums and ahs. When someone speaks English too rapidly, my mom's eyes cloud with confusion. I instantly recognize her I-don't-get-it look, and I know it's time to explain something.

In the airport before we departed for China, my parents' friends herded around me. "Your parents so proud of you," said one man. "Always talking about you."

His words surprised me. I felt like I barely spoke with my parents. Did they really know who I was? Then another question, the one I always managed to skirt, surfaced in my conscience: did I even come close to understanding *them*?

The tour was a 17-day whirlwind. We visited lakes laden with lotus flowers, snapped pictures of jagged mountains rising out of the Yellow River, and hiked up stone stairs to intricately painted temples.

But the best part of the trip was watching my parents. They carried themselves with an ease unfamiliar to me. They blended into the throngs of Chinese people instead of sticking out in the crowd. Their voices swelled with authority. My mom translated the tour guide's Chinese in her unwavering voice, whispering historical anecdotes she'd learned in school.

Often during the tour, my own face resembled my mom's I-don't-get-it look. At meals, my parents answered my constant questions about each colorful bowl that would rotate by on the Lazy Susan.

My experience in China pieced together the puzzle I knew about my parents. For the first time, I saw them in their entirety. I saw them in their culture, not in mine.

I realized that many things I found embarrassing or frustrating about my parents were normal in China. I understood why my parents talked and acted the way they did—and why my dad constantly reminded me I was lucky.

One day, my parents and I sat on a bench overlooking stone monoliths. "Too bad I don't speak fluent Chinese," I said. "I should have listened when you tried to teach me."

I wanted to tell my parents that if I could go back in time, I would accept myself for who I was and them for who they were.

My dad looked at me with understanding. "It's okay," he said. "You learning it now."

My mom smiled supportively. "Never too late," she said.

The trip to China changed my life. Now when I speak to my parents, there is a mutual understanding. Our conversations extend past questions about where they went to eat or how my job is going. I talk about my life. My parents talk about what they were doing when they were my age, and I can imagine them with crystal clarity, fresh young students at universities.

And I realize my dad has been right about something all along: I am very lucky indeed.

(Adapted from S. Liao: A Very Lucky Daughter, in *Reader's Digest*, June 2001)

Notes

stature 身高，身材
envision 想象
domestic 一心照顾家庭的
itching 渴望的
materialize 使具体化，实现
glimmer 闪烁，微微闪烁
whine 哀诉，发牢骚
squirm 扭动，蠕动
Mandarin 官话，普通话
stink 让人讨厌透了
lecture 教训，训斥
standardized test 标准化测试
contemplate 思忖
shuffle 翻阅
douse 浸泡；浇洒
ketchup 番茄酱
herd 成群聚集
whirlwind 旋风
lotus flower 莲花
jagged 高低起伏的
intricately 精细复杂地
blend 交融
unwavering 坚定的
anecdote 轶事
Lazy Susan(餐桌上盛食物便于取食的)旋转餐盘
monolith 石柱

Questions

1. How are the views of the author and of her parents influenced by their different experiences?

2. Why did the author's parents stick to the traditional Chinese lifestyle and send her to learn Chinese?

3. Why did the author refuse to learn Chinese and "pushed away my parents' culture"? What did she mean by being "normal"? What did the author's father mean when he said that she is "lucky"?

Summary

1. The differences between generations are now a particularly acute problem in the daily communication of people's life throughout the world.

2. Communication between people born and brought up at different times is very much the same kind of problem as communication between people born and brought up in different places. It is actually a form of intercultural communication.

3. Every generation is a "melting pot" of different kinds of people, yet every generation is united in an "age location" in history. Fads, fashion, and politics reflect specific attitudes about each generation's interpretation on life. Many generations have been labeled with a name reflecting their attitudes and actions.

4. In the case of different generations within the same society or even the same family, each side tends to believe that its interpretation of communicated messages is the same as that of the other side.

Chapter 11 Gender Differences in Communication

More is meant than meets the ear.

—English proverb

Chapter 11 Gender Differences in Communication

Preview Questions

1. What are the basic differences between males and females?
2. Have you ever had problems communicating with people of the other gender?
3. What do you think is the proper way a male or female should talk?

Text A

Rapport-Talk and Report-Talk

I was sitting in a suburban living room, speaking to a women's group that had invited men to join them for the occasion of my talk about communication between women and men. During the discussion, one man was particularly talkative, full of lengthy comments and explanations. When I made the observation that their husbands don't talk to them enough, this man volunteered that he heartily agreed. He gestured toward his wife, who had sat silently beside him on the couch throughout the evening, and said, "She's the talker in our family."

Everyone in the room burst into laughter. The man looked puzzled and hurt."It's true," he explained. "When I come home from work, I usually have nothing to say, but she never runs out. If it weren't for her, we'd spend the whole evening in silence." Another woman expressed a similar paradox about her husband: "When we go out, he's the life of the party. If I happen to be in another room, I can always hear his voice above the others. But when we're home, he doesn't have that much to say. I do most of the talking."

Who talks more, women or men? According to the stereotype, women talk too much. Linguist Jennifer Coates notes some proverbs:

A woman's tongue wags like a lamb's tail.

Foxes are all tail and women are all tongue.

The North Sea will sooner be found wanting water than a woman be at a loss for word.

Modern stereotypes are not much different from those expressed in the old proverbs. Women are believed to talk too much. Yet study after study finds that it is men who talk more—at meetings, in mixed-group discussions, and in classrooms where girls sit next to boys.

Who talks more, then, women or men? The seemingly contradictory evidence is reconciled by the difference between what I call public and private speaking. More men feel comfortable doing "public speaking," while more women feel comfortable doing "private speaking." Another way of describing these differences is by using the terms report-talk and rapport-talk.

For most women, the language of conversation is primarily a language of rapport: a way of establishing connections and negotiating relationships. Emphasis is placed on displaying similarities and matching experiences. From childhood, girls criticize peers who try to stand out or appear better than others. People feel their closest connections at home, or in settings where they feel at home—with one or a few people they feel close to and comfortable with—in other words, during private speaking. But even the most public situations can be approached like private speaking.

For most men, talk is primarily a means to preserve independence and negotiate and maintain status in a hierarchical social order. This is done by exhibiting knowledge and skill, and by holding center stage through verbal performance such as story-telling, joking, or imparting information. From childhood, men learn to use talking as a way to get and keep attention. So they are more comfortable speaking in larger groups made up of people they know less well—in the broadest sense, "public speaking." But even the most private situations can be approached like public speaking, more like giving a report than establishing rapport.

Once again, the seeds of women's and men's styles are sown in the ways they learn to use language while growing up. In American culture, the center of a little girl's social life is her best friend. Girls' friendships are made and maintained by telling secret. For grown women too, the essence of friendship is talk, telling each other what they're thinking and feeling, and what happened that day: who was at the bus stop, who called, what they said, how that made them feel. When asked who their best friends are, most women name other women they talk to regularly. When asked the same question, most men will say it's their wives. After that, many men name other men with whom they do things such as playing tennis or baseball (but never just sit and talk) or a chum from high school whom they haven't spoken to in a year.

Men and women often have very different ideas of what's important and at what point "important" topics should be raised. A woman told me of a conversation with her boyfriend. Knowing he had seen his friend Oliver, she asked, "What's new with Oliver?" He replied, "Nothing." But later in the conversation it came out that Oliver and his girlfriend had decided to get married. "That's nothing?" the woman gasped in frustration and disbelief.

For everyone, home is a place to be offstage. But the comfort of home can have opposite and incompatible meanings for women and men. For many men, the comfort of home means freedom from having to prove themselves and impress others through verbal display. At last, they are in a situation where talk is not required. They are free to remain silent. But for women home is a place where they are free to talk, and where they feel the greatest need for talk, with those they are closest to. For them, the comfort of home means the freedom to talk without worrying about how their talk will be judged.

The difference between public and private speaking, or report-talk and rapport-talk, can be understood in terms of status and connections. It is not surprising that women are most comfortable talking when they feel safe and close, among friends and equals, whereas men feel comfortable talking when there is need to establish and maintain their status in a group. But the situation is complex, because status and connection are bought with the same currency. What seems like a bid for status could be intended as a display of closeness, and what seems like distancing may have been intended to avoid the appearance of pulling rank. Hurtful and unjustified misinterpretations can be avoided by understanding the conversational styles of the other gender.

(Adapted from D. Tannen: You Just Don't Understand—Women and Men in Conversation)

Notes

paradox 自相矛盾
contradictory 相矛盾的
reconcile 调解;调和
rapport 和睦关系;联系
negotiating 协调,处理
peer 同龄人,同辈
hierarchical 等级的,等级森严的
gasp 气喘,倒抽气
frustration 受挫;失望
offstage 幕后的;在私生活中的
incompatible 不相容的;不一致的
pull rank 以权势压人

Questions

1. How do men and women usually talk and why do they talk so differently?

2. Can we say there exist similar differences between men and women in our Chinese society? Why or why not?

Text B

He Says... She Says...

Do you sometimes suspect your better half lives on another planet? Have you ever wondered whether he's being thick on purpose—or whether it just comes naturally? The truth may be that he's not merely acting dumb—he really can't help it!

It is simply that men and women are programmed to receive, process and impart information in quite different ways. Scientists have found that, although women's brains are smaller, they have far more grey matter in those parts which control verbal fluency, initiative, short term memory and listening skills.

Upbringing and peer pressure continue to reinforce this natural disparity. The sexes are treated differently right from the cradle. Girl babies are crooned over, talked to and stroked more than boys. As a result, girls learn to talk earlier, they're better at languages and have a better memory for detail. They also pick up on and respond better to facial expressions and body language.

Boys and girls play differently, too. Girls tend to play in small groups; they usually have a "best friend" with whom they share their secrets. Boys, on the other hand, tend to form looser attachments, often belonging to "gangs" rather than having one special buddy. They bond through physical rather than verbal play.

Women never lose the need for a best friend with whom they can exchange confidences. Perhaps because women have this need for verbal intimacy, we also make better listeners. Men, who feel no such need in the first place, rarely form the same kind of one-to-one close friendships, so they're less practiced at giving and receiving "intimate" messages.

To a woman, communication and verbal reassurance are vital. She needs to be told that she's loved, that she looks good, that the dinner she's been slaving over is wonderful. He takes the obvious for granted—after all, if he didn't loved her he wouldn't be there; she bought that new frock, so she must know it looks O. K. And if the dinner was a disaster, he wouldn't have eaten that much. To him, this is all quite reasonable.

It's reasonable, too, to assume that if she has something to say, she'll say it, right? Wrong! A woman wants to be asked. To her it's a signal that he's interested, that he cares.

Being logical creatures, men tend to take things at face value. Ask him a question and he'll answer it. Ask a woman and she'll probably reply with another question (guaranteed to drive him mad!)

Women tend to look for the meaning behind the words. They're experts at reading non-verbal cues like body language and tonal inflections; they're more attuned to insinuation and innuendo. This can be a mixed blessing: on the one hand it makes them more sensitive and intuitive, on the other, they can sometimes read things which aren't there.

Men tend to stick to factual stuff like current affairs, sport, business and so on, while women like to talk about their feelings, families and other people. Men are notoriously bad at discussing their feelings. They're brought up to believe that boys don't cry, that it's "sissy" to talk about emotions.

Women remember exactly what has been said, when, how and by whom. They use more terms of endearment and they're more apologetic and self-critical, (as in "that's only my opinion—for what it's worth.") And, while women may make a request in the form of a polite question ("Darling, would you mind passing the newspaper, please?"), men are more likely to issue a direct command ("pass the paper!").

Studies show that women do interrupt more, but usually only to murmur encouraging prompts like "I see" and "Really." Men interrupt in order to hijack the conversation altogether!

Men are less likely to confront problems in a relationship on the basis that if they ignore it, it will go away. When they can ignore it no longer, men often deal with problems internally. Women, on the other hand, need to talk things out.

Men and women have very different ways of dealing with anger. Boys are considered more naturally aggressive, so displays of anger are "permissible" and, throughout life, it remains the one emotion men feel comfortable about expressing. Anger in girls, however, is deemed unfeminine and unacceptable, and they learn to suppress it.

Say a woman has a problem. What she needs is a good old grumble to her nearest and dearest. Only, instead of offering comfort and reassurance, he weighs in with all kinds of practical advice. This may or may not be useful, but, to a woman, it's deeply unsatisfying. It's sympathy she is after, not solutions. But, in his logical way, he gives her what he thinks she is asking for. And can she really blame him? She may be sending all kinds of hidden messages, but what he hears is: "please help me with this problem"—so he does.

The danger when dealing with the opposite sex is in assuming that, since we both use more or less the same words, there's no room for misunderstandings. But remember, while one may be speaking plain English, the other's probably listening in foreign!

(Adapted from V. Jones: Mutual Misunderstanding, in *Ladies First*)

Notes

thick 愚钝的，理解力差
dumb 沉默寡言的；愚钝的
grey matter（脑的）灰白质，智力
initiative 主动性
reinforce 加强
disparity 不同，不一样
croon 低声哼唱，轻声地说
pick up on 理解；注意到
tonal inflection 语调变化
attuned 与……合拍的，协调的
insinuation 暗示，迂回表达
innuendo 暗讽，影射
notoriously 众所周知地
grumble 抱怨，咕哝

Questions

1. Why do misunderstandings often arise in male-female communication?

2. What do you think we should do to avoid such misunderstandings in communicating with people of the opposite sex?

Exploration

We may find some differences between men's and women's speech in China just the same as those in English-speaking countries. For instance, men and women have different ideas of what is important to talk about and which topics deserve talking, and therefore what men and women frequently talk about are often very different from each other. However, we have to realize that the situation in China may not be exactly the same as that in the U.S.A. and other English-speaking countries. Many men in China seem to be not quite good at talking in public places, because our traditional culture, unlike English-speaking cultures, has seldom encouraged people to talk much in public and made many people feel uncomfortable when they are asked to talk on public occasions.

As men and women are becoming equal in many aspects of our social life, there will be some changes in the so-called characteristics of gender in people's verbal behaviors. Some distinctions between men and women in the way they talk may blur or even disappear. The social expectation about the appropriateness of men's and women's speech may change to such an extent that gender will no longer play very important role in determining how one should talk.

However, so long as men and women are socially as well as biologically different, there may still exist differences between men and women. Achieving understanding in cross-gender communication remains to be difficult today. What can we do to improve it?

Cases for Discussion

Case 1

Even where men and women base their communications on the exchange of information, the types of information communicated are likely to be different. There is an old joke on the subject.

A man says, "My wife and I have agreement: I make all the big decisions, but she gets to make the little ones. I decide what the United Nations should do, how to solve the world energy crisis, and who will win the next World Cup; she decides where we should live, how we should eat, how to educate the kids, and where we'll retire."

The joke is based on observation of the fact that what men consider "information" is what we might call pubic affairs or news; what women consider "information" is more likely to be the close and important details of their daily lives.

A man is more likely to say he had had a good talk with someone if the talk had ranged over broad subjects like the economy, politics, and sports. The more general and abstract the discussion, the more it would count as a good "talk." Women, on the other hand, are likely to consider it a good "talk" when close details of individual lives are brought out, particularly where those details show people's characters, their feelings, and their reactions to the events of their ongoing lives. What women call a good talk, men might dismiss by saying it is nothing but gossip.

Questions

1. What do you think of this joke? Does it tell us much about gender differences?
2. Why do men often consider what women call a good talk as nothing but gossip?

Case 2

The conversation below is not at all unusual in our life.

He: What would you like for your birthday?

She: I don't care, anything's OK.

He: No, really, what do you want? I'd like to get you something nice.

She: You don't have to get me anything, besides we can't afford much right now.

He: Well, how about if we just go out for dinner together then?

She: Sure, that's fine. I don't really want anything. You always give me whatever I want anyway.

Both the man and the woman in this conversation feel frustrated by this situation. He really wants to give her something nice, unusual, something she would not otherwise buy for herself because they do not usually spend much money on special things for each other or for themselves. But from this conversation he is not able to figure out what she would like, and he gives up and settles for just going out for dinner—something they have always done and which carries no special meaning for either of them. What has frustrated him is that while he has asked quite clearly and specifically what she wants, she has told him nothing.

The woman in this conversation is also frustrated. She would very much appreciate a special and unusual gift as a symbol of the strength of their relationship. What the gift would be is not the consideration for her at all; what is important to her is that he should know her well enough to be able to tell what would be just the right gift. The fact that he has asked outright indicates to her that he, like all men, is unobservant, is unable to interpret her feelings, or in the worst case does not really care for her as much as he says.

Questions

1. Why do both the man and the woman feel frustrated by this situation?
2. What can we learn about communication differences between males and females from this conversation?

Case 3

A man's boss calls him into the office to discuss with him the possible transfer to an overseas assignment.

Supervisor: You've done well for us here. Do you think you could adjust to working in Frankfurt?

Employee: Well, of course, I've never been there, but I see no reason why I could not perform as well there as anywhere.

When he goes home he says to his wife, "I've been given a transfer to Frankfurt. Maybe you should start looking into schools for the kids."

Throughout these situations he has quite unconsciously used a language of exclusion. Although this transfer is a transfer for not just him but for his entire family, he has never thought to use a pronoun to include them. He has not said, "We've never been there," or, "We're going to go to Frankfurt and maybe we should start looking into schools." A woman in the same situation might be quite concerned in the first place with not just how she would be able to perform her work, but how the whole family might get along in such a transfer. She would most likely feel it quite natural to want to discuss it with the family before saying that she was quite sure that it would work out well.

Of course, a woman who takes such an inclusive stance in discussing the transfer with her boss might be thought to be a weak employee who could not make such crucial decisions on her own. While the man with his exclusive language communicates to his boss that he is quite independent and able to stand on his own (whether or not his family will get along), the woman communicates dependence and even suggests the possibility that if things did not go well with the family, she would not be able to perform her work up to standards.

The language of exclusion which a man uses will tend to emphasize his autonomy and independence while the language of inclusion used by a woman is more likely to play up the intimacy and relationships, recognizing them as significant factors.

Note

Frankfurt(德国城市)法兰克福

Questions

1. What would you do if you were the employee in the same situation?
2. What do you think this difference between males and females illuminates?

Readings for Further Study

1
Miscommunication

When we speak we try to say the minimum we can, but yet get the hearer to draw a rich set of inferences that will fill out our meaning. Thus, much of what we say merely constitutes "cues" or "clues" to guide the hearer in drawing the right inferences. What I communicate goes far beyond what I have literally said.

Users of different languages, and different social or ethnic groups speaking the same language, often differ in how they handle these cues. This fact gives rise to a great deal of miscommunication between people. For example, in a discussion of conversations between speakers of American English and those of Indian English (from India), a sociolinguist points out that speakers of Indian English formulate their turns at talk rather differently than speakers of American English. In a single turn at talk in a conversation, Indians tend to take a good deal of time to provide background information for their main point, and they use increased stress (higher pitch and increased loudness) to mark this background information. Then they shift to low pitch and low amplitude on their main point. However, Americans hear their background information, given its length and its increased stress, as their main point, assume they are finished when this background information is done, and go to make their own contribution, feeling that the Indian has said nothing original. The Indian feels he or she is always interrupted and never allowed to make his or her point.

Miscommunication can occur in any encounter, even between members of the same social group or for that matter, the same family. Consider the following conversation between a husband and wife.

A husband and wife are talking about whether they should accept an invitation to visit the wife's sister:

Wife: Do you want to go to my sister's?

Husband: Okay.

Wife: Do you really want to go?

Husband (angry): You're driving me crazy! Why don't you make up your mind what you want?

What is going on here is this: the wife assumes she can say outright what she wants and that her husband will say outright what he wants. The wife feels she is perfectly willing to do what the husband wishes, and, in fact, feels confident in her kindness in being willing to do so. When she asks her question, "Do you want to go to my sister's?", she means the question literally; she is asking for information about the husband's preferences to that she can accommodate them.

The husband wants to be accommodating as well. But he assumes that people—even married people—don't directly say outright what they want. To him, such direct statements are coercive because he finds it hard to deny direct requests. So he assumes that people hint at what they want and in turn pick up hints from others. And a good way to hint is to ask a question, rather than making a statement. Thus, when his wife asked her question ("Do you want to go to my sister's?"), he assumed that his wife was not really asking a question, but hinting that she wanted to go to her sister's. Wishing to be accommodating, he gives in to her wishes, as he perceives them, and says "Okay."

But the wife follows up with a second question ("Are you sure you want to go?"). The husband hears this equally as a hint about what the wife wants, rather than a genuine question. He now assumes she doesn't want to go and is asking him to let her **off the hook**. He sees his wife as **irrational**. First she lets him know that she wants to go, and then when he gives her what she wants, she changes her mind and lets him know that she doesn't want to go.

However, from the wife's perspective, the husband's answer ("Okay") to her initial question ("Do you want to go to my sister's?") does not sound enough like an answer to the question. It seemed to her to indicate that he was going along with something, not really saying what he wanted. Since she simply wanted to please him by doing what he wanted to do, she presses him further with her second question, "Do you really want to go?" When he explodes with "You're driving me crazy! Why don't you make up your mind what you want?", she finds him totally irrational.

Because of their different backgrounds, these two people have different ways of signaling what they mean (the wife is an American native New Yorker of East European Jewish **extraction**; the husband is Greek). And they each misjudge the other's signals. However, they are not aware that they have a language problem, for people are rarely consciously aware of their linguistic practices, and have, in fact, great difficulty bringing them to consciousness. Therefore, they tend to blame problems not on the other person's use of language, but on the person's character, personality, or intentions.

There are also gender differences in using such cues. Many men and women in the U.S. differ in how they use "minimal responses" like *yes* and *mm hm* in conversation (these are sometimes called "channel feedback cues"). Women tend to mean by these responses *I'm listening to you; please continue*. For men, however, these minimal responses have a somewhat stronger meaning, such as *I agree with you* or at least *I follow your argument so far*. The fact that women use these minimal responses more often than men do is, in part, due simply to the fact that women are listening more often than men are agreeing. This difference, of which men and women are consciously aware, can lead to repeated misunderstandings. Since the woman is sending more minimal responses than the man would in the same circumstance, he assumes she agrees with everything he says. Since the man is sending fewer such responses than the woman would in the same situation, she assumes the man is not listening.

(Adapted from J. P. Gee: An Introduction to Human Language)

Notes

inference 推论，推断
ethnic 种族的
off the hook 脱离困境
irrational 无理性的，荒谬的
extraction 血统，家世

Questions

1. Could you give some examples to illustrate the point that what we communicate goes far beyond what we literally say?

2. Are you sometimes aware that misunderstandings may result from differences in people's use of language instead of their personalities or intentions?

2
Learning to Become Male or Female

Family, peer group, and school are considered to be three major influences on children's **socialization**. Each of these worlds has its own organization and messages about gender.

The family usually provides the most important speech model for young children; it is where most of us learn our ideas about gender as well as race and class. Gender identity is a basic concept of maleness or femaleness that children develop early in life. As they mature, children acquire increasing knowledge of their society's gender stereotypes and the expressions associated with male and female roles from interacting with parents, **siblings**, and peers, as well as through playing with certain types of toys, dressing or being dressed in ways typical of their sex, and through images in children's books, television, and so on.

The family is generally seen as a central site where children construct their sense of self. Many families are still traditional in terms of their division of labor by sex. Chores given to children or performed by parents provide clues about what adults consider appropriate for each sex. At a young age children are already practicing for adult roles of male and female.

From the time their children are born, mothers and fathers treat males and females differently. We have different expectations of boys and girls. Boys learn that they shouldn't cry. "Real men" keep their emotions to themselves. To express feelings openly in front of others is to risk embarrassment and to be **vulnerable**, a sign of weakness for men. Girls, on the other hand, are expected not to engage in **rough-and-tumble** play. They are supposed to be little ladies, to be quiet and nice. A little boy who cries after fighting with a girl is likely to be told "Don't cry," but the girl who cries after the fight is more likely to be told "Don't fight."

Schools too show patterns of gender separation, some of which continue patterns already learned at home, whereas others are introduced in the school setting. Studies show that children who are heavy television viewers tend to give more sex-typed responses when asked about their preferences for toys and appropriate gender roles. Most of the personal things children bring to school already divide along gender lines, for instance. Girls bring makeup, little stuffed animals, and jewelry but boys bring little toy truck, plastic dinosaurs, and such. Such findings have led some researchers to argue that boys and girls live in different worlds in which separate cultures are developed and transmitted, each with quite different patterns of the differences in men's and women's ways of speaking.

Although women predominate in both the home and the early school years as the primary caretakers and teachers of children, their presence diminishes in the higher levels of education and practically disappears by the time students are in universities. The higher the position, the more dramatic the gap between the number of men and women. The absence of women from the highest levels of specialized knowledge and prestige professions communicates a clear message that what women do is not important, or that they are not suited to these positions.

Peer groups also exert powerful pressure on children. As a girl points out, "You always try to be the same as everyone else."

Gender differences are observed in their early years when children play in same-sex peer groups. Boys tend to talk about being buddies and being tough, whereas girls tend to talk about being "best friends" and being nice. Boys tend to have a larger network than girls, who usually have one or two girlfriends with whom they play regularly. To some extent, the size of these groups may be determined by the different types of activities they engage in. It takes only three girls to **skip rope** or two to play house, whereas more boys are needed for team sports such as football. To some degree, the kinds of activities chosen may also determine the nature of the verbal interaction in them. Traditional girls' games such as **hopscotch** and jump rope rely on turn-taking more than some of the team sports played by boys, which depend on rules.

Girls' play was once described as "immature" by comparison with that of boys. Some scholars suggested that girls' games like playing house are less complex than those of boys and teach "meaningless **mumbo-jumbo**" rather than rules. Thus, the kinds of play activities girls engage in do not lead to the development of the kind of skills such as performing under competitive stress, which will be potentially useful later in life. Boys' games, on the other hand, have been seen as adaptive to the demands of corporate life, with its emphasis on hierarchy and competition.

It has been claimed that girls use language to create and maintain cohesiveness, and their activities are generally more cooperative and noncompetitive. Differentiation between girls is not made in terms of power. When conflicts arise, the group breaks up. Bossiness tends not to be tolerated, and girls use forms such as *let's*, *we're gonna*, and *we could* to get others to do things instead of appealing to their personal power or issuing direct commands. When they argue, girls tend to phrase their arguments in terms of group needs rather than in personal terms. They also stroke or comb their friends' hair, express interest in each other's clothing and haircuts, and so on. Best friends share secrets with one another. By early adolescence some girls spend their playground time talking rather than playing. Stories may also provide a substitute for fighting.

Boys, on the other hand, tend to have more hierarchically organized groups than girls, and status in the hierarchy is paramount. They also tend to play more outdoors and with higher levels of physical activity, often involving rough-and-tumble play as well as fighting, but rarely any touching that could be termed affectionate. In boys' groups, speech is used to assert dominance, to attract and maintain an audience when others have the floor. Boys issue commands to other boys rather than suggest what should be done. Certain kinds of speech events, such as joking and storytelling, are valued in boys' groups, and are turned into competitions. A boy has to learn how to get the floor to perform so that he can acquire prestige.

Of course there are many competing pressures on children from their peers. Boys, in particular, feel they have to talk "rough" with other boys in order not to be ridiculed. Although girls are under the same pressure to fit in with a group, they have to be careful not to go too far or people will judge them negatively.

(Adapted from S. Romaine: *Communicating Gender*, Chapter 7)

Notes

socialization 社会化过程
sibling 兄弟姐妹
vulnerable 易受攻击的，脆弱的
rough-and-tumble 乱作一团地打闹
skip rope 跳绳
hopscotch "造房子"游戏
mumbo-jumbo 莫名其妙的东西
cohesiveness 凝聚力
bossiness 专横，爱指挥人
adolescence 青春期
affectionate 出于柔情的
assert 维护，坚持

Questions

1. Of family, school, and peer group, which do you think has the strongest influence on children today? And why?

2. Are there any other things that may contribute to children's acquisition of gender concepts and stereotypes?

Summary

1. Men and women are believed to receive, process and impart information in quite different ways. The danger in communicating with people of the other gender is in assuming that, since we both use more or less the same words, there's no room for misunderstandings.

2. For most women, the language of conversation is primarily a language of rapport: a way of establishing connections and negotiating relationships. Emphasis is placed on displaying similarities and matching experiences.

3. For most men, talk is primarily a means to preserve independence and negotiate and maintain status in a hierarchical social or order. This is done by exhibiting knowledge and skill, and by holding center stage through verbal performance such as story-telling, joking, or imparting information.

4. The difference between public and private speaking, or report-talk and rapport-talk, can be understood in terms of status and connections. Women are most comfortable talking when they feel safe and close, among friends and equals, whereas men feel comfortable talking when there is need to establish and maintain their status in a group.

Chapter 12 Culture and Business

God gave to every people a cup, cup of clay, and from this cup they drank their life. They all dipped in the water, but their cups were different.

—Anonymous

Chapter 12 Culture and Business

Preview Questions

1. What should businesspersons do if they want to be successful in international trade?

2. Is management the same all over the world? Why or why not?

3. Does globalization mean that local and cultural differences no longer count in today's business exchanges?

Text A

Cultural Views toward Management

Many leaders and managers involved in international business activities do not have sufficient intercultural skills to be successful. Managers are often sent abroad with little, if any, training. The real challenge is developing the ability of management from different countries and cultures to think and work together—a primary factor for the success of global organization. This challenge exists because even a seemingly universal concept like "management" can be viewed differently from culture to culture.

To understand the management behavior of other cultures, we need to have an appreciation of North American management styles. Hofstede describes management in the American sense:

"It refers not only to the process but also to the managers as a class of people. This class (1) does not own a business but sells its skills to act on behalf of the owners and (2) does not produce personally but is responsible for making others produce, through motivation. Members of this class carry a high status and many American boys and girls aspire to the role. In the United States, the manager is a cultural hero."

Dominant managerial values in the United States include achievement and success, belief in hard work, pragmatism, optimism, Puritanism, rationality, impersonality in interpersonal work relationships, equality of opportunity, acceptance of competition, and individualism. This set of values is not cross-culturally consistent.

In Germany, the manager is not a cultural hero. In fact, Germans do not have a very strong concept of management. The reason for this is that Germany has historically honored the worker who possesses exceptionally high occupational skills and qualifications. As such, Germany has an apprenticeship system that culminates in a skill certificate recognized throughout the country. The highly skilled and responsible German workers do not necessarily need a manager, American-style, to motivate them. They expect their boss to assign their tasks and to be the expert in resolving technical problems. Germany has one of the world's lowest rates of personnel in leadership and staff roles. As such, managers are usually vice presidents or department heads. Their dominant values include a strong sense of professional calling and pride in work, a tendency toward an authoritarian leadership style, and a paternalistic commitment to the country's welfare. From a German perspective, effective managers are self-confident, energetic, open-minded, and particularly competitive.

As was the case with the Germans, the Japanese do not share a strong sense of management. For them, the key component of the organization is the "worker group." This worker group can expect lifelong employment and advancement according to seniority. American CEOs are primarily concerned with doing right by their shareholders. In contrast, a Japanese manager's constituency is his or her employees. Japan's top corporate managers are not—and never will be—slaves to shareholders. Japanese CEOs can thus try to abide by the country's lifetime-employment gospel without driving away shareholders. Instead of growth, an important focus for Japanese managers is keeping men in good-paying jobs in order to maintain social stability. Because of this system of lifetime employment that focuses on the worker group the Japanese are to a large extent controlled by their peer group rather than by their managers. Managers—section chiefs or department heads—value groupism, harmony, acceptance of hierarchy in work relationships, sense of obligation, and debt of lower level personnel to superiors, and consensual decision making. While American managers emphasize supervisory style, decision making, and control mechanism, the Japanese are more concerned with communication process, interdepartmental relations, and paternalistic approach.

Management style in France also differs from the style in the United States. Whereas in the Unites States it is assumed that managers and employees have a fair contract between themselves, in France each class is honored in what has been labeled a "stratified society." That is, managers act in very superior roles. In France, employees not only accept rigid role positions, but expect them. That is, subordinates are aware of their place in the societal hierarchy. They do, however, feel honor toward their own class. Hofstede further clarifies the issue of class honor as it applies to management in France:

"French do not think in terms of managers vs. nonmanagers but in terms of cadres vs. non-cadres; one becomes a cadre by attending the proper schools and one remains it forever; regardless of their actual task, cadres have the privileges of a higher social class, and it is very rare for a non-cadre to cross the ranks."

Obviously, the French value this high power differential. Additional values include individualism and authority based on absolutism. Because French managers or cadres are well paid, have attended the best schools, and come from well-established families, they tend to have an elitist approach to management.

This elitism is very different from the perspective in mainland China. Hofstede summarizes the Chinese view:

"Overseas Chinese American enterprises lack almost all characteristics of modern management. They tend to be small, cooperating for essential functions with other small organizations through networks based on personal relations. They are family owned, without the separation between ownership and management typical in the West, or even in Japan and Korea... Decision making is centralized in the hands of one dominant family member, but other family members may be given new ventures to try their skill on. They are low-profile and extremely cost-conscious, applying Confucian virtues of thrift and persistence. Their size is kept small by the assumed lack of loyalty of non-family employees, who, if they are any good, will just wait and save until they can start their own family business."

Because of the impact of social history, business management in China is affected by interpersonal connections (*guanxi*), which overpower the formal organizational structure in many cases. Business contracts are often specified in legal terms but implemented relying on trust and relationships between the parties involved.

From this examination of various cultural views regarding management styles and managers, you can appreciate how a business procedure, often thought of as universal, can differ from culture to culture. Because of the cultural diversity in the global economy, you may soon find yourself employed by an organization that transacts business with people from many different cultures. You may find yourself managing, being managed by, or co-managing with members of other cultures. Your ability to succeed in these situations will very much depend on your skills as an intercultural business communicator.

(Adapted from L. A. Samovar: *Communication between Cultures*, Chapter 7)

Notes

Puritanism 清教徒的习俗，清教主义
apprenticeship 学徒
culminate 达到顶点；告终
calling（做某事的）内心倾向
paternalistic 家长式的
seniority 年长；资深
constituency 选区选民；相关人员；支持人员
abide by 遵守，信守
gospel 准则，信条
consensual 大家同意的
stratified 分阶层的
subordinate 部属，下级
absolutism 专制主义；绝对主义
cadre 干部
elitist 精英的；上等的
low-profile 低姿态的
cost-conscious 很在意费用的

Questions

1. Why is it incorrect to say that business procedures are universal in today's world?
2. What do you think of the Chinese view on business management as described in the text?
3. What does one need to learn in order to be successful in international business?

Text B

Cross-Cultural Negotiation

The art of negotiating is hard enough in your own country, dealing with colleagues who think like you, process information as you do, share a common set of values and speak the same language. Now consider a situation where there is little shared knowledge, few common values and a different language is spoken and you can readily see just how complicated negotiating international transactions can become. What is the likely outcome when the Japanese, who expect deference for rank meet with the Americans who expect equality across the board? The chances of conflict, error and misunderstanding because of basic cultural differences are huge.

People from different cultures use different negotiating styles and approaches. They have different strategies for persuasion and a different set of protocols. Differences occur in the way a conflict is viewed, managed, and resolved.

Negotiating is all about attitude. There are two basic approaches to how a final outcome is viewed. Some cultures view the negotiating process as a "win-win" situation—a process through which both sides gain. Other cultures adopt a zero sum mentality where someone's gain must always equal someone's loss. The sum of the net gain and net loss is always zero. Individuals from cultures with this "win-lose" view see the process of negotiation as a series of confrontational battles to be either won or lost. Individuals from the "win-win" perspective instead view negotiations as a collaborative effort seeking to maximize total gain. Trying to convince win-lose practitioners that a win-win strategy is possible is usually difficult. Sellers, of course, prefer to project a win-win approach while buyers tend toward the zero sum game.

Most international businesspeople would probably associate the concept of "face" with Asian and Middle Eastern cultures. The reality, however, is that "face" is a universal concept. It's just that other cultures call it something different. In the West, for example, it is self-respect, self-esteem or dignity. All individuals need it, and all individuals resent it when it is damaged by their own actions or those of others.

In many Asian cultures "face" is a deeply held value. Indeed, Confucian societies will go to extremes to avoid pointing out errors, faux pas, or indiscretions that would cause themselves or another to lose face in front of a group. The value placed on saving and giving face is closely linked to the preservation of group harmony in Confucian societies as well as deep respect for the existing social order. To cause someone to lose face is seen as a challenge to their position within the hierarchy —and thus a threat to the group order.

In Western cultures, the loss of face really means "personal" failure and is limited to the individual. In Asian and Middle Eastern cultures, however, loss of face is a group concept that brings shame not only to the individual but also to the company or organization he or she represents. Since most Asian cultures are collectivists with high risk-avoidance, saving face or giving face is the preferred way to resolve conflict and avoid embarrassing the parties involved.

Collectivist cultures tend to avoid open conflict (most collectivist cultures are high risk-avoidance ones as well) while individualistic cultures meet confrontation head-on, often believing that confrontation is the quickest route to problem solving. In cross-cultural negotiations, conflict may be evident even before the two parties sit down to talk, for the goals of the negotiations may be at odds with the task-driven, low risk-avoidance culture wanting to cut a deal at all costs and in a great hurry and the relationship-driven high risk-avoidance culture seeking to build a relationship first for future business transactions.

When locked in negotiations it is important to take into consideration the differences in the decision-making process between cultures. In some cultures, where power is decentralized (United States, Australia), decisions can be made quickly—and often by a single individual. However, in cultures with collectivist values (Japan, China), decisions are made by consensus and can take longer. (However, implementation of decisions is quicker in collectivists cultures as opposed to individualistic cultures that often demand the right to question the decision handed down.) Consider the examples of the United States and Japan, where values and cultural influences play a major role in the decision-making process. The contrast begins with the basic objective a business decision is meant to achieve. In Japan, that objective is preservation of group harmony. In the United States, it is usually maximum profit or operating efficiency.

Now consider a decision as to whether or not to buy out a competitor, say, in the steel-making industry. In Japan, where decision-making is decentralized, the process would be a bottom-up one. In the United States, it is centralized and top-down. The Japanese will start with trying to define the question or problem, beginning with input from the lower ranks—the people who may be directly affected by the decision. From these lower groups, the decision is passed upwards or laterally until it eventually reaches senior management who are already aware of the consensus built from below. Once completed, the merger would go fairly smoothly because the consensus came from the bottom up and workers, not wishing to disturb group harmony, work hard to make it successful.

In the United States, senior management would begin the process, not by defining the problem, but rather by seeking a solution to the question of how to maximize profit from this acquisition. The route of the decision is purely top-down. Keeping in mind that the American objective is economic efficiency, the problem is framed as one of maximizing resources and return on capital. The decision would be objective and impersonal. If maximizing efficiency involves layoffs at both companies, so be it. The workers had no input on the decision and will question what is in it for them if they go along.

(Adapted from C. Mitchell: *International business Culture*, Chapter 13)

Notes

deference 遵从，敬重	hierarchy 等级制度
protocol 礼仪	head-on 迎头地；不妥协地
mentality 心态	at odds 不一致
confrontational battle 遭遇战	consensus 一致意见
collaborative 合作的，协作的	implementation 贯彻，执行
practitioner 实践者	buy out 买下全部产权
Confucian 孔子的，儒家的	laterally 侧面地，横向地
faux pas 有失检点的话或行为	acquisition 获得
indiscretion 轻率；不明智行为	

Questions

1. What does the author mean when he says that negotiating is all about attitudes?

2. Why is "face" a deeply held value in Asian societies? How will it influence the way business is conducted?

3. What do you think of the culturally different processes in decision making?

Exploration

Lack of cross-cultural awareness may result in failures in international marketing. In the following, there are a few Chinese brand names translated into English that have failed to be accepted by English-speaking customers.

White Elephant　FangFang　Golden Cock　Red Light

Why do you think they have failed in global marketing? What has to be done for the improvement?

In translating from one language into another, it seems necessary to be faithful to the original. However, it also has to be appropriate and acceptable in the target language and culture.

How would you translate the following brand names into Chinese if you were asked to do the job for the companies?

1. Safeguard (toilet soap)
2. BMW (automobile)
3. Benz (automobile)
4. Chanel (cosmetics)
5. Poison (perfume)
6. Malboro (cigarette)
7. Gold Lion (tie)
8. Carrefour (supermarket)
9. Sprite (soft drink)
10. Hazeline (toilet soap)
11. Bush & Lomb (contact lens)
12. Crest (toothpaste)

Try to find out how they have been translated and see if the translations have helped promote the sale of the products in China.

Cases for Discussion

Case 1

An American manager, who was working in Japan, arrived at a hotel some twenty minutes before the expected arrival time of his vice president, who was flying in from the States. He checked at the desk and was alarmed to discover that the reservation for his superior had been switched to another hotel. He was angered at the change made without his approval, but he did not immediately attempt to find out why. He dashed to the second hotel, where he met his vice president. Although the second hotel was equal to the first one, the change seemed capricious. He wanted to find out why the switch had been made. Later, he asked his Japanese assistant to inquire. The inquiry soon became bogged down with explanations of procedures on how the reservations were made. The American arrived at the conclusion that his question was not going to be answered, and it was not.

Note

bog down 陷入困境

Questions

1. Why do you think the American manager could not get a direct answer to his question?

2. What can we learn from this case about the communicative differences between American and Japanese?

Case 2

As the export manager for a Danish manufacturer, Danmark Widgets (DMW), Lars Larsen's market research reveals that his company's product line has strong sales potential in two major markets, the USA and Japan.

Since DMW markets abroad through exclusive distributors, Lars next works up a shortlist of three potential importers in each of the two markets. These are firms which already distribute related products to the main end-users of widgets in the United States and Japan.

Now Lars needs to get in touch with these potential distributors. He has to meet each importer personally in order to evaluate them and select the firm which will do the best job for DMW. How does he go about getting in touch with the prospective importers in each of these two contrasting markets?

Lars contacts the U.S. candidates directly. He puts together a set of English-language brochures about DMW and its product line, writes a brilliant cover letter requesting an appointment for a meeting, and mails the package to his three American prospects.

Then a week or so later he picks up the telephone. "Good morning, this is Lars Larsen of Danmark Widgets. How are you today? Thanks, I'm fine too."

"Have you received the information we sent you last week? Oh good. Well, I'm going to be in the U.S. in a few weeks and would you like to meet for a discussion? Yes, Well, would the 14th be convenient for you?"

"Splendid! We'll see you at nine o'clock then. I will confirm everything by fax today. See you on the 14th."

And that's all there is to it. Lars makes two more calls to set up meeting dates with the other candidates, and his USA itinerary is complete.

Now it's time to tackle his Japanese schedule. What will Lars do then? Is he going to send each of them that packet of information and then follow it up with a phone call?

Notes

exclusive distributor 独家专营的销售商或批发商

prospective 预期的，可能的

brochure 小册子

itinerary 行程计划

Questions

1. What do you think Lars will do with his Japanese prospects?
2. What can you learn from this case and the previous one?

Case 3

A Chinese software company wanted to cooperate with an American software company, so they invited the American company to China to have a negotiation. The latter was very interested in this invitation because they all knew that nowadays China is the would-be largest potential market in the world. Therefore, the American company sent three persons to China, of whom Mr. Green was the group leader. On the other hand, Mr. Wang, as the group leader of fifteen people, was in charge of this matter for this Chinese company.

When finally Mr. Wang saw Mr. Green at the airport, he smiled, "you must be very tired!" Mr. Green was somewhat puzzled, but he did not pay much attention to that. Then, when they arrived at the hotel, Mr. Wang treated Mr. Green a big dinner. Mr. Green was at a loss when he saw that so much food was served. "That is impossible to eat out all that food," said Mr. Green. But Mr. Wang said, "I'm very sorry that we've just prepared some poor food, I hope you don't mind about it." Mr. Green was totally puzzled, "Who said that China is a developing country and Chinese are poor? If the poor live in this way, there must be no God!" He also considered Mr. Wang as an insincere guy apologizing for this big dinner.

Next day when Mr. Green suggested that they should begin the negotiation. Mr. Wang just laughed, "There is no need to hurry after all, and you three come to China for the first time, so just see around our city for several days. First enjoy yourselves, and then talk about business. Would that be all right?"

But Mr. Green was a little unpleasant, "If we don't begin our negotiation, what on earth did we come to China?"

"I know that our business is negotiation, but we also hope that you can enjoy yourselves. We can start our negotiation several days later," said Mr. Wang.

"Business is business, we really appreciate you good will, but we came to China not for ourselves but for the company," said Mr. Green.

Mr. Wang was a little embarrassed hearing this. But finally they began their negotiation. When they were all seated, Mr. Green felt very strange, he just couldn't understand why the Chinese company sent so many persons to this negotiation. After all, this was a business negotiation, but not a big fight.

After Mr. Wang introduced all his members to Mr. Green, the latter finally found out that these persons included sales manager, technician and some other similar people. "I can't see why these people come." thought Mr. Green. Then he introduced his members to Mr. Wang, "This is my secretary, and this is the lawyer of our company." When hearing the word "lawyer," all Chinese people present felt somewhat disappointed and angry. Mr. Wang frowned and totally got no idea what to say. "Why lawyer? It's just like calculating family property in preparation for a divorce at a time when we are just beginning to fall in love." thought Mr. Wang.

During the negotiation, Mr. Green recommended several articles, but each time Mr. Wang would just say, "Oh, that's very good, but I have to talk with my boss." Mr. Green was very unpleasant, for he couldn't understand why the company sent Mr. Wang if he couldn't make any decision. What's worse, sometimes Mr. Wang would give some puzzling answers, like "I can fully understand this, but I am afraid there are many problems about this. It's very complex."

"Then what are the problems?" asked Mr. Green. This made Mr. Wang embarrassed and he just kept silent.

At last, Mr. Green couldn't help losing this temper any more, "I don't think that your company really wanted to cooperate with our company!"

Mr. Wang also felt angry, but he just said "Take it easy. In fact, we do want to cooperate with you, but you can see that things are complex."

Mr. Green was so angry to these cloudy words that he accidentally fell back onto the seat. All the Chinese people present laughed and asked, "Are you OK?" Mr. Green said nothing and left the room for he thought he was not respected.

The next day, he left China with his members.

Notes

potential 潜在的

recommend 建议

article 条款

Questions

1. Why was Mr. Green so angry?
2. How can we avoid such failures in international business?

Readings for Further Study

1
Two Casts of Mind

Perhaps the most difficult aspect of the Japanese for Westerners to comprehend is the strong orientation to collective values, particularly a collective sense of responsibility.

Let me illustrate with an anecdote about a visit to a new factory in Japan owned and operated by an American electronics company. An American electronics company, a particularly creative firm, frequently attracts attention within the business community for its novel approaches to planning, organizational design, and management systems. As a consequence of this corporate style, the parent company determined to make a thorough study of Japanese workers and to design a plant in Japan that would combine the best of East and West. In their study they discovered that Japanese firms almost never make use of individual work incentives, such as piecework or even individual performance appraisal tied to salary increases. They concluded that rewarding individual achievement and individual ability is always a good thing.

In the final assembly area of their new plant, long lines of young Japanese women wired together electronic products on a piece-rate systems: the more you wired, the more you got paid. About two months after opening, the head foreladies approached the plant manager. "Honorable plant manager," they said humbly as they bowed, "we are embarrassed to be so forward, but we must speak to you because all of the girls have threatened to quit work this Friday." (To have this happen, of course, would be a great disaster for all concerned.) "Why," they wanted to know, "can't our plant have the same compensation system as other Japanese companies? When you hire a new girl, her staring wage should be fixed by her age. An eighteen-year-old should be paid more than a sixteen-year-old. Every year on her birthday, she should receive an automatic increase in pay. The idea that any one of us can be more productive than another must be wrong, because none of us in the final assembly could make a thing unless all of the other people in the plant had done their jobs right first. To single one person out as being more productive is wrong and is also personally humiliating to us." The company changed its compensation system to the Japanese model.

Another American company in Japan had installed a suggestion system much as they have in the United States. Individual workers were encouraged to place suggestions to improve productivity into special boxes. For an accepted idea the individual received a bonus amounting to some fraction of the productivity savings realized from his or her suggestion. After a period of six months, not a single suggestion had been submitted. The American managers were puzzled. They had heard many stories of the inventiveness, the commitment, and the loyalty of Japanese workers, yet not one suggestion to improve productivity had appeared.

The managers approached some of the workers and asked why the suggestion system had not been used. The answer: "No one can come up with a work improvement idea alone. We work together, and any ideas that one of us may have are actually developed by watching others and talking to others. If one of us was singled out for being responsible for such an idea, it would embarrass all of us." The company changed to a group suggestion system, in which workers collectively submitted suggestions. Bonuses were paid to groups which would save bonus money until the end of the year for a party at a restaurant or, if there was enough money, for family vacations together. The suggestions and productivity improvements rained down on the plant.

One can interpret these examples in two quite different ways. Perhaps the Japanese commitment to collective values is an anachronism that does not fit with modern industrialism but brings economic success despite that collectivism. Collectivism does not seem to provide the individual incentive to excel which has made a great success of American enterprise. Entirely apart from its economic effects, collectivism implies a loss of individuality, a loss of the freedom to be different, to hold fundamentally different values from others.

The second interpretation of the examples is that the Japanese collectivism is economically efficient. It causes people to work well together and to encourage one another to better efforts. Industrial life requires interdependence of one person on another. In the Japanese mind, collectivism is neither a corporate or individual goal to strive for nor a slogan to pursue. Rather, the nature of things operates so that nothing of consequence occurs as a result of individual effort. Everything important in life happens as a result of teamwork or collective effort. Therefore, to attempt to assign individual credit or blame to results is unfounded.

Industrial life, however, is essentially integrated and interdependent. No one builds an automobile alone, no one carries through a banking transaction alone. In a sense the Japanese value of collectivism fits naturally into an industrial setting, whereas the Western individualism provides constant conflicts. The image that comes to mind is of Chaplin's silent film *Modern Times* in which the apparently insignificant hero played by Chaplin successfully fights against the unfeeling machinery of industry. Modern industrial life can be aggravating, even hostile, or natural: all depends on the fit between our culture and our technology.

The "bullet train" speeds across the rural areas of Japan giving a quick view of cluster after cluster of farmhouses surrounded by rice paddies. This particular pattern did not develop purely by chance, but as a consequence of the technology peculiar to the growing of rice, the staple of the Japanese diet. The growing of rice requires construction and maintenance of an irrigation system, something that takes many hands to build. More importantly, the planting and harvesting of rice can only be done efficiently with the cooperation of twenty or more people. Thus the Japanese have had to develop the capacity to work together in harmony, no matter what the forces of disagreement or social disintegration, in order to survive.

For centuries and generations, these people have lived in the same village next door to the same neighbors. Living in close proximity and in dwellings which gave very little privacy, the

Japanese survived through their capacity to work together in harmony. In this situation, it was inevitable that the one most central social value which emerged, the one value without which the society could not continue, was that an individual does not matter.

Now consider a flight over the United States. Looking out of the window high over the state of Kansas, we see a pattern of a single farmhouse surrounded by fields, followed by another single homestead surrounded by fields. In the early 1800s in the state of Kansas there were no automobiles. Your nearest neighbor was perhaps two miles distant; the winters were long, and the snow was deep. Inevitably, the central social values were self-reliance and independence. Those were the realities of that place and age that children had to learn to value.

To the Western soul, Japanese society presents a chilling picture. Subordinating individual tastes to the harmony of the group and knowing that individual needs can never take precedence over the interests of all is repellent to the Western citizen. But a frequent theme of Western philosophers and sociologists is that individual freedom exists only when people willingly subordinate their self-interested individuals is a society in which each person is at war with the other, a society which has no freedom.

(Adapted from W. Ouchi: Japanese Workers and American Workers—Two Casts of Mind)

Notes

corporate 公司的;社团的
piecework 计件工作,按件付酬的工作
appraisal 评估,估量
forelady 女工头,女工监督
humiliating 羞辱性的
bonus 奖金,红利
anachronism 不合时代的人或事
incentive 刺激,奖励
bullet train 子弹头高速火车
rice paddy 稻田
stapie 主食;大宗出产
proximity 邻近,接近
Kansas(美国)堪萨斯州
homestead 家宅

Questions

1. Why are the Japanese and the U.S. Americans culturally so different?

2. Can you find something in the traditional living situations in China that will help explain certain characteristics of the Chinese culture?

2
The Globalization of Business

Globalization, for better or for worse, has changed the way the world does business. Though still in its early stages, it is all but unstoppable. The challenge that businesses and individuals face is learning how to live with it, manage it and take advantage of the benefits it offers. The International Monetary Fund defines globalization as the growing economic interdependence of countries worldwide through increasing volume and variety of cross-border transactions in goods and services and of international capital flows, and also through the more rapid and widespread diffusion of technology.

The current era of globalization began shortly after the end of World War II with the victorious Western powers supporting a worldwide "open" trade and investment policy. Technology is one reason for the globalization phenomenon. Computers, which have eased telecommunication burdens, are cheaper now than they have ever been—and more powerful, too. New technology will lead to even further global business integration, as the Internet becomes more accepted as a business medium worldwide.

Those who argue that globalization is a good thing say that companies dealing on the world stage will eventually become that much more efficient as they benefit from large economies of scale. Productivity will be boosted and living standards everywhere have the potential to rise as the world becomes richer and more prosperous because of globalization.

The naysayers take the opposite view, claiming that globalization has, in effect, triggered a "race to the bottom." Countries with low wages are attracting jobs from higher wage-paying nations, thus dragging everyone down to their level.

Globalization creates more jobs than it actually destroys, but they are in different sectors and in different geographic regions. It takes more skill, education and mobility to be employable. The jobs lost in Europe and North America over the decades have generally been those requiring relatively uneducated workers. Indeed, wage differentials between the skilled and unskilled will likely increase. Both sides can point to ample examples to support their cases. But in the end, both are probably exaggerating to some extent. What is irrefutable is that the world economic pie is indeed bigger because of globalization—and it is being sliced differently than before.

The whole concept of effective globalization of a company presents a paradox: the more global a company becomes the more reliant it must become on local resources—people and management and marketing talent—to distribute its products or services to new markets. The nationality of companies is becoming less important. British Airways is one of the first major global companies to recognize this trend. The airline has removed the British national flag from its aircraft livery and instead is using designs and art forms from across the world.

Successful companies, both large and small, are dealing with the globalization paradox by learning to think globally and act locally and by encouraging a diversity of management and giving subsidiary operations in different countries a higher degree of autonomy than ever before.

One obvious impact of globalization is that the number of business travelers, and the amount of miles they fly to conduct business across borders, has exploded. Business travelers are constantly coming in contact with new and different cultures—but sometimes they find some awfully familiar sights to remind them of home. Some would argue that the globalization of trade is moving us toward a common international standard in many aspects of business—from accounting standards to unofficial dress codes. In many cases the quest for a "one-size-fits-all" set of standards for global business behavior has progressed quite far.

Many international businesspeople will argue that when talking about the globalization of business standards people really mean the Americanization of such standards. In some cases this may be true. The area of corporate management is one such case. However, this is not true in scores of other areas, from accounting to pollution standards to the finer points of human resources management. However, the current success of U.S. multinational companies has triggered global interest in American management practices. Many companies worldwide are adopting proven American management techniques. These include a strong customer and service orientation, streamlining of information systems, stock options for senior executives, and corporate stock buybacks.

However, there is a large school of global executives who believe that the Americanization of companies not only goes against the basic cultures of many nations, but that it is simply the latest management fad—not unlike the 1970s and 1980s when everyone tried to copy Japanese management techniques.

Management styles come and go on a global basis, but each time one of these management techniques comes into vogue and is copied, it brings the world closer to a global standard or really a global style of business management. People all over the world still use many of the techniques borrowed from the Japanese. And when the American fad ends, they will still use some of those techniques. Each time companies copy something from another culture, management styles on a global basis converge just a little more.

Though we will probably never see a single global management style, there are some basic principles being adopted. Local differences remain too large and few can agree on an absolute standard.

(Adapted from C. Mitchell: *International Business Culture*, Chapter 4)

Notes

the International Monetary Fund 国际货币基金组织
diffusion 扩散;传播
boost 推动;增加
naysayer 否定者,反对者
differential 差别,差异
irrefutable 无可辩驳的,不可否认的
subsidiary 附属公司,子公司
autonomy 自治,自主权
dress code 衣着规范
streamlining 合理化;提高效率
stock option 股票期权
buyback 购回
vogue 时尚,风行
converge 会聚;趋同

Questions

1. Do you think that globalization will greatly reduce the cultural differences?
2. Why do many people argue that globalization really means Americanization?

Summary

1. The concept of management can be viewed differently from culture to culture, although it is often thought as universal.

2. Many leaders and managers involved in international business activities have to gain intercultural skills and develop the ability of management from different countries and cultures to think and work together.

3. Cross-cultural negotiation is complicated because people from different cultures use different negotiating styles and approaches, and have different strategies for persuasion and a different set of protocols. They are also different in the decision-making process.

4. Globalization, for better or for worse, has changed the way the world does business. Successful companies, both large and small, are dealing with the globalization paradox by learning to think globally and act locally and by encouraging a diversity of management.

Chapter 13 Intercultural Perception

Everyone thinks that all the bells echo his own thoughts.

—German proverb

Chapter 13 Intercultural Perception

Preview Questions

1. How would you call a foreigner whose name and nationality you do not know?

2. Will a person's nationality often influence your view of him or her?

3. Are you free of prejudice against other people? If you don't think you are, whom are you sometimes prejudiced against?

Text A

Differing Images

Members of different cultures look differently at the world around them. Some believe that the physical world is real. Others believe that it is just an illusion. Some believe everything around them is permanent while others say it is transient. Reality is not the same for all people.

Now we will examine the influence that one's perception of the world, its people, things, and events has on intercultural communication. Understanding and appreciating differences in perception are crucial if we are to improve our ability to get along with people of other cultures.

Perception is the process by which we maintain contact with the world around us. Because we usually are capable of hearing, seeing, smelling, touching, and tasting, we can sense our environment; we can be aware of what happens outside of us. In actuality, what we do is create internal images of the physical and social objects and events that we encounter in our environments.

An important phase of perception involves our giving meaning to the objects and events in our environment. Objects and events can vary considerably in their ability to elicit meaning, and the meaning extended varies according to the individual and the individual's culture. Although identification and naming is a part of meaning attribution often referred to as the objective part—there also is a subjective aspect. When encountering a tree, almost everyone agrees on the objective part of meaning, but what a tree means to any unique individual varies according to that individual's experiences and culture. Thus, a vegetarian who sees a slice of raw meat might become ill or find it unsavory, while a meat eater can hardly wait to place it on a barbecue. Each one attaches a personal subjective meaning to the object. Although the object is outside both of them, they have learned and internalized different personal meanings and responses for the external world.

We must keep in mind, that all individuals do have specialized and unique differences that force them to perceive the external world in highly personalized fashions. And, the greater the differences between people, the greater the disparity in their perceptions is likely to be. Consequently, two people with similar experiences tend to share a similar view of the world. Conversely, as was the case with the meat eater and the vegetarian, dissimilar backgrounds can call forth vastly different responses to the same object or event.

Culture, by exposing a large group of people to approximately similar experiences relative to other cultures, often has the effect of being a unifying force in the perception of the environment. A culture that values kindness above all else, for example, will perceive acts of violence differently than will a culture that stresses a survival-of-the-fittest orientation toward life. The members of a culture share common experiences and, therefore, learn common behavior patterns. Through this cultural learning, they come to share common perceptions. Individual differences within a culture tend to be considerably less variable than differences that occur between cultures.

The intercultural communicator normally is confronted with people who do not share his or her perceptions of the external world, and who may respond to that world in a manner that is often hard to understand. The more diverse the cultures, the more bizarre the behaviors may appear. In England, for example, a person with good manners is perceived as someone with no aggressive behavior in an interpersonal setting—someone who does not speak to strangers. In other cultures, such as the Arab, Italian, or Jewish, aggressive behavior during interaction is normal and, consequently, is perceived as highly desirable while a reserved attitude is a sign of bad manners.

Even our nonverbal actions can be perceived differently from one culture to another. In the United States it is not uncommon to see men without their shirts walking in the streets or eating at public restaurants. In Hong Kong China, on the other hand, shirts are never taken off in public places. The meaning attributed to a shirtless person is quite different in Hong Kong than in the United States. To many Chinese, a semi-dressed person in public is uncouth.

Two people could disagree over a single event or an object because they actually perceived it differently. Disagreement about an event can occur within a culture as well. Who caused an accident, or which team played the hardest are typical events over which witnesses can and often do disagree. Our individual psyches cause us to see that which fits in with our personal perceptual sets. In these instances no amount of talking will alter the fact that two people, viewing the same external happening, "saw" two different events.

(Adapted from L. A. Samovar: *Understanding Intercultural Communication*, Chapter 5)

Notes

transient 短暂的，易逝的	personalized 个人化的
crucial 至关重要的	survival-of-the-fittest 适者生存
elicit 引出，引起	bizarre 稀奇古怪的
identification 识别	reserved 沉默寡言的，矜持的
attribution 归于	psyche 心理；精神
unsavory 没滋味的，难吃的	

Questions

1. How do we form our images of the world and people in it?

2. In what ways does culture influence people's perception of their environment?

3. Why do you think it is often difficult to achieve understanding in communicating with other individuals?

Text B

Who Is *Gaijin* and Who Is Not?

Gaijin is undoubtedly one of the first words the newcomers to Japan learn to recognize. It is usually translated as either "outsider""non-Japanese""alien", or "foreigner." Not only are non-Japanese called *gaijin* by the Japanese, but the word quickly becomes part of the active vocabulary of most *gaijin* who have been in Japan for even a short period of time—to refer to themselves and other non-Japanese but almost never to refer to Japanese.

Conversations, in English, like the following are common:

Jack: Hi, Tom. Did you see that *gaijin* at the train station this morning?

Tom: No. What did he look like?

Jack: Tall, blond, and blue eyed.

Tom: God, some *gaijin* have all the luck.

The above dialogue not only reflects the adoption of the word by native speakers of English, but also the three most remarkable physical characteristics of *gaijin*: tall, blond and blue eyes. However, despite the common use of this word by native speakers of English, most *gaijin* do not like being called *gaijin* because they feel that the Japanese use the word in a derogatory manner.

The negative feelings toward the word probably reflect the situations in which most *gaijin* encounter it. It is not uncommon to see groups of school children pointing and screaming, "*gaijin*, *gaijin*." I remember walking down a street in Kyoto a few years ago. My presence was a particular surprise to one small child who ran, screaming, from house to house raising the alarm that the *gaijin* were coming.

Before *gaijin* slips into Websters along with *typhoon*, sushi, and kamikaze, I thought it would be interesting to find out a bit more about this would-be loan word. With this in mind, I passed out a multiple-choice answer questionnaire (in Japanese) to 40 Japanese third-year senior high school students (i.e. they would be entering college in less than six months), at a Japanese public, coeducational high school. These students had never had a *gaijin* teacher.

In sharp contrast to most *gaijin*, the students said that they associated positive (32 students) rather than negative things with the word *gaijin*, which they tended to translate as "non-Japanese" (27). They also felt that the word was neutral (32) rather than impolite (4). They also said that if they knew the nationality of individual, especially in the case of Chinese, Koreans, and Indians, they would prefer to use the term for the nationality rather than the word *gaijin*. However, in the case of Americans, British, French, and other Europeans, there was only a slight preference for the nationality term over the use of *gaijin*. One question in particular is of interest because it shows and inverses relationship between the use of the two terms. It read: circle which word you would most likely use to refer to a person from the following countries. The results were as follows:

Country	*use nationality*	*use* gaijin
Republic of Korea	38	2
China	38	2
India	34	6
Philippines	31	9
Africa	30	10
Saudi Arabia	29	11
France	27	14
Italy	24	15
England	22	19
America	20	21

Although the students said (29) that they did not think of any particular nationality when they heard the word *gaijin*, the story was quite different when they were presented with a list of nationalities and asked to select which people came to mind when they heard the word *gaijin*. They overwhelmingly tended to think of Americans (34), with Europeans a distant second (10), and Asians (3), and Africans (1) very low on the scale. It also indicated that when race or skin color cannot be used, country plays a decisive factor in determining whether to use the nationality term or the word *gaijin*.

When the students were asked to select essential physical characteristics of *gaijin*, they thought that hair color and eye color were especially important (to most Japanese a *gaijin* is an individual with blond hair and blue eyes). With regard to personality, they thought that *gaijin* were "outgoing." In talks with adult Japanese English-language students, I have found that "outgoing" usually means energetic, young, and talkative. One question asked the students to select words which they associate with the word *gaijin* and another question listed the same words and asked them to indicate which they would include a description of a "typical Japanese." In order of preference, the two lists appear as follows:

Typical Japanese	Gaijin
1. hard-working (22)	1. outgoing (20)
2. honest (16)	2. exotic (16)
3. happy (7)	3. strong (12)
4. lazy (6)	4. unknown (11)
5. exotic (5)	5. impressive (8)
6. impressive (5)	6. hard-working (6)
7. dishonest (4)	7. lazy (5)
8. troublesome (4)	8. honest (4)
9. outgoing (3)	9. strange (4)
10. strange (3)	10. troublesome (4)
11. strong (2)	11. happy (4)
12. unknown (2)	12. dishonest (3)

Even a cursory examination shows that, in general, items which are higher on the Typical Japanese scale will be found to be lower on the *gaijin* scale and vice versa.

Length of time in Japan did not seem to have any effect on the term; however, most of the students felt that *gaijin* do not stay in Japan for more than a few weeks. This may have been true in the past but it is no longer so. More and more people are staying for not one or two years but much longer periods of time.

(Abridged from P. Duppenthaler: Gaijin, in *English Today*, Vol.5, No.3)

Notes

derogatory 贬义的

sushi(日本)寿司

kamikaze(第二次世界大战日军驾驶神风飞机的)神风突击队队员

cursory 粗略的

Questions

1. Why do you think the Japanese use *gaijin* to refer to foreigners, especially Westerners?

2. What do you think of those descriptions of typical Japanese and *gaijin*?

3. Will you associate the personality characteristics of *gaijin* with foreigners you see in China? Why or why not?

Exploration

We have a tendency to make a claim that often goes beyond the facts, with no valid basis. It may be based on the truth, but it is an exaggerated statement regarding our belief about what a group of people are or should be. For example, imagine that your wallet was stolen by "a" Korean when you were traveling in Republic of Korea last summer. The incident ruined your whole trip there. When you came back, your friends asked how your trip to Republic of Korea was. You might have said, "Those Koreans are thieves. They stole my wallet."

Making very general statements about other cultures is unwise and risky. One possible risk is that you tend to apply the same criteria to all the people from the culture. You are most likely to be frustrated when you think "Americans are friendly" but the American you meet does not appear very friendly as you have expected and this may make you jump to the other extreme and make a reverse but again very general statement "Americans are so unfriendly." Another possible risk is that general statements are usually misleading. When we say "The French are rude," we should also find out in what circumstances and to what extent this statement has its grounds.

Brainstorm to find out the biased views you may hold against people of other races or nations or even the Chinese who seem to be different from you are in certain aspect and how such views would affect your communication with other people.

Cases for Discussion

Case 1

Many years ago, several international businessmen were on a conference cruise when the ship began to sink. "Go tell those fellows to put on life jackets and jump overboard," the captain directed his first mate.

A few minutes later the first mate returned. "Those guys won't jump," he reported.

"Take over," the captain ordered, "and I'll see what I can do."

Returning moments later, he announced, "They're gone."

"How'd you do it?" asked the first mate.

"I told different things to different people. I told the Englishman it was the sporting thing to do, and he jumped. I told the Frenchman it was stylish; the German that it was a command; the Italian that it was forbidden; the Russian that it was revolutionary, so they all jumped overboard."

"And how did you get the American to jump?"

"No problem," said the captain, "I told him he was insured!"

Questions

1. If there had also been a Chinese businessman onboard, what should the captain say in order to make him jump overboard?

2. What do you think of the story? Does it tell you something that is true of people of those different nations?

Case 2

Here are the results of Gallup Polls taken in 1966 and March 1972, indicating the qualities, positive and negative, that Americans attributed to Chinese people. The following table shows the numbers who chose particular adjectives in the two years.

Quality	1966	1972
Hardworking	37	74
Honest	—	20
Brave	7	17
Religious	14	18
Intelligent	14	32
Practical	8	27
Ignorant	24	10
Artistic	13	26
Progressive	7	28
Sly	20	19
Treacherous	19	12
Warlike	23	13
Cruel	13	9

It can be seen that, in 1966 when the cultural revolution began, the dominant images were mostly negative. But by the time Nixon had returned from China in 1972, the main images of Chinese among Americans had changed greatly, and the dominant images were all of them positive.

Questions

1. Why did the image of Chinese people in the United States change so much within those six years? Did we Chinese actually change very much?

2. What do you think the Chinese image would be like in the U.S.A. now?

Case 3

The following is a list of cultural stereotypes, which Spaniards between age 15 and 21 who have never been to the U.S. or who have never had any American friends, might have about Americans.

- Men in the U.S. have muscular builds; they resemble Arnold Schwarzenegger or Sylvester Stallone. America men like to wear short, sleeveless T-shirts to show off their physiques.
- American women are either unusually fat or unusually thin, never of normal build.
- Americans wear very bright colors and mixed patterns, and they wear summer clothes even in winter. They have no sense of style.
- The typical American "native dress" is jeans, cowboy boots, and a cowboy hat.
- Americans spend almost all day at work; they have very little free time.
- The first two things an American wants to discuss are salary and age.
- The two favorite leisure-time activities in the U.S. are movies and rodeos.
- Most Americans live either in skyscrapers or on farms.
- In big cities everyone has a large car like a Cadillac, but outside of cities people usually travel on horseback.
- Americans divorce repeatedly and have very complicated private lives.
- In marriages in the U.S., the wife always dominates.
- American cities are so dangerous that a person has a good chance of being killed in the street; therefore, American men either know *kung-fu* or carry a gun.
- Americans eat almost nothing but hamburgers, hot dogs, popcorn, and Coke.
- Americans generally eat fast food Monday through Saturday, but never on Sunday.
- American men are always drinking beer, even at breakfast.
- Americans speak very quickly and very loudly. They use their hands a lot, often gesturing in an exaggerated way when they talk. Their strange intonation makes their speech sound like singing.
- The typical American is very rude, often putting his feet on a desk or table and frequently belching in public. He yawns a lot, never trying to hide it. In international affairs as in personal life, Americans do whatever they want and don't care what other people think.

Questions

1. Which of those statements do you think are stereotypes and which, if any, are accurate descriptions of American culture?

2. What do you think of the following ways that people sometimes respond to stereotypical questions or statements? Can you think of any other ways?

a. deny them

b. joke about them

c. indicate their stereotypical nature

d. ask why the statement was made

e. become angry

f. ignore the statement

g. try to defend the statement

Readings for Further Study

1
Culture and Perception

We now open our discussion of perception with a few questions that are intended to direct you toward the topic of perception. The moon is a rocky physical sphere that orbits the earth; yet when looking at this object, many Americans often see a man in the moon, many Native Americans perceive a rabbit, the Chinese claim a lady is fleeing her husband, and Samoans report a woman weaving—why? In Japan and China people fear the number four, in the United States it is the number thirteen. For Americans, a "V" sign made with two fingers usually represents victory. Australians equate this gesture with a rude American gesture usually made with the middle finger—why? Most Asians respond negatively to white flowers because white is associated with death. For Peruvians, Iranians, and Mexicans, yellow flowers often invoke the same reaction—why? In all these examples, the external objects (moon, hands, flowers) were the same, yet the responses were different. The reason is perception, and that is what we are about to discuss—more specially, how distinct cultures have "taught" their members to look differently at the world around them.

Defining perception

Perception is the means by which you make sense of your physical and social world. As the German-born Swiss novelist Hermann Hesse states, "There is no reality except the one contained within us"—and it has been placed in us, in part, by our culture. The world inside of us includes symbols, things, people, ideas, events, ideologies, and even faith. Your perceptions give meaning to external forces. Perception is the process of selecting, organizing, and interpreting sensory data in a way that enables us to make sense of our world. In other words, perception is a process by which we make what we sense into a meaningful experience by selecting, categorizing, and interpreting internal and external stimuli to form our view of world. Internal stimuli include our nervous system, desires, interests, and motivations. External stimuli are the sensations that come from the way we see, smell, touch, hear, and taste. We experience everything in the world not as it is—but only as the world comes to us through our sensory receptors.

Human perception is usually thought of as a three-step process of selection, organization, and interpretation. Each of these steps is affected by culture.

1) Selection

The first step in the perception process is selection. Within your physiological limitations you are exposed to more stimuli than you could possibly manage.

Needs affect what we are more likely to attend to. When we need something, have an interest in it, or want it, we are more likely to sense it out of competing stimuli. When we're hungry, we're more likely to attend to food advertisements.

2) Organization

The second step in the perception process is organization. Along with selecting stimuli from the environment, you must organize it some meaningful way. Remember that language provides the conceptual categories that influence how its speakers' perceptions are encoded and stored.

Far from being simply a technique of communication, language is itself a way of directing the perception of its speakers and it promotes for them habitual modes of analyzing experience into significant categories.

3) Interpretation

The third step in the perception process is interpretation. This refers to attaching meaning to sense data and is synonymous with decoding. People do not always have similar interpretations of the world around them. The same situation can be interpreted quite differently by diverse people. A police officer arriving at a crime scene can be experienced by the victim as calming and relief giving but by the criminal as fearsome and threatening.

Many interpretations, however, are learned within a person's culture. Therefore, those who share a common culture will probably perceive the world more similarly than those who do not share a common culture.

Whether you feel delighted or ill at the thought of eating the flesh of a cow, fish, dog, or snake depends on what your culture has taught you about food. Whether you are repulsed at the sight of a bull being jabbed with sharp swords and long steel spears or believe it is a poetic sport depends on culture. By exposing a large group of people to similar experiences (such as foods or sports), culture generates similar meanings and similar behaviors. This does not mean, of course, that everyone in a particular culture is exactly the same. Here is a serious example of how culture affects perception and communication. In a classic study, Mexican children from a rural area and children from the dominant culture in the United States viewed, for a split second, stereograms in which one eye was exposed to a baseball game while the other was exposed to bullfight. In the main, the children reported seeing the scene according to their culture; Mexican children tended to report seeing the bullfight and American children tended to report the baseball game. What should be obvious is that the children made selections based on their cultural backgrounds; they tended to see and to report what was most familiar. This study would, of course, yield different results with Mexican children from a large city, for they are familiar with baseball.

In yet another experiment demonstrating how culture influences perception, Caucasian mothers tended to interpret as positive those aspects of their children's speech and behavior that reflected assertiveness, excitement, and interest. Navajo mothers who observed the same behavior in their children reported them as being mischievous and lacking discipline. To the Navajo mothers, assertive speech and behavior reflected discourtesy, restlessness, self-centeredness, and lack of discipline; to the Caucasian mothers, the same behaviors reflected self-discipline and were, therefore, beneficial for the child.

Personal credibility is another perceptual trait that is touched by culture. People who are credible inspire trust, know what they are talking about, and have good intentions. Americans usually hold that expressing one's opinion as openly and forcefully as possible is an admirable trait. Hence, someone is perceived as being highly credible if he or she is articulate and outspoken. For the Japanese, a person who is quiet and spends more time listening than speaking is more credible because they regard constant talking as a sign of shallowness. Among Americans, credible people seem direct, rational, decisive, unyielding, and confident. Among the Japanese, credible persons are perceived as being indirect, sympathetic, prudent, flexible, and humble. In Japan, social status is a major indicator of credibility, but in the United States it has only modest import. Even the perception of something as simple as the blinking of one's eyes is affected by culture. Blinking while another person talks may be hardly noticeable to North Americans, but the same behavior is considered impolite in China.

We are now ready to summarize how culture is implicated with the process of perception in two ways. First, perception is selective. This simply means that because there are too many stimuli impinging on your senses at the same time, you "allow only selected information through your perceptual screen to our conscious mind." What is allowed in, as discussed earlier, is in part determined by culture. Second, your perceptual patterns are learned. Everyone is born into a world without meaning, and it is culture that gives meaning to most of our experiences. Perception is culturally determined. We learn to see the world in a certain way based on our cultural background. As is the case with all of culture, perceptions are stored within each human being in the form of beliefs and values. These two, working in combination form what are called cultural patterns.

(Based on L. A. Samovar & R. E. Porter: *Communication between Cultures*, Chapter 2)

Notes

perception 理解;感知
rocky 坚固的
Samoan 萨摩亚人
Peruvian 秘鲁人
Hermann Hesse 赫尔曼·黑赛(1877—1962),德国出生的瑞士小说家和诗人
ideology 意识形态
sensory 感觉的
receptor 感受器
repulse 排斥;憎恶
jab 猛刺
poetic 富有诗意的
classic 经典的
stereogram 立体图
bullfight 斗牛
Caucasian 欧洲血统的白人
discourtesy 无礼
restlessness 不平静
credibility 可信性
trait 特点,特性
articulate 清晰明白的
outspoken 坦率直言的
unyielding 不屈服的
prudent 谨慎的
impinging 碰撞(impinge 的现在分词)

Questions

1. How does culture influence each step of our perception?

2. What should we be aware of when we know that everybody's perception is greatly affected by his or her own culture?

2
Ethnocentrism

If we accept the belief that our past influences our view of reality and the corresponding tenet that each of us may have similar but not identical personal histories, then it should follow that another person's picture of the universe will not be exactly like ours. Yet most of us act as if our way of perceiving things is the correct and only way.

In our daily activities these differences in perception appear between different groups. Various generations, minorities, occupations, and cultures have conflicting values and goals that will influence their orientation and interpretation of reality.

Our culture is a major factor in perceptual discrepancies. Culture helps supply us with our perspective of reality. For example, if our cultures admire thin women, then we would tend to have negative reactions (at least concerning appearance) to cultures that venerate the stout female. Undoubtedly, we evaluate them by our group's cultural standards. Our cultural tells us, in a variety of ways, how to judge others and what to use as criteria for those judgments. The danger of such evaluations is that they are often false, misleading, and arbitrary. It is truly a naive view of the world to believe and behave as if we and our culture have discovered the true and only set of norms.

When our perceptions and subsequent communication behavior are characterized by this narrow and rigid orientation, we are guilty of ethnocentrism, that is, negatively judging aspects of another culture by the standards of one's own culture. The word "ethnocentrism" is derived from two Greek words: *ethnos*, or "nation"; and *kentron*, or "center." It is the technical name for the view of things in which one's own group is the center of everything, and all others are scaled and rated with reference to it. This suggests that ethnocentrism occurs when our nation is seen as the center of the world.

In other words, ethnocentrism refers to our tendency to identify with our in-group (e.g., ethnic or racial group, culture) and to evaluate out-groups and their members according to its standard. Because of ethnocentrism, we tend to view our own cultural values and ways of doing things as more real, or as the "right" and natural values and ways of doing things. The major consequence of the view is our in-group's values and ways of doing things are seen as superior to the out-groups' values and ways of doing things.

The above should not be taken to suggest ethnocentrism is always deliberate. Often the expression of ethnocentrism is a function of how we are socialized. People born and raised in the Untied States, for example, are taught many subtle cues suggesting the Untied States is the center of the world. Consider the major league baseball championship series played between the winners of the two leagues. Is it called the United States Series? No, obviously not; it is called the World Series, implying that no other nation has baseball teams (granted there are now Canadian teams in the World Series, but no Japanese, Republic of Korea's, or Mexican teams). Another example of the tendency for people in the United States to view their country as the center of the world is in the use of the term "American." We must remember that citizens of the other members of the Organization of American States (OAS) from North, Central, and South America are also "Americans."

The existence of ethnocentrism is not limited to recent historic times or to the United States. The early Greeks used the term *barbariskos* ("barbarians") to refer to those people living around them who did not speak Greek. Because they did not speak Greek, the ancient Persians and Egyptians were considered by the Greeks to be inferior. In current times many languages have a word with very similar meanings. The Japanese word *gaijin*, for example, means "foreigner, a person who is not Japanese," and is sometimes used with a condescending overtone.

As has often been pointed out, ethnocentrism often is expressed in the way people draw their maps. The Chinese, who called their country the Middle Kingdom, were convinced that China was the center of the world. Similar beliefs were held by other nations. The British drew the Prime Meridian of longitude to run through Greenwich, near London. Europeans drew maps of the world with Europe at the center, and North Americans with the New World at the center.

Ethnocentrism can all too easily lead to "us" versus "them" thought and language. It seems as people create a category called "us," another category of "not-us" or "them" is created. The collective pronouns "us" and "them" become powerful influences on perception. The names given to "them" can be used to justify their suppression and even their extermination. Sometimes people call this "the language of oppression." For instance, the words "chicks" and "babes" labeled women as inferior. People still remember that the Nazis labeled Jews "bacilli," "parasites," "disease," "demon," and "plague." Why do the words used to refer to "them" matter? It's because although killing another human being may be unthinkable, "exterminating a disease" is not. In the history of the United States, segregation was justified when Blacks were considered "chattel" or property. And the subjugation of Native Americans was defensible when the word "savage" was used.

Opposite to the attitude of ethnocentrism is the attitude of cultural relativism. Cultural relativism involves the view that all cultures are of equal value and the values and behavior of a culture can only be judged using that culture as a frame of reference.

Cultural relativism suggests that the only way we can understand the behavior of others is in the context of their culture. Evaluations must be relative to the cultural background out of which they arise. No one cultural trait is "right" or "wrong"; it is merely "different" from alternative cultural traits. This is not to say we must never make value judgments of people in other cultures. Making them is often necessary. Postponing these value judgments, or recognizing their tentative nature, until adequate information is gathered and we understand the people from the other culture, however, greatly facilitates understanding and effective communication.

(Based on L. A. Samovar et al.: *Understanding Intercultural Communication*, Chapter 4 & F. E. Jandt: *Intercultural Communication—An Introduction*, Chapter 3)

Notes

perspective 视角,观点
venerate 尊敬,推崇
barbarian 野蛮人,原始人
Persian 波斯人
Egyptian 埃及人
the Prime Meridian of longitude 本初子午线
Greenwich 格林尼治
bacilli 病菌
parasite 寄生虫
demon 恶魔,恶棍
plague 瘟疫
exterminate 根除,消灭
chattel 有形财产,动产
subjugation 征服
savage 野蛮人,未开化的人

Questions

1. How does the way people draw their maps reflect their views of the world?
2. What might be the consequences of ethnocentrism in intercultural communication?
3. Do you think education and intercultural exchange may help eradicate ethnocentrism?

Summary

1. People attach meanings to the objects and events in our environment, so individuals have specialized and unique differences that make them perceive the external world in highly personalized fashions.

2. Culture, by exposing a large group of people to similar experiences relative to other cultures, has the effect of being a unifying force in the perception of the environment.

3. Members of different cultures look differently at the world around them. And it is crucial for us to understand and appreciate differences in perception in order to improve our ability to get along with people of other cultures.

4. In intercultural communication people are often confronted with those who do not share the same perception of the external world, and who may respond to that world in a manner that is often hard to understand.

Chapter 14 Culture Shock and Adaptation

The gentleman pursues harmony instead of homogeneity; the vulgar man seeks uniformity at the sacrifice of harmony.

—Confucian saying

Chapter 14 Culture Shock and Adaptation

Preview Questions

1. How do you usually feel when you begin to live in a new place?
2. Do you like to move from place to place or to stay in a place for long? Why?
3. What should we do when we find ourselves in cultural conflicts?

Text A

Two Views of Culture Shock

Culture shock is caused by the anxiety that results from losing all our familiar signs and symbols of social contact. Those cues or signs include various ways in which we adapt ourselves to the situation of daily life: when to shake hands and what to say when we meet people, when and how to give tips, how to buy things, when to accept and when to refuse invitations, when to take statements seriously and when not. These cues, which may be words, gestures, facial expressions, or customs, are acquired by all of us in the course of growing up and are as much a part of our culture as the language we speak or the beliefs we accept. All of us depend for our peace of mind and our efficiency on hundreds of these cues, most of which we do not carry on the level of conscious awareness.

When an individual enters a strange culture, all or most of these familiar cues are removed. He or she is like fish out of water. Edward Hall describes an example of an American living abroad for the first time:

At first, things in the cities look pretty much alike. There are taxis, hotels with hot and cold running water, theaters, neon lights, even tall buildings with elevators and a few people who can speak English. But pretty soon the American discovers that underneath the familiar exterior there are vast differences. When someone says "yes" it often doesn't mean yes at all, and when people smile it doesn't always mean they are pleased. When the American visitor makes a helpful gesture he may be rebuffed; when he tries to be friendly nothing happens. People tell him that they will do things and don't. The longer he stays, the more puzzling the new country looks.

There are two major views of culture shock: the disease view and self-awareness view.

One perspective on culture shock is *the disease view*. The culture-shocked person experiences a breakdown in communication, is unable to cope, and feels isolated and lost. The culture-shocked person thus develops a number of defensive (and sometimes offensive) attitudes and behaviors to protect the mind from the confusion of an entirely new situation. In this view, the culture-shocked person is a helpless victim. The only things this victim can do to "get well" are to adjust to the new culture somehow, or else to leave the culture quickly.

In this disease view, people can experience many different emotional and mental difficulties. They can become extremely frustrated, angry, and rejecting of the new culture. They consider the host country bad, ridiculous, stupid, or hopeless—precisely because they themselves feel bad, ridiculous, stupid, or hopeless. Culture-shocked person may start to **glorify** the home country; suddenly everything about the native land is wonderful compared to this terrible new place! Some culture-shocked people fear physical contact with anyone or anything from the new culture, no matter how safe or clean. Feelings of helplessness about delays and confusions can turn rapidly into **resentment**. People in culture shock may feel harmed, tricked, deceived, injured, or ignored—or all of these.

People can become physically ill from the stress of culture shock. **Ulcers**, headaches, stomach aches, back aches, dizziness, excessive sleepiness—these and hundreds of other symptoms can often be traced back to an underlying culture shock condition.

The disease view of culture shock, in which the person is an unwilling victim, is not the only view of culture shock. There is another, much more positive concept of culture shock. This is called the *self-awareness view of culture shock*. Culture shock can be part of a positive learning experience. Culture shock, if handled well, can lead to profound self-awareness and growth.

Day-to-day living in another culture is undoubtedly an educational experience. While traveling, and living abroad people learn second language, observe different customs, and encounter new values. Many people who have lived in other countries feel that **exposure** to foreign cultures enables them to gain insight into their own society. When facing different values, beliefs, and behavior, they develop a deeper understanding of themselves and of the society that helped to shape their characters. The striking contrasts of a second culture provide a mirror in which one's own culture is reflected.

Peter Adler, a well-known expert on culture shock, says that positive cross-cultural learning experiences typically:

- involve change and movement from one cultural **frame of reference** to another;
- are personally and uniquely important to the individual;
- force the person into some form of self-examination;
- involve severe frustration, anxiety, and personal pain, at least for a while;
- cause the person to deal with relationships and processes related to his or her role as an outsider;
- encourage the person to try new attitudes and behaviors; and

- allow the person to compare and contrast constantly.

The strong, creative person can deal with culture shock positively, instead of sinking into steady complaints about the culture, wallowing in very real physical ailments, or running away at the first opportunity. Culture shock can become an opportunity for growth.

(Based on R. L. Oxford & R. C. Scarcella: Two Views of Culture Shock, in *Patterns of Cultural Identity*)

Notes

cue 暗示,线索
neon light 霓虹灯
exterior 外部,外表
rebuff 遭到拒绝或冷遇
glorify 颂扬,赞美
resentment 愤恨,不满
ulcer 溃疡
exposure 接触
frame of reference 参考系,行为准则
wallow 翻滚;沉迷

Questions

1. What do you think of the two views of culture shock? What is their major difference?

2. What should we do to deal with culture shock positively? And what can we gain through such experiences?

Text B

Adjustment and Reentry Processes

"Culture shock" occurs as a result of total immersion in a new culture. It happens to people who have been suddenly transplanted abroad. Newcomers may be anxious because they do not speak the language, know the customs, or understand people's behavior in daily life. Language problems do not account for all the frustrations that people feel. When one is deprived of everything that was once familiar, difficulties in coping with the new society may arise.

When an individual enters a strange culture, he or she is like fish out of water. Newcomers feel at times they do not belong and consequently may feel alienated from the native members of the culture. When this happens, visitors may want to reject everything about the new environment and may glorify and exaggerate the positive aspects of their own culture.

Reactions to a new culture vary, but experience and research have shown that there are distinct stages in the adjustment process. When leaving the comfortably secure environment of home, a person will naturally experience some stress and anxiety. The **severity** of culture shock depends on visitors' personalities, language ability, emotional support, and duration of stay. It is also influenced by the extent of differences, either actual or perceived, between the two cultures.

The adjustment stages during prolonged stays may last several months to several years. The following W-shaped diagram illustrates periods of adjustment in a second culture. The stages in the cycle do not always occur in the same order and some stages may be skipped:

The Adjustment Process in a New Culture

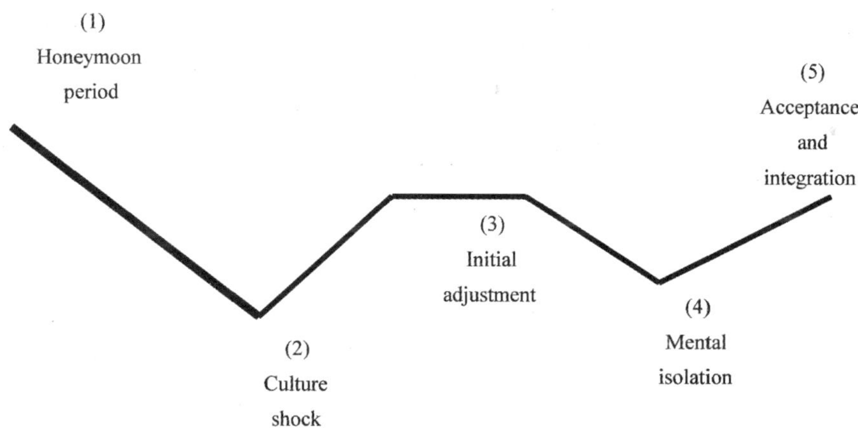

Each stage in the process is characterized by "symptoms" or outward signs typifying certain kinds of behavior:

(1) Honeymoon period. Initially many people are fascinated and excited by everything new. The visitor is elated to be in a new culture.

(2) Culture shock. The individual is immersed in new problems: housing, transportation, shopping, and language. **Mental fatigue** results from continuously straining to comprehend the foreign language.

(3) Initial adjustment. Everyday activities such as housing and shopping are no longer major problems. Although the visitor may not yet be fluent in the language spoken, basic ideas and feelings in the second language can be expressed.

(4) Mental isolation. Individuals have been away from their family and good friends for a long period of time and may feel lonely. Many still feel they cannot express themselves as well as they can in their native language. Frustration and sometimes a loss of self-confidence result. Some individuals remain at this stage.

(5) Acceptance and integration. A routine (e.g., work, business, or school) has been established. The visitor has accepted the habits, customs, foods, and characteristics of the people in the new culture. The visitor feels comfortable with friends, **associates**, and the language of the country.

People who have spent considerable time outside of their home cultures may experience a similar process when they return to their native countries, although the stages are often shorter and less intense. The following W-shaped diagram illustrates reactions and emotions experienced when a person steps back into his or her own country.

The Reentry Adjustment Process

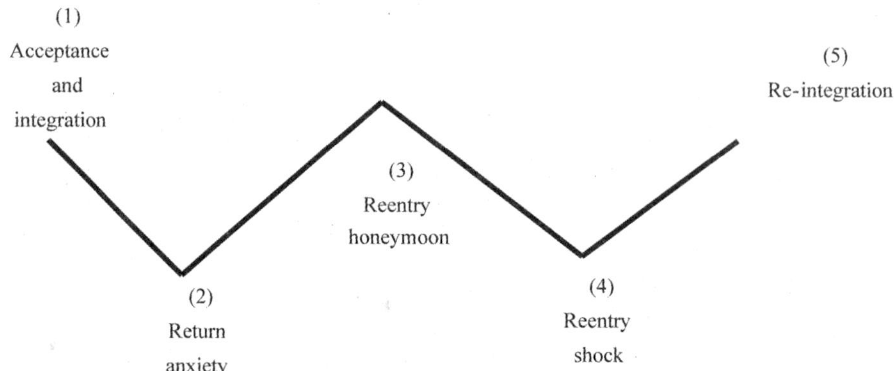

As in the first diagram, each stage in the reentry process is characterized by symptoms and feelings:

(1) Acceptance and integration. See description given for the preceding diagram.

(2) Return anxiety. There may be confusion and emotional pain about leaving because friendships will have to be disrupted. Many people realize how much they have changed because of their experiences and may be nervous about going home.

(3) Return honeymoon. Immediately upon arrival in one's own country, there is generally a great deal of excitement. There are parties to welcome back the visitor and renewed friendships to look forward to.

(4) Reentry shock. Family and friends may not understand or appreciate what one has experienced abroad, and the native country or city may have changed in the eyes of the person who has returned.

(5) Re-integration. The person becomes fully involved with friends, family, and activities and feels once again integrated in the society. Many people at this stage realize the positive and negative aspects of both home and foreign countries and have a more balanced perspective about their experiences.

Individuals experience the stages of adjustment and reentry in different ways. When visitors have close relatives in the new culture or speak the foreign language fluently, they may not experience all the effects of culture shock or mental isolation. Certain individuals have difficulties adapting to a new environment and perhaps never do; others seem to adjust well from the very beginning of their stay.

Day-to-day living in another culture is undoubtedly an educational experience. While traveling, and living abroad people learn second languages, observe different customs, and encounter new values. Many people who have lived in other countries feel that exposure to foreign cultures enables them to gain insight into their own society. When facing different values, beliefs, and behavior, they develop a deeper understanding of themselves and of the society that helped to shape their characters. The striking contrasts of a second culture provide a mirror in which one's own culture is reflected.

(Adapted from D. R. Levine & M. B. Adelman: *Beyond Language*, Chapter 10)

Notes

immersion 沉浸,陷入	associate 同事
transplant 迁移,移居	reentry 重返,重新进入
severity 严重程度,严峻性	integration 结合,整合
mental fatigue 精神疲劳	disrupt 打乱,破坏

Questions

1. What do you think would be your reactions to a new culture if you were to live abroad for a considerable period of time?

2. Why do different people experience the stages of adjustment and reentry processes in different ways?

Exploration

If you go to a foreign culture, you may experience something exciting and interesting, but also encounter many difficulties and problems. For instance, you may feel very lonely and homesick in a completely new environment. It may be comparatively easy for you to get accustomed to some foreign habits, e.g. drinking black tea instead of green tea, or making appointments for almost everything you have to do with others, but it can be rather hard for you to adapt yourself to other things, e.g. the way the foreign people communicate or the manners in which they deal with interpersonal relationships.

Certain skills, attitudes, ways of responding, and styles of behaving are often considered to be helpful in the overseas adaptation process. Now try to rate yourself in the following on a scale of 1 (very low), 2 (low), 3 (medium), 4 (high), and 5 (very high), to see if you are well equipped to adapt to new cultural environments.

________ motivation

________ self-reliance

________ tolerance for ambiguity

________ tolerance for differences
________ non-judgementalness
________ open-mindedness
________ sense of humor
________ perceptiveness
________ warmth in human relationships
________ flexibility, adaptability
________ empathy
________ communicativeness
________ curiosity
________ ability to fail
________ low goal/task orientation
________ strong sense of self (not self-centeredness)

Now total your score. If you score higher than 65, you are probably well equipped to live in a different culture. However, if you scored less than 55, you've got some serious homework to do before you go abroad for a considerable length of time.

Cases for Discussion

Case 1

Mr. Kim went to San Francisco from ROK about five years ago, together with three other Korean men. Being hard working and adaptable to a new life, he soon found work in a big American firm, where he was working as a salesman. So one year later, he was able to bring the rest of his family over and hence, lived with his family. Although his family members spoke little English, they could still get along well in the community. They had new friends who gladly helped them to adjust to various aspects of the new culture. In addition, they enjoyed their company, accepted their invitations to dinner or to birthday celebrations. They had also found some other Korean immigrants and joined some of their organizations.

However, Mr. Kim's family members still did not feel comfortable in this new society. They felt that people were always so busy and had no time for one another. They missed the days in ROK, where people often stopped by to chat and stay for hours. Although they also had friends here in San Francisco, everyone seemed so business-oriented and they were not like friends at all. When Mr. Kim mentioned this to one of his American friends, he responded by an invitation to dinner. Although he accepted the invitation, he still seemed to be disappointed. And his American friend was totally bewildered and frustrated about what to do.

Questions

1. Why do Mr. Kim and his family feel uncomfortable even though they have some new friends in the U.S.?

2. Can you figure out from this case some differences between Koreans and Americans in socializing with one another?

Case 2

The following account by a Peruvian illustrates the distressing experience of culture shock.

Soon after arriving in the United States from Peru, I cried almost everyday. I was so tense that I heard without hearing, and this made me feel foolish. I also escaped into sleeping more than twelve hours at a time and dreamed of my life, family, and friends in Lima. After three months of isolating myself in the house and speaking to no one, I ventured out. I then began to have severe headaches. Finally I consulted a doctor, but she only gave me a lot of drugs to relieve the pain. Neither my doctor nor my teachers ever mentioned the two magic words that could have changed my life: culture shock! When I learned about this, I began to see things from a new point of view and was better able to accept myself and my feelings.

I now realize most of the Americans I met in Lima before I came to the U.S. were also in one of the stages of culture shock. They demonstrated a somewhat hostile attitude toward Peru, which the Peruvians sensed and usually moved from an initially friendly attitude to a defensive, aggressive attitude or to avoidance. The Americans mostly stayed within the safe cultural familiarity of the embassy compound. Many seemed to feel that the difficulties they were experiencing in Peru were specially created by Peruvians to create discomfort for foreigners. In other words, they displaced their problem of adjustment and blamed everything on Peru.

Notes

Peru 秘鲁 compound 大院

Questions

1. Do you agree that some knowledge about culture shock can be helpful to us when we are

actually experiencing it?

2. What can we learn from the case of the Peruvian?

Case 3

What the life of a Chinese student in the U.S.A. would be like and how he or she would feel about it? Read the following letters written by a Chinese girl studying in the U.S.A. to her grandmother in Shanghai.

Letter 1 September 6

Dear Grandmother:

...I love it in America and everyone is wonderful with me. I have a really nice roommate, Gabriela, who is from Mexico and has been here for three years already. She is very kind and helpful to me. We share many things. We often sit up late at night talking.

...Americans are so friendly that they smile at you even when they don't know you. Strangers at bus stops talk to one another about personal things like what you're studying or what year you are in school.

...I like my classes very much. Some of my classmates and I have lunch together and practice our English every day. And Brian, an American boy in the class, sometimes eats with us and helps us. My cross-cultural teacher, Miss Joy, is very nice and always helps us and gives us advice. And this is a most beautiful city with lots of new things to try out and places to visit. And everything is so modern and new...

Your granddaughter

Letter 2 September 30

Dear Grandmother:

...All I know is that my heart is breaking. I think of you and Mother and my friends all the time. I'm always looking at my watch and counting on my fingers to see what time it is back in China and imagining what you and Mother and Father are doing at that very moment. I always carry the photo of all of us in front of the Great Wall tucked in my book. Even in class, my mind is back in China. It seems that things got worse right after I wrote the last letter. Gabriela and Brian are now too busy with their other classes to spend much time with us—everybody is so busy. And I'm losing weight—the food here has no taste. How I would love to have some of your *jiaozi* right now. And I'm sleeping much more; I can't seem to get started. And I'm worried about my studies.

I just have no desire to go anywhere or do anything. Time just pushes me here and there and my money is going so fast. Everything costs money here! I'm so surprised at how much everything costs. There are so many things to learn—not just English language but how to take the bus, how to wash clothes, and a thousand other things and I make so many mistakes...

I miss you so much.

Your... granddaughter

Letter 3 October 14

My dear Grandmother:

...I am feeling much better than I did in my last letter to you. One thing that helped a lot was that one night Gabriela and I sat and talked for a long time and I told her how I felt. She told me that she went through the same thing and that I was just fine. She suggested that I do some physical exercise and make an effort to get out and meet people. And now in class, Miss Joy is teaching us a lot about American culture and I'm beginning to understand a little about why they act the way they do. And I guess time helps. One day, it just seemed like I was better. I still miss you and everyone else but I feel like I'm going to be OK now...

Your happier granddaughter

Letter 4 November 20

Honorable Grandmother:

...I'm afraid I made a serious mistake in coming here. After all back home, I had a good job and now everyone will be ahead of me. To tell you the truth, I can't remember now why I thought it would be so great to come to America to study. And the Americans, now that I know them better, I discover that I don't like them very much at all. In fact, the longer I am here the more proud I am to be Chinese. It's easier to be with other Chinese. We understand one another...

Americans are not as advanced as we have been told. The professors don't know how to teach at all. They're more interested in being our friends than in teaching...

Your disappointed granddaughter

Letter 5 January 9

Dear Grandmother:

The new semester has started. I'm in the same dorm room and am very happy that Gabriela and I are roommates again. I'm also helping new students to adjust. I give them a tour of the campus and show them which books to buy. It seems strange to think that only a few months ago I was like them. I feel like I have come very far in a short time. Last night I cooked Chinese food for some of my old classmates. I think that we will always have a special relationship with one another. I think, Grandmother, that I have finally arrived in America. I have not lost my Chinese roots. In fact, they're stronger than ever.

Respectfully, your granddaughter

Questions

1. Do you think there are stages of adjusting to a foreign culture? If so, what are the stages in Li Li's experiences?

2. What can you learn from Li Li's experiences and how should we cope with culture shock?

Readings for Further Study

1
Qualities of Mindfulness

When Napoleon invaded Russia, he appeared to the world as a brilliant conquering hero, yet again proving his military genius by daring to march against a giant. But behind the proud banners and eagles, he carried a dangerous mindset, a determination to have Russia, no matter what the cost in human life. As Tolstoy describes him in *War and Peace*, Napoleon had no use for alternatives; his determination was absolute.

Opposite Napoleon stood the old Russian bear of a general, Kutuzov, a veteran who liked his vodka and had a habit of falling asleep at state occasions. An uneven match, or so it would appear.

As Napoleon's army advanced, Kutuzov let his army fall back, and then fall back some more. Napoleon kept coming, deeper into Russia, farther from his supply lines. Finally, as Kutuzov knew would happen, a powerful ally intervened: the Russian winter. The French army found itself fighting the cold, the wind, the snow, and the ice.

When Napoleon at least achieved his single, obsessive goal—Moscow—there was no one there for him to conquer. Everyone had left. The Russians had set their holy city on fire to greet the invader. Once more Kutuzov played the seeming loser.

At that moment, when Napoleon had no choice but to retreat—from the burned city, from the winter—the mindful old general attacked. He appealed to the people to save their land, and that appeal revived all of Russia. The French had everything against them.

In the character of Kutuzov we can find the key qualities of a mindful state of being: (1) creation of new categories; (2) openness to new information; and (3) awareness of more than one perspective.

In each case, Napoleon's blind obsession provides a vivid mirror image, a portrait of mindlessness. First of all, Kutuzov was flexible: evacuating a city would usually fall under the category of defeat, but for him it became the act of setting a trap. Second, his strategy was responsive to the news of Napoleon's advance, while Napoleon did not seem to be taking in information about Kutuzov's moves. Finally, while Napoleon saw his rapid advance and march on Moscow only from the point of view of conquering enemy terrain, Kutuzov could also see that an "invasion" in the contest of winter and distance from supplies could be turned into a bitter route.

Creating new categories

Just as mindlessness is the rigid reliance on old categories, mindfulness means the continual creation of new ones. Categorizing and recategorizing, labeling and relabeling as one masters the world are processes natural to children. The child's best-loved and most intense occupation is with his or her play or games. Might we not say that every child at play behaves like a creative writer, in that he or she creates a world of his or her own, or rather, re-arranges the things of his or her world in a new way which pleases him or her?

The child's serious recreation can become the adult's playful recreation.

As adults, however, we become reluctant to create new categories. Our orientation to outcome tends to deaden a playful approach. If I asked you to make a list of what you did yesterday, what would you say? Think about it for a moment, then think of what you would say if I offered you money for each item in your answer. Did you list your day in large **chunks** at first-breakfast, work, lunch, phone calls? Most people will say, for example, that they "ate breakfast" rather than "bit, chewed, and swallowed a piece of toast" and so on, even when offered a reward for a longer list of activities.

Most strong opinions rest on **global** categories. If we describe someone we dislike intensely, a single statement usually does it. But if, instead, we are forced to describe the person in great detail, eventually there will be some quality we appreciate. This is true of objects or situations as well, and is one way of changing an intolerable situation: we can try to have the good without the bad.

Welcoming new information

A mindful state also implies openness to new information. Like category making, the receiving of new information is a basic function of living creatures. In fact, lack of new information can be harmful.

Mindfully engaged individuals will actively attend to changed signals. Behavior generated from mindful listening or watching, from an expanding, increasingly differentiated information base, is, of course, likely to be more effective.

Consider a relationship between two business partners, Mr. X and Mrs. Y. Perhaps they sense that although the business is growing, misunderstandings are multiplying as well. Mr. X notices that Mrs. Y is categorizing him as rigid. Attuned to subtleties, he feels a lack of approval. Realizing that he and Mrs. Y are very different, but that she may see his style as inappropriate rather then different, he explains his behavior from his own point of view, saying how hard he tries to be consistent and predictable. Mrs. Y accepts Mr. X's depiction of his behavior, now realizing the value of a business partner she can depend upon, instead of seeing these same qualities as rigid. Mrs. Y was able to make this switch because she, too, was open to cues, to another point of view.

More than one view

Openness, not only to new information, but to different points of view is also an important feature of mindfulness. For years, social psychologists have written about the differences between the perspective of an actor [or actress] and that of an observer. For instance, we are likely to blame circumstances for our own negative behavior: "The subway always makes me late." If the very same behavior is engaged in by someone else, however, we tend to blame that individual: "He [or she] is chronically behind schedule."

Once we become mindfully aware of views other than our own, we start to realize that there are as many different views as there are different observers. Such awareness is potentially liberating. For instance, imagine that someone has just told you that you are rude. You thought you were being frank. If there is only one perspective, you can't both be right. But with an awareness of many perspectives, you could accept that you are both right and concentrate on whether your remarks had the effect that you actually wanted to produce.

This list should not give the impression that for every act there are two set, polarized interpretations. As we said, there are potentially as many interpretations as there are observers. Every idea, person, or object is potentially simultaneously many things depending on the perspective from which it is viewed. We can see how one set of circumstances gives rise to more than one view. "I go regularly to visit my mother—every week, for years now, every week—like clockwork," says a grown-up son. His elderly mother sees things differently: "He's so unpredictable, I never even know what day of the week he's coming. For years now, sometimes it's Monday, sometimes it's not until Friday. I never know."

The consequences of trying our different perspectives are important. First, we gain more choice in how to respond. A single-minded label produces an automatic reaction, which reduces our options. Second, when we apply this open-minded attitude to our own behavior, change becomes more possible.

(Adapted from E. J. Langer: The Nature of Mindfulness)

Notes

Napoleon 拿破仑(1769—1821)
mindset 心态
Tolstoy 托尔斯泰(1982—1910),俄国批判现实主义作家
Kutuzov 库图佐夫(1745—1813),俄国元帅
vodka 伏特加酒
evacuate 撤离,腾空
global 总括的,整体的
polarized 完全对立的
simultaneously 同时地

Questions

1. Why does the author mention Napoleon's defeat in his invasion of Russia?
2. According to the author, what are the important features of mindfulness?
3. How can we be mindful in intercultural communication?

2

Managing Conflict in Communication

Conflict is inevitable in any relationship; it is going to happen whether we want it to or not. Many of us, nevertheless, view conflict negatively. Conflict itself, however, is not positive or negative. How we manage the conflicts we have, in contrast, can have positive or negative consequences for our relationships.

Conflict is sometimes defined as the process which begins when one party perceives that the other has **frustrated**, or is about to frustrate, some concern of his or hers. This definition covers a broad range of phenomena. Conflicts can arise from differences in goals or practices or from other sources (i.e., tension often generated from hostile or negative feelings).

As indicated above, it is not conflict itself that is positive or negative. How we manage the conflict, however, can have positive or negative consequences for our relationships. In managing conflict with strangers, or with people who are similar, it is important that we establish what is often called a **supportive** climate.

The first characteristic of a supportive climate is description rather than evaluation. We cannot understand others if we evaluate them before we understand their positions. Using evaluative speech brings up our defenses. Descriptive speech, in contrast, does not make the other person uneasy and, in addition, it allows us to find out how they are interpreting what is happening.

Taking a problem orientation is the second characteristic of a supportive climate. Defining a mutual problem and expressing a willingness to **collaborate** in finding solution imply that we have no **predetermined** outcome we want to see. If we have a predetermined outcome in mind and try to force this outcome on the other person, we are trying to control her or him. Attempts to control others are inevitably met with resistance.

Being **spontaneous**, as opposed to being **strategic**, is the third characteristic of a supportive climate. If we appear to have a hidden motive and are acting in what appears a strategic way to others, it will arouse defensiveness in others. If others appear spontaneous and not strategic to us, on the other hand, we will not get defensive.

Empathy is also important in establishing a supportive environment. Others will know that we are concerned with their welfare. If others appear neutral toward us, we will become defensive.

The fifth characteristic of a supportive climate is communicating that we are equal. If we talk in a way that others perceive as sounding superior, others will become defensive. If we truly want to manage conflicts with strangers, we must avoid communicating with **indifference**, avoidance, and **disparagement**, and communicate with sensitivity or equality.

The final characteristic of a supportive climate is open-mindedness. If we communicate to others that we are open to their viewpoint and willing to try to change our behavior if needed, others will not become defensive. If, on the other hand, we communicate in such a way that indicates that we think we are right and certain of our attitudes and behavior, others will become defensive.

Many of these characteristics of a supportive climate should sound familiar. While the words are not exactly the same, the attitude to resolve conflict is very similar to becoming mindful. In becoming mindful, we have to create new categories (which is necessary to be descriptive), be open to new information, and not be certain that we already know the answers. The focus is on the process, not the outcome.

If we change the way we react to others, they will change the way they react to us. The objective of change is developing a relationship that can deal with differences. Achieving change requires that we separate relationship and substantive issues and pursue goals in each arena separately.

Some scholars offer us an approach to effective negotiations. Stated most simply, their belief is that we should always be unconditionally constructive. According to them, we must do only those things that are both good for the relationship and good for us, whether or not they reciprocate.

1. Rationality. Even if they are acting emotionally, balance with reason.

2. Understanding. Even if they misunderstand us, try to understand them.

3. Communication. Even if they are not listening, consult them before deciding on matters that affect them.

4. Reliability. Even if they are trying to deceive us, neither trust nor deceive them; be reliable.

5. Noncoercive modes of influence. Even if they are trying to coerce us, neither yield to that coercion nor try to coerce them; be open to persuasion and try to persuade them.

6. Acceptance. Even if they reject us and our concerns as unworthy of their consideration, accept them as worthy of our consideration, care about them, and be open to learning from them.

Few, if any, of us follow the six guidelines in our normal, everyday communication with others. In order to apply the guidelines, we must be mindful. What is unconscious is not within a person's control but what is made conscious is available for human beings to understand to change, or to reinforce.

Effective communication involves minimizing misunderstandings. To be an effective communicator requires that we be motivated, and have the appropriate knowledge and skills.

Conflict is inevitable at some point when we communicate with others. Conflict, in and of itself, is not positive or negative. How we manage the conflict is critical. To manage the conflict constructively and communicate effectively, we must be unconditionally accepting of the person with whom we are in conflict and set up a supportive environment to resolve the conflict.

(Adapted from W. B. Gudykunst & Y. Y. Kim: *Communicating with Strangers*, Chapter 12)

Notes

frustrated 挫败，阻挠	empathy 同感；感情移入
supportive 支持性的，维持的	indifference 不关心，冷淡
collaborate 协作，合作	disparagement 轻视，轻蔑
predetermined 预先确定的，事先就有一定倾向的	unconditionally constructive 无条件地具有建设性、积极性
spontaneous 自发的，无意识的，自然的	reciprocate 回报，回应
strategic 战略性的	noncoercive 非强制的，非胁迫的

Questions

1. What did you usually think of conflicts in communication? What is your opinion now after reading the article?

2. Are there any other things that we have to pay attention to apart from those mentioned in the article for dealing with conflicts in intercultural relationships?

Summary

1. Culture shock is caused by the anxiety that results from losing all our familiar signs and symbols of social contact.

2. Different people may view culture shock differently. Some considering it as a disease perspective may sink into steady complaints about the new culture and become an unwilling victim, while others looking at culture shock in the self-awareness view will deal with problems positively and learn much about the new culture and themselves.

3. Reactions to a new culture vary, but there are distinct stages in the adjustment process. The severity of culture shock depends on visitors' personalities, language ability, emotional support, and duration of stay. It is also influenced by the extent of differences, either actual or perceived, between the two cultures.

4. Exposure to foreign cultures will enable us to gain insight into our own society. When facing different values, beliefs, and behavior, we will develop a deeper understanding of ourselves and of the society that helped to shape our characters. The striking contrasts of a second culture provide a mirror in which one's own culture is reflected.

Chapter 15 Intercultural Understanding

It is a luxury to be understood.

—Ralph W. Emerson

Chapter 15 Intercultural Understanding

Preview Questions

1. How would you feel if you find it very difficult to make other people understand you?

2. Why do you think it is often said that intercultural communication is vital to human survival in this world?

3. What should we do to improve our communication with people of other cultures?

Text A

Improving Intercultural Communication

So far we have already discussed many cases of intercultural communication in which problems arise because people involved are culturally different. All this suggests that intercultural communication is difficult. Now you may ask what we can do about it if intercultural communication to us is inevitable in our times. In the following there are just some suggestions offered by scholars working in this field for improving intercultural communication.

Know yourself

Although the idea of knowing yourself is common, it is nevertheless crucial to improving intercultural communication. The novelist James Baldwin said it best when he wrote, "The questions which one asks oneself begin, at last, to illuminate the world, and become one's key to the experience of others."

Your first step toward introspection should begin with your own culture, regardless of what that culture might be. Remember, we are products of our culture—and that culture helps control communication.

You should identify those attitudes, prejudices, and opinions that we all carry around and that bias the way the world appears to us. Knowing our likes, dislikes, and the degrees of personal ethnocentrism enables us to place them out in the open so that we can detect the ways in which these attitudes influence communication.

The third step in knowing ourselves is learn to recognize your communication style—the manner in which you present yourself to others. It involves discovering the kind of image we portray to the rest of the world. Ask yourself, "How do I communicate and how do others perceive me?" If you perceive yourself in one way, and the people with whom you interact perceive you in another way, serious problems can arise.

Seek to understand different languages

Since language is so important to successful communication, whenever possible, both parties involved in intercultural communication should seek a common language and attempt to understand cultural differences in using the language. If you plan to spend some time around people from other cultures, try to learn their language. You would be far more effective if you could speak Spanish when doing business in Mexico. Moreover, you should keep in mind that there is more to language than vocabulary, syntax, and dialects. Language is more than a vehicle of communication; it teaches one a culture's lifestyle, ways of thinking, and different patterns of interacting. In addition, you should also realize there are different styles of "talk." One is not right and the others wrong—they are only different.

Develop empathy

The next suggestion for improvement is to develop empathy—be able to see things from the point of view of others so that we can better know and adjust to the other people.

Perhaps the most common of all barriers to empathy is a constant self-focus. It is difficult to gather information about the other person, and to reflect on that information, if we are consumed with thoughts of ourselves.

Many of the hindrances to empathy can be traced to a lack of motivation. This problem might well be the most difficult to conquer. We are most motivated to respond to people who are close to us both physically and emotionally. We are primarily concerned about our families. As our personal circle widens, it includes relatives and friends. Interest in other people then moves to neighbors and other members of the community. As we get further and further away from people in our immediate circle, we tend to find it hard to empathize. Think for a moment about your reaction to the news that someone you know had been seriously injured in an automobile accident versus your response to reading that 700,000 people were suffering from severe famine in the Sudan. In most instances you would be more motivated to learn about your friend than about the people thousands of miles away in Africa. Although this is a normal reaction, it often keeps us from trying to understand the experiences of people far removed from our personal sphere.

For intercultural communication to be successful, we must all learn to go beyond personal boundaries and try to learn about the experiences of people who are not part of our daily lives. We must realize that we live in an interconnected world, and we must therefore be motivated to understand everyone—regardless of how much we seem separated from them by either distance or culture.

To be successful as an intercultural communicator, you must develop empathy, and that can be cultivated only if you become sensitive to the values and customs of the culture with which you are interacting. Empathy can be increased if you resist the tendency to interpret the other's verbal and nonverbal actions from your culture's orientation. Learn to suspend, or at least keep in check, the cultural perspective that is unique to your experiences. The action or words of others may appear unusual (or even downright ridiculous). However, you can avoid conflict by understanding and respecting their viewpoint. This does not mean that you have to agree with them. When you can see their perspective, you are better able to understand the situation. So you are better equipped to provide a mutually agreeable solution to the problem.

(Adapted from L. A. Samovar et al.: *Communication between Cultures*, Chapter 10)

Notes

James Baldwin 鲍德温(1924—1987),美国小说家
introspection 内省,反省
bias 使有倾向性,使有偏见
(be) consumed with 一心想着
hindrance 障碍
Sudan 苏丹
interconnected 相互联系的
downright ridiculous 十分地荒谬可笑

Questions

1. Is knowing oneself less difficult than knowing others? Why or why not?
2. Could you give some examples of hidden personal premises in our life?
3. Is the way you present yourself exactly the same as the way you perceive yourself? How does this affect your communication with others?
4. Why is developing empathy important to intercultural communication?

Text B

Communicating Effectively with Strangers

To say we communicated does not imply an outcome. Communication is a process involving the exchange of messages and the creation of meaning. No two people ever attach the same meaning to a message. Whether a specific instance of communication is effective or not depends on the degree to which the participants attach similar meanings to the message exchanged. Stated differently, communication is effective to the extent that we are able to minimize misunderstandings. To say that meaning in communication is never totally the same for all communicators is not to say that communication is impossible or even difficult—only that it is imperfect.

When we communicate, we attach meaning to (or interpret) messages we constructed and transmit to others. We also attach meaning to (or interpret) messages we receive from others. We are not always aware of this process, but we do it nevertheless. To say that two people communicated effectively requires that the two attach relatively similar meanings to the messages sent and received (i.e., they interpret the message similarly).

Ineffectively communication can occur for a variety of reasons when we communicate with strangers. We may not encode our message in a way that it can be understood by others, strangers may misinterpret what we say, or both can occur simultaneously. The problems that occur may be due to pronunciation, grammar, familiarity with the topic being discussed, familiarity with the other person, familiarity with the other person's native language, fluency in the other person's language, and/or social factors.

When we are communicating with strangers and basing our interpretations on our symbolic systems, ineffective communication often occurs. Consider a white teacher interacting with a black student raised in the lower-class subculture in the United States. The teacher asks the student a question, in answering the question, the student does not look the teacher in the eye. The teacher, in all likelihood, would interpret the student's behavior as disrespectful or assume that the student is hiding something. Establishing eye contact is expected in the white middle-class subculture in the United States when you are telling the truth and being respectful. The student's intent, on the other hand, may have been to show respect to the teacher, given that children in the lower-class black subculture in the Untied States are taught not to make eye contact with people they respect. Situations like this lead to misunderstanding and ineffective communication.

The obvious knowledge factors influencing our effectiveness in communicating with strangers are our ability to speak the other language and the knowledge we have about the strangers' culture.

One other aspect of knowledge that is critical to effective interaction with strangers involves the way in which we are taught to talk about human behavior.

There are at least three interrelated cognitive processes involved here: description, interpretation, and evaluation. Effective communicators distinguish among these three processes, while ineffective communicators probably do not make a distinction. By description we mean an actual report of what we have observed with the minimum of distortion and without attributing social significance to the behavior. Description includes what we see and hear and is accomplished by counting and/or recording observations.

In order to clarify these processes, we offer the following example:

Description The teacher is sitting on the desk in torn, faded jeans.

This statement is descriptive in nature. It does not attribute social significance; it merely tells what the observer saw. If we were to attribute social significance to this statement, or make an inference about what we saw, we would be engaged in interpretation. In other words, interpretation is what we think about what we see and hear. The important thing to keep in mind is that multiple interpretations can be made for any particular description of behavior. Returning to our example, we have the following:

Description The teacher is sitting on the desk in torn, faded jeans.

Interpretation

The teacher likes to be informal.

The teacher doesn't care about his or her appearance.

The teacher doesn't engage in behavior appropriate to his or her role.

The teacher isn't paid enough to dress in fashion.

Each of these interpretations can have several different evaluations. Evaluations are positive or negative judgments concerning the social significance we attribute to behavior. To illustrate this, we can use the first interpretation given above:

Interpretation The teacher likes to be informal.

Evaluations

I like that; it makes it easier for student and teacher to get to know each other.

I don't like that; teachers should dress and use appropriate manners for their occupation.

Of course, several other evaluations could be made, but these two are sufficient to illustrate potential cross-cultural differences. In the United States, the first evaluation might be common because of the informality of the education system. In many other cultures, however, the second evaluation would predominate. In Japan, for example, it is expected that teachers will dress appropriately for their position, and, in addition, it is unacceptable for a teacher to sit on a desk.

If we are unable to distinguish among these three cognitive processes, it is likely that we will skip the descriptive process and jump immediately to either interpretation or evaluation when confronted with different patterns of behavior. This leads to misattributions of meaning and, therefore, to ineffective communication. Being able to distinguish among the three processes, on the other hand, increases the likelihood that we are able to see alternative interpretations that are used by strangers, thereby increasing our effectiveness. Differentiating among the three processes also increases the likelihood of our making more accurate predictions of strangers' behavior.

(Adapted from W. B. Gudykunst & Y. Y. Kim: *Communicating with Strangers*, Chapter 12)

Notes

construct 构建，形成	distortion 歪曲
disrespectful 无礼的，不尊重的	social significance 社会意义，社会含意
cognitive 认知的	

Questions

1. What evaluations can you make of the other interpretations of the example "The teacher is sitting on the desk in torn, faded jeans"?

2. Why do we have to distinguish the three cognitive processes if we want to be effective in communication?

3. According to the article, what are the essential factors in an effective communication?

Exploration

It is said that the city of New York is in a sense very much international, a miniature of the "global village," for one of the three New Yorkers is foreign-born, two of five residents speak English as a second language and more than 600,000 people living in it barely speak English at all.

To some extent this is also the case with some of the cities in China. Do you find the population of the city where you live becoming more and more diversified, with a lot of the residents who were born somewhere else and who do not speak the local dialect?

Since we tend to overemphasize the disparities between people categorized as "we" and those categorized as "others," those "others" who are very different from us may be considered as strange, unnatural, disgusting, and even inferior. However, we should be aware of the fact that we are also "others" in their eyes and learn to view them in their own perspectives.

Now try to decide what and how we should do now to improve our relation with all those who we have categorized as "others," if we are to be up to the task of creating communication adequate for an interdependent world.

Cases for Discussion

Case 1

It is a story about a Chinese mother, Mrs. Zhang and her American daughter-in-law, Susan.

At the airport, Susan and her husband, Mrs. Zhang's son, would fly back to New York and she was talking to her mother-in-law. Since Mrs. Zhang doesn't know any English and Susan can speak little Chinese, Susan's husband had to act as the interpreter.

Susan：Mrs. Zhang, come to New York if you want.

Husband：妈妈，您可一定要来纽约看看。

Mother：不去了，给你们添麻烦。

Husband：Oh, it depends on the physical condition.

Susan：Yes, oh thanks for your delicious food, I like them very much.

Husband：谢谢妈妈给我们做了那么多的好吃的。

Mother：自家人谢什么。苏珊，你以后可不要再减肥了，身体健康才最重要哪！

Husband：It's my pleasure. Susan, I hope you become even more beautiful.

Susan：Thank you! The same to you.

Husband：谢谢妈妈，我祝您身体健康。

Mother：啊，谢谢，谢谢！

Questions

1. How would you translate for the mother and the daughter-in-law if you were asked to play the role of the husband?

2. What do you think of the husband's actual translation? Is it very different from your translation? If it is, what are the differences? And why are they different?

Case 2

This dialogue occurs between a Chinese employee (C) and his American boss (A). A wants C to do extra work on Saturday, but C doesn't want to work on Saturday because it's going to be his son's birthday.

A：It looks like we're going to have to keep the production line running on Saturday.

C：I see.

A：Can you come in on Saturday?

C：Yes, I think so.

A：That'll be a great help.

C：Yes, Saturday is a special day, did you know?

A：What do you mean?

C：It's my son's birthday.

A：How nice. I hope you all enjoy it very much.

C：Thank you. I appreciate your understanding.

Questions

1. What does the Chinese employee mean by saying "I see"? Does it mean agreement, acceptance or promise?

2. Why does the American boss fail to understand what the Chinese employee implies by saying "It's my son's birthday"? Why does the Chinese fail to say "no"?

Case 3

This is an interaction between a supervisor from the United States and a subordinate from Greece.

American: How long will it take you to finish the report?

(*Interpretations*) *American: I asked him to participate.*

Greek: His behavior makes no sense. He is the boss. Why doesn't he tell me?

Greek: I do not know. How long should it take?

American: He refuses to take responsibility.

Greek: I asked him for an order.

American: You are in the best position to analyze time requirements.

American: I press him to take responsibility for his own actions.

Greek: What nonsense! I better give him an answer.

Greek: 10 days.

American: He lacks the ability to estimate time; this estimate is totally inadequate.

American: Take 15. It is agreed you will do it in 15 days?

American: I offer a contract.

Greek: These are orders. 15 days.

(*In fact the report needed 30 days of regular work. So the Greek worked day and night, but at the end of the 15th day, he still needed one more day's work to finish the report*).

American: Where is the report?

American: I am making sure he fulfills his contract.

Greek: He is asking for the report.

Greek: It will be ready tomorrow.

American: But we agreed that it would be ready today.

American: I must teach him to fulfill a contract.

Greek: The stupid, incompetent boss! Not only did he give me wrong orders, but he does not appreciate that I did a 30-day job in 16 days.

(*In the end, the Greek hands in his resignation.*)

Questions

1. Why are the interpretations so different from each other?

2. The misunderstanding obviously comes from the fact that the American supervisor wants the employee to participate in decisions, while the Greek subordinate expects to be told what to do. What can we do about it? How to resolve such problems in communication in which participants hold different cultural expectations?

Readings for Further Study

1
Overcoming Ethnocentrism in Communication

The ethnocentric impression that one's communication style is natural and normal **predisposes** Americans to evaluate other styles negatively. Such evaluation is likely to elicit a defensive reaction, forming a mutual negative evaluation that stems from blindness toward differences between cultures. For instance, Americans may evaluate Japanese indirect communication style as "ambiguous," while American directness may be received by Japanese as "immature." When communicators engage in mutual negative evaluation, the **recriminatory** interaction may be enough to block communication. If the communicators then attempt to overcome the difficulty through ethnocentric procedures, the communication event may **deteriorate** even further. The American, sensing Japanese reluctance to confront a problem, becomes even more personal and aggressive. The Japanese, reacting to an embarrassing social **indiscretion**, becomes even more formal and indirect. With each turn of this **regressive spiral**, negative evaluations are intensified; "ambiguity" may spiral to "evasion" "deviousness" "deception," and finally to "dishonesty." On the other side of the culture curtain, "immature" may spiral to "impolite" "brash" "**impertinent**," and finally to "offensive."

Negative evaluations and spirals are not limited merely to American-Japanese interactions. The following situations illustrate regressive spirals common to Americans communicating with people of a variety of other cultures.

An American student listens with growing impatience to a Nigerian student, who is responding to a simple question about his religion with several long stories about his childhood. Finally, the American breaks in and makes her own point clearly and logically. The American evaluates the Nigerian negatively as being stupid or devious (for talking "in circles"). The Nigerian evaluates the American as being childish or unsophisticated (for being unable to understand subtlety). The American urges the Nigerian to state his point more clearly, and in response the Nigerian intensifies his efforts to provide more context.

To avoid appearing "status conscious," the American manager requests that a Thai employee address him by his first name. The employee agrees but continues to use the manager's formal title in conversations. The American evaluates this action as unduly **subservient** and unfriendly. The Thai evaluates the American as naive and disrespectable (of the special place held by the employee in the organization's hierarchy). The American insists on pursuing casual friendliness, **engendering** even more formality in the employee's behavior.

An American trainer presents a proposal to her British counterpart. The Briton states that it is the most ridiculous **hogwash** she has ever seen. The American responds by saying that her feelings are hurt (by the attacking tone of her counterpart). The British woman enlarges on her original statement by pointing out the specific shortcomings of the proposal. The American says she must have been mistaken about considering the woman her friend, and the Briton becomes silent.

The main factor in these and endless other examples of intercultural communication spirals is a lack of awareness of specific cultural differences in communication style. In the first case of the Nigerian, both people are unaware of the American preference for a direct and explicit style in contrast to the more **contextual** African style. Both these communicators are likely to leave the situation less inclined to ask or answer questions of each other again. In the Thai case, there might be an ironic conclusion: the Thai may eventually **acquiesce** in calling the supervisor by his first name but rather than the action being one of the American **egalitarianism**, it will be a confirmation of the higher-status person's right to demand **compliance**. The misunderstanding will go underground.

The British situation illustrates a particularly troublesome clash of American personal and European intellectual styles, and it deserves closer attention. Europeans tend to use a low-context approach to intellectual confrontation—they state their points explicitly and without the ambivalence considered polite by Americans in intellectual matters. In personal matters of feeling and relationship, however, Europeans use a more high-context style, relying on suggestion and nonverbal nuance. Americans, on the other hand, treat a relationship in a low-context manner. They verbalize emotions far more often, including direct expressions of how they feel about the person with whom they are communicating. But Americans are more likely to handle intellectual confrontation in a high-context manner. They tend to indicate disagreement nonverbally with tone of voice or facial expression, for example, "Well (pause), that idea certainly has *some* merit." Americans commonly stereotype Europeans as being adamant in intellectual matters, while Europeans stereotype Americans as lacking strong convictions (or as being ignorant). On the other side of the coin, Americans often think Europeans are unnecessarily coy about interpersonal relationships, while Europeans see Americans as lacking subtlety in personal affairs.

To avoid complicating the already difficult task of intercultural communication, participants in a cross-cultural situation need to consider first the possibility that a negative evaluation might be based on an unrecognized cultural difference. Each person needs to be aware that he or she is evaluating the other, often on similarly ethnocentric grounds.

Americans can overcome the tendency to stereotype and generate negative evaluations by approaching every cross-cultural situation as a kind of experiment. They should assume that some kind of cultural difference exists but that the nature of the difference is unclear. Using available generalizations about the other culture, they can formulate a **hypothesis** and then test it for accuracy. Lacking a generalization about the other culture, the hypothesis can be based on possible contrasts to a typical American pattern in the situation. The hypothesis should be tested by acting **tentatively** as if it were accurate and by watching carefully to see what happens, as illustrated in the following example:

An American student in a homestay in Germany is sitting down to her first dinner with the host family. (The family speaks English.) She avoids the initial pitfall in a cross-cultural encounter by treating the occasion as a chance to learn. And she does not fall back on her American behavior patterns, which might involve somewhat nervous chatter about what happened during the day and how she felt about it. By allowing the family to initiate the conversation, the student may be able to ascertain the pattern of topics that are appropriate for dinner conversation. But what if they wait for her? One hypothesis she might consider is that Germans typically do not engage in conversation during a meal. Thinking over what she knows about Europeans in general, she decides that this is not likely (although it is typical in some other cultures). The student is unaware of the generalization that Germans prefer to discuss intellectual or political issues over meals (and at other times as well). But the student does remember her mother telling her never to discuss politics and religion at the dinner table. Perhaps the German pattern is a contrast to this American social norm? She tentatively begins a discussion of the political problems of American forces stationed on German soil, ready to back off from the topic if it seems uncomfortable. However, the family engages this subject heartily, the student is relieved, and the homestay is off to a good start.

Generating and using cultural generalizations effectively while avoiding stereotyping is one of the most demanding skills of intercultural communication. Cultural self-awareness is necessary, as is some knowledge of predominant patterns in the target culture and their variations (e.g., generational, gender, ethnic group). Although this knowledge is usually limited, it can still be used to hypothesize likely areas of contrast and possible communication problems. As more knowledge of relevant cultural differences is acquired, generalizations can become more specific, hypotheses more particular, and communication difficulties more predictable.

(Adapted from E. C. Stewart & M. J. Bennett: *American Cultural Patterns*, Chapter 8)

Notes

predispose 使人形成某种倾向	hogwash 废话，胡说
recriminatory 互相责备的	contextual 根据上下文的，有来龙去脉的
deteriorate 恶化	acquiesce (无奈地)接受，(勉强地)同意
indiscretion 轻率的言行	egalitarianism 平等主义
regressive spiral 恶性循环	compliance 顺从，依从
impertinent 鲁莽的	hypothesis 假设
subservient 恭顺的，低三下四的	tentatively 试探性地
engender 造成	

Questions

1. Why do people involved in intercultural communication often evaluate the other(s) negatively?

2. Is it possible to overcome the tendency to stereotype? If it is, what should we do?

3. If we cannot help making generalizations, how to use cultural generalizations effectively?

2
A Matter of Survival

There is, perhaps, no more important topic in the social sciences than the study of intercultural communication. Understanding between members of different cultures was always important, but it has never been as important as it is now. Formerly, it was necessary for empire, or trade. Now it is a matter of the survival of our species.

We stand at the beginning of the global age in human affairs, and the development of our human powers to affect each other and the planet we share has been so rapid and so great that we threaten our own survival. Whatever the solutions to the problems created by our inventiveness and fecundity, they cannot be found or implemented unless we are able to create intercultural understanding and cooperation on a scale never before achieved. Only effective intercultural communication can enable us to achieve cooperation and understanding on a global scale.

The key to an adequate understanding of intercultural communication is a simple one. We have no choice. We must succeed in doing it, we have succeeded in doing it in the past (here and there), and we must recognize the imperative of extending our capacity to do it to a global level .

But we already know this. One glance is all it takes. Whether it was the glance of Melanesian people, gathered around a satellite television set in the Highlands of Papua New Guinea, or that of a group of African executives gathered around the same pictures in a boardroom in Nairobi, or the gaze of an American family in their living room—one glance was enough. The picture was the picture the planet Earth, viewed from space.

It did not show the boundary line of nations, the net of political alliances among them—the colored patchwork of the maps of power and control. It showed one, fragile but beautiful blue-green world—*Spaceship Earth* it has been called. Once this image became part of the common heritage of humankind, we knew what we needed to do and be.

Events have conspired to point to the same destiny. We have witnessed problems of pollution, increased trade and economic interdependence, greater levels of travel and migration, accelerating population growth, and increased electronic means for communication across planetary distances.

At the same time, we see everyday evidence of a terrible paradox. While we are clearly more involved in each other's lives than ever before, we appear no less deeply involved in brutal rejection of each other. While more people from more cultures are communicating and cooperating across differences, as many, it seems, are killing and maiming each other in the name of cultural and religious identity. At the same time, still virulent remnants of the forces of 19th and 20th century imperialism are at work among nations. The dilemma of the global age is that, while we have finally discovered that we are one people who must share one precarious world, we are profoundly divided by race, culture and belief and we have yet to find a tongue in which we can speak our humanity to each other.

To find that tongue must be our first and last endeavor, for the pursuit of peace and freedom from pollution and poverty are merely means to an end and the end is the celebration of our human possibilities. To peace, freedom from poverty and pollution we may add a more fundamental need—finding a voice in which to speak, first, in reaching the understanding on which we will assure peace, share wealth and live cleanly, and then, in the speech with which we will freely utter our own becoming.

We must make a wager—we will be able to find common ground while preserving genuine difference and diversity. If we do not succeed in this we will fail as a species. We *must* assume we will succeed. If we still fail, we will have lost nothing in the attempt. If we assume that will fail, and we *could* have succeeded, we will have lost everything. We will wager that success in finding a common tongue but preserving difference is possible.

The alternatives are not pleasant to contemplate. Basically there are two possibilities: the first is that we, or our descendants, will all be members of a single, world culture, perhaps clinging lovingly to minor regional differences in cuisine or folk music and this single culture will either be a genuinely new global culture, no doubt influenced by many prior cultures, but not a mere amalgam of them, or it will be a heavily American (or Chinese) imperial culture. Either way, we will have lost something precious—our diversity—and life will be less interesting for this loss.

The second possibility is that we remain roughly where we are or have been, with intercultural misunderstanding as common as it is at present, or, spurred on by population growth, pollution, scarcity of resources and war, more common and more deadly.

Neither of the two possibilities is worth contemplating. The notion of a new culture which is influenced by all cultures is attractive in some ways, but history tells us that we do not have enough time for this to come about. It is also highly improbable. Most cultural blending has come about by conquest and has only achieved the kind of mellowness which partially hides ancient imperialism by the passage of a great deal of time—as is the case in the United Kingdom, for instance.

The imperial solution is even less attractive although entirely possible. The problem with this solution is that the structural and other violence necessary to bring it about appear unlikely to permit us to solve our planetary problems. An imperial culture is a culture blind to the conditions necessary for its own survival.

The second possibility—do nothing, or continue recent trends toward accentuation of difference—provides the most probable scenario, but is holds out very little promise of yielding the harvest of understanding and cooperation we must reap if we are to survive the winter of scarcity and bitterness that may be just ahead of our present world wide Indian summer.

The wager we must make is that it is possible and desirable for all cultures to change, but not to change by blending with one another or being submerged by a single culture. Each culture must change to the extent necessary for it to recognize difference, to acknowledge the validity of other cultures, to incorporate some degree of tolerance of cultural diversity, and to discover some common ground in the new intercultural space thus created ground upon which a conversation about intercultural understanding and cooperation can be built. The apparent paradox of this change is that there must be room in it not only for tolerance but also for critique, including critique of other cultures.

(Abridged from R. Young: *Intercultural Communication—Pragmatics, Genealogy, Deconstruction*, Chapter 1)

Notes

our species 人类

fecundity 多产;繁殖力

Melanesian people (西南太平洋岛群的) 美拉尼西亚人

Papua New Guinea (大洋洲岛国)巴布亚新几内亚

Nairobi(肯尼亚首都)内罗毕

alliance 结盟,同盟

conspire 共同发生作用

planetary 行星的,全球的

maim 使受重伤

wager 赌注,担保

contemplate 凝视;沉思	mellowness 柔和,温和宜人
descendant 子孙后代	accentuation 强调
amalgam 混合物	scenario 方案,设想;事态
spur 刺激,推动	Indian summer 小阳春,兴旺而短暂的晚期

Questions

1. Why is the study of intercultural communication important in today's world?

2. What should people in different cultures do to find a solution to problems of intercultural communication?

3. Why is it a fundamental need to find a common tongue? Does the common tongue here refer to a particular language?

Summary

1. To improve intercultural communication, we have to know ourselves. We should understand our own culture, by identifying those attitudes, prejudices, and opinions that we carry and that bias the way the world appears to us.

2. We should also learn to develop empathy, to be able to see things from the point of view of others so that we can better know and adjust to the other people.

3. To achieve better communication effects with people of different cultural backgrounds, we have to distinguish at least three interrelated cognitive processes: description, interpretation, and evaluation. This ability enables us to see alternative interpretations that are used by other people and make more accurate predictions of their behavior.

4. All cultures have to change, but not to change by blending with one another or being submerged by a single culture. Each culture must change to the extent necessary for it to recognize difference, to acknowledge the validity of other cultures, to incorporate some degree of tolerance of cultural diversity, and to discover some common ground upon which a conversation about intercultural understanding and cooperation can be built.

References

Chen, G.M. & W. J. Starosta. *Foundations of Intercultural Communication*. Boston: Allyn & Bacon, 1998.

Davis, L. *Doing Culture: Cross-Cultural Communication in Action*. Beijing: Foreign Language Teaching and Research Press, 2001.

Dodd, C. H. *Dynamics of Intercultural Communication* (5th ed.). New York: McGraw Hill Higher Education, 1998.

Gregg, J. Y. *Communication and Culture: A Reading-Writing Text*. Boston: Heinle & Heinle Publishers, 1998.

Gudykunst, W. B. & Y.Y. Kim *Communicating with Strangers: An Approach to Intercultural Communication* (4th ed.). New York: McGraw Hill Higher Education, 2003.

Hall, E. T. *The Silent Language*. New York: Doubleday & Co, 1959.

Hirschberg, S. *One World, Many Cultures*. Boston: Allyn & Bacon, 1995.

Jandt, F. E. *Intercultural Communication: An Introduction*. Thousand Oaks: Sage Dublication, Inc, 1998.

Knepler, H. & M. Knepler *Crossing Cultures*. New York: Macmillan, 1991.

Kluckhohn, C. *Mirror for Man*. Greenwich: Fawcett Publications, 1965.

Levine, D. R. & M. B. Adelman *Beyond Language: Cross-Cultural Communication* (2nd ed.). Englewood: Prentice Hall, 1993.

Levine, R. *The Geography of Time*. New York: Basic Books, 1997.

Lustig, M. W. & J. Koester *Intercultural Competence: Interpersonal Communication Across Cultures* (5th ed.). New York: Pearson Education, Inc, 2006.

Samovar, L. A. & R. E., Porter *Communication between Cultures* (5th ed.). Belmont: Wadsworth Publishing Company, 2004.

Scollon, R. & S. W. Scollon *Intercultural Communication: A Discourse Approach*. Oxford: Blackwell, 1995.

Steward, E. C. & M. J. Bennett *American Cultural Patterns*. Yarmouth: Intercultural Press, Inc, 1991.

Ting-Toomey, S. *Communicating across Cultures*. New York: The Guilford Press, 1999.

Varner, I. & L. Beamer *Intercultural Communication in the Global Workplace* (3rd ed.). Columbus: McGraw-Hill Companies, Inc, 2005.

图书在版编目(CIP)数据

跨文化交流入门/许力生主编. —杭州：浙江大学出版社，2018.7

ISBN 978-7-308-17492-3

Ⅰ.①跨… Ⅱ.①许… Ⅲ.①文化交流—研究—英文 Ⅳ.①G115

中国版本图书馆 CIP 数据核字（2017）第 246931 号

跨文化交流入门

主编　许力生

责任编辑　李　晨　徐　瑾

责任校对　刘序雯

封面设计　春天书装

出版发行　浙江大学出版社

（杭州市天目山路 148 号　邮政编码 310007）

（网址：http://www.zjupress.com）

排　　版　杭州林智广告有限公司

印　　刷　嘉兴华源印刷厂

开　　本　787mm×1092mm　1/16

印　　张　15.75

字　　数　510 千

版 印 次　2018 年 7 月第 1 版　2018 年 7 月第 1 次印刷

书　　号　ISBN 978-7-308-17492-3

定　　价　45.00 元